Turn Here Sweet Corn

ATINA DIFFLEY

University of Minnesota Press
Minneapolis
London

Map by Teresa Diffley

Published by the University of Minnesota Press
111 Third Avenue South, Suite 290
Minneapolis, MN 55401-2520
http://www.upress.umn.edu

Library of Congress Cataloging-in-Publication Data

Diffley, Atina.
    Turn here sweet corn : organic farming works / Atina Diffley.
    ISBN 978-0-8166-7771-9 (hc : alk. paper)
    ISBN 978-0-8166-7772-6 (pb : alk. paper)
    1. Diffley, Atina. 2. Women farmers—United States—Biography.
3. Organic farming—United States—Anecdotes. I. Title. II. Title: Organic farming works.
    S417.D48D54   2012
    631.5'84—dc23

                                                        2011051422

Printed in the United States of America on acid-free paper

The University of Minnesota is an equal-opportunity educator and employer.

18 17 16 15 14 13 12   10 9 8 7 6 5 4 3 2 1

Chase says, "Do you want to go farming?" Like it's an invitation to come outside and play.

Emma holds a strand of her hair together with mine and sighs, "The same."

Blake loves kale and open-mindedly tastes anything I say is edible.

This story is for you, your generation, and those to come.

Contents

Cold, Hard Water

An explosion of light rips me out of deep sleep. Behind the flash is a deafening boom. The sky sparks again, a fused web of tearing lines. Wind jumps in, straight on from the west, driving hard rain against the house. I crank the window closed but not quickly enough—the bed and I are drenched. I hear tiny pings against the glass.

Damn. I look at the date on the clock, June 8, 2005. Not now.

Maybe if I go back to sleep, I'll find I'm just having a nightmare. I curl into a ball at the foot of the bed and squeeze my eyes tight. If I can't see it, maybe it isn't true. I pinch my ears closed between my forefingers and thumbs. Maybe if I don't hear it. But it just grows louder, harder, and faster.

I sit up and peer out the window trying to see how big it is, but it's completely black outside, then blinding light. The sound is huge now, thumping, bouncing, and rolling off the steel roofs of the out-buildings and echoing between them. Loose metal on equipment is banging and slapping. Small branches are pelting the glass of the window and the wall of the house. I slide out of bed and find Martin standing at the open kitchen door.

Light spills out onto the deck and illuminates the hail. He takes my hand. We would have to shout to talk. The hailstones are hitting the deck and ricocheting, flat three-inch saucers with rough, serrated edges and opaque white centers. I feel a sharp burning on my leg, look down at my calf, and see a long scratch. Blood wells up along the line.

The sound changes from a wide thumping to a hammerhead

pounding, and the hail becomes perfectly clear, smooth balls, as big as a B-size potato. They hit and bounce upward, fall and bounce again. The pounding beats in the thought of everyone and every-thing exposed to the storm. Laura and Adam in their first year start-ing out, did they ever think about hail when they were dreaming about farming? The pounding says think: think about the baby birds in their nests with only leaves for a roof. Think about the Hmong family down the road; sometimes they sleep overnight in plywood shacks alongside their vegetable plots. What about the twin fawns that bed down in the bush willows? Are they crying?

A hailstone is just hard, cold water. I love water. I need water. I imagine water flowing and plants drinking. More than half of my body is water. What happens when I am cold and hard? I think about winter and snow and trees sleeping. But this is June and everything is growing. I don't know what purpose hail has.

The deck is completely white now. No wood is showing. I can see Meagan's and Sarah's lights on. Their cabins have metal roofs; the sound inside must be terrifying. I wish they were up here in the safety of the brick house. It is impossible to travel between the homes. I can only wait until it is over.

Martin makes a nest of blankets on the floor, and we crawl into it. His arms are calm strength. I imagine the parent birds with their sheltering wings wrapped around their babies. If only we could together be a shield around our fields. I remind myself that we've survived storms before. I say, "Remember the one-hundred-mile-an-hour, straight-line wind that blew out of Saint Peter?"

We had been doing routine spring work—I was in the green-house, Martin was fixing tractors—when it raced in. In just a few short minutes it knocked over four of the biggest bur oaks on the farm, three-hundred-year-old trees that had previously survived prairie fires and lightning strikes. And then it left, just blew out and on east as abruptly as it came.

"Remember July 23, 1987, when it rained eleven inches?" Martin says.

I will never forget that image. The clouds were dense and black and boiling in deep cups shaped like the bottom of an egg carton. We had our heads bent to the ground planting broccoli so we didn't notice it coming until the light changed and Bobby Mueller Junior said, "We're going to get floored." We tried to finish the row, but the rain came down in one solid sheet instead of drops. We had to just leave the equipment in the middle of the field. Everywhere was instantly running mud. We couldn't drive or even see the ground. All we could do was trudge with tiny, careful steps through the muck toward the house, holding hands in a line. We put the kids in the middle. The lightning and thunder were right there, we didn't dare stop, and we were fools to be in it.

That was the storm where I gained a true understanding of the word *saturated*, when soil has absorbed water to its full capacity, and what happens when it simply can't take any more. I wonder what happens when people can't take any more?

"Remember, that broccoli turned out gorgeous," Martin says.

That's true. It was also the last broccoli we harvested off that land, before it was destroyed. It seems so many storms ago now, safe to talk about, but neither of us is willing to talk about this storm. I have a specious superstition that if we pretend the positive, then everything will be fine. As long as we don't verbalize our fears, maybe they aren't true. But I know we are both thinking the same thing: our crops are shredded, we will spend years catching up financially, it is a complete disaster. Or maybe we aren't thinking—just feeling. I can't tell the difference right now.

"Tell me about your hail disaster in the '70s," I say. Maybe there is encouragement in the story. This is an unspoken rule of our relationship; we take turns being the discouraged and the supporter. Only one of us goes down at a time.

"It was 1977, my fifth year farming. I thought I had enough experience and market developed to expand production and take more risk. I went to the Rosemount bank and borrowed $25,000 at 11 percent interest to purchase tractors and equipment. It was the perfect spring, gentle rains and no late frost, plenty of sun. Everything looked fantastic. Ten days early for the most part. I was just getting into the harvest, had been picking zucchini for a week, the tomatoes were starting to turn pink, when we got hit. The only crops that survived were underground, potatoes, beets, and carrots."

"You must have replanted."

"It was too late in the season. Remember? We paid off that debt in '88 with the drought assistance check." Martin hands me earplugs and adds, "We better get to sleep; the crew will be here early."

He drops right off. I can feel the deep fall and rise of his sleep—breathing against my chest. It used to be the other way around; he was the one who stayed awake thinking about the crops. My mind is stuck repeating the same words. We should have quit last fall. Quit while we were ahead. This is followed with, now we're in the clear for another twenty-five years. Lightning doesn't strike twice in the same place.

But I know that is not true. The big oak in the front yard has been hit seven times. I picture the fields as they were last night on our ritual evening walk. Rows of broccoli and kale with dark green leaves broadly touching in the aisles, fields of sweet corn in different stages, from just emerging—the teeny spike, powerful with the strength of new growth, bursting through the soil—to knee-high plants, melodramatic leaves furling out of the center whirl. It only makes me feel worse.

I decide to think about seeds germinating and visualize the moment when the hypocotyl emerges from the seed coat. I see the radicle shooting down. Then lateral roots with tender white hairs spinning out, searching for water and nutrients. I picture the cotyledon slowly cracking open and the first foliage leaves emerging.

The image changes. I am the seed. My legs become a radicle. My arms spread into laterals. Fine root hairs grow off my limbs. The pounding rain softens the closed kernel of my mind and opens it up into the center of a giant blue sky. Air floods in, opening it more.

My intelligence stretches in the sunshine. Pale green leaves of new understanding sprout above my cotyledon.

And then I am deep—in dreamless sleep.

We both awake as the sunrise is starting. It is absolutely still. There is no rain or hail or wind. The birds are not singing. We lie without moving, eyes locked. Like the truth is in the silence if only we listen, or maybe each other is just the safest place in the world. After a while I gesture my head toward the window. We pull on yesterday's work clothes, walk down the stairs and out the door without shoes. The sky is deep, clean blue and cloudless, brimming with calm and peace. Our kitchen garden is a raised bed, nestled snug against the house. We stand next to it, translating what we see into the scale of destruction that we know is in the fields.

The earth is soggy and beaten, speckled with bits of green leaves and pockmarked with craters where the hail hit. Yesterday a proud line of fresh sweet beets ornamented the garden; all that is left now are ragged sawn-off roots, old-blood red against the black soil. The bed of dense romaine lettuce is shredded; the fleshy cores stand in the center of minced leaves. The Spicy Globe basil is simply gone. Martin grabs the camera, and we move toward the fields.

The top layer of soil is loose, slick mud; underneath, the ground is compacted hard from the driving rain. We keep our balance low and slide our feet instead of step. The first field we come to holds the broccoli and cabbage seedbeds. These are outdoor nurseries where we produce field-grown vegetable transplants. Last night it was a dense, green sea of vibrant leaves, pulsing with life. I was so proud. They are my responsibility and were the best we'd ever grown. Now the seedlings are jammed into the soil in a tangled, muddy mass. I pull out a plant and wipe the mud off on my shirt to look closer, but I can't make out roots from stems, stems from leaves. I can't tell if it's alive or dead. I always knew if we kept farming, sooner or later this was inevitable. We were just gambling as to when.

I try not to think about money, but my mind is making calculations of the harvest we had projected months from today. Two hundred thousand plants, minus 25 percent margin for general field loss, at a very conservative average of a dollar per plant, is somewhere around $150,000 dollars. This is just two crops out of fifty acres of mixed organic vegetable production. I think of my grandmother repeatedly reminding me as a child, "Don't count your chicks before they hatch." I was already banking these, and it's not just the money. People were counting on this food.

Normally, Martin and I vie for who talks the most; we are both passionate and excitable, and silence is rare between us. But we are in a bizarre state, taking in information but not processing it, not drawing conclusions, not making decisions, and not sharing thoughts.

I still don't hear any birds. We slide from field to field. I can see the mud packed like clown-sized clogs on Martin's bare feet and splattered on his legs, but I don't feel it on myself. The sun has risen above the tree line and is throwing long rays of morning light. We come to a field that yesterday hosted tidy rows of bushy, green tomato plants. Now there is a naked chain of three-inch stems, bare of any leaves, a line of short nubs. I realize what feels so surreal. The hail has not only destroyed the foliage, but their shadows have been erased as well.

I dig up a tomato and find the root ball is pulsing thick with fine, white hairs. New lateral roots have sprouted and pushed deep. Above ground there is nothing but a stripped stem, but below, in the soil, they seem very much alive.

We keep moving. The kale as a whole looks battered. The leaves are torn, and many of the centers are gone. They'll grow back, but the leaves will be small, limp, and scattered, not a crisp, round crown perfect for bunching. The cabbage is the same. Where the hail hit the center, the meristem, which would have grown into a main head, is sliced off. Now instead of a big, solid cabbage, these plants will grow only a cluster of loose-leaved chouchou, miniature French delicacies, of no value in our market.

Cabbage is our workhorse, but I didn't realize I was emotionally attached to it. The touch of Martin's hand on the small of my back brings tears to my eyes. He whispers in my ear, "Mon petit chouchou."

Nothing could be more romantic than "You are beautiful my little cabbage," but there is nothing endearing about this hail. I can't take the camera out of its bag. Pictures would make this permanent. I want to be able to forget.

The sweet corn is twisted and pushed into the mud. The leaves are mostly gone. Now it's Martin's turn. I can see many of the plants will recover. He can see only the loss. I dig a plant out of the mud and show him that the core is still intact. "They will stand up and grow again," I say. "In two months you'll be out here harvesting by the truckload." He just stares.

We come to the cucumbers planted inside of slotted row tunnels. The plastic has a few holes punched in it, but for the most part the tunnels and the plants look unscathed, calm and composed. Last winter we spent $5,000 on equipment to lay these tunnels. I argued with Martin when he proposed it. It was an awful lot of money for an implement we would use for one week of the year, even if it would make harvest two weeks longer. But now, first season in use, it has just protected $14,000 worth of crop from destruction. Finding these obvious survivors perks me up. "We'll be swimming in cucumbers."

The crew joins us. I realize they are even more shocked than we are. Their loss as employees is less financial than ours as owners, but they have been working hard all spring. They are emotionally invested. Farming is tactile work, and they made the beginner's assumption that the reward for their efforts would be a bountiful harvest. We've at least experienced crop loss before and knew the gamble. Sooner or later hail of this magnitude was likely to happen. I always say after we finish planting a field, "It will be a gorgeous crop—if it makes it." They always laugh, but I don't think they understood until now. It's not a joke. It isn't real until the food is on the table.

I know in my head that many of the plants will grow back. The roots are strong. The soil is fertile. I tell myself this can somehow be a positive experience for the crew. But I don't believe it. Right now I just feel like we are hung. It is impossible to make any decisions until we know what will recover. Ideally we'd all just go away for a week; when we returned, things would look so much better, but I need to stick around to water the greenhouse. I tell them, "Take the day off. Go to town and have some fun. I'll call and give you a report."

They just look at me. Everyone hangs around, reading, napping, and taking brief forays into the fields to look again. When we see each other, we laugh and make jokes, then wander off. We aren't comfortable together, but we don't want to be apart.

Meagan and I walk over to see Laura and Adam in their incubator field. We find them holding hands in a bed that was salad mix. Now there is nothing. I look at them and remember Martin and me in the first field we planted together. How proud and accomplished we felt. How in love we were, with each other, with the land, with the plants and the work. I imagine how they must have felt yesterday, before the hail, and how devastated they must feel now. They look at me and open their mouths, but nothing comes out.

"Congratulations, you are real farmers now," I say. "It looks much worse than it is. In a week you'll be amazed. Even this lettuce will grow back. The roots aren't damaged. As long as the growing tips are intact, they will grow new leaves. They'll come back even stronger than before." I'm happy I have them to encourage. I say it all over again because they look like they don't believe me, but really, it's myself I'm trying to convince.

I know this is true. Why can't I feel it? Why don't I believe it?

Maybe helping them see the humor in it would help. "Do you know the Mark Twain quote?" I ask. They don't respond. " 'Everyone talks about the weather, but no one does anything about it.' " Just deadpan. "Hail is like a thief in the night—stealing without warning. But unlike a quiet thief, this one rolled in with full announcement."

Meagan says, "I can tell when you are stressed, you laugh a lot."

"Gallows humor," I say.

This is just wrong. June is supposed to be bursting green and lush, the bounty of the universe in full evidence. This is squalor and violence. Instead of spring-fresh, the air is a stench of decay and rot. I can intellectualize. No one is hurt. We won't starve, go broke, or lose the farm. Many plants will recover. But when I stop distracting myself and notice how I feel, I am vulnerable and exposed, like I have been beaten by a merciless sky and left to survive on my own wits. I know this is just emotion, but I feel completely isolated despite so much support. I look for reality. I know it's out there somewhere. I can't see it. I don't understand the purpose. Maybe there is none. Maybe hail just exists.

A few days later we are working on wagons outside the greenhouse, reseeding broccoli plants to replace the hail loss. "Hey, the birds stopped singing," Meagan says.

I look up. The tree leaves are hanging limp. "It's really still."

"Too still," Sarah says.

The sky looks fine, blue with a few puffy, white clouds. We keep seeding. Then Meagan points and says in a low, slow voice, "Look—west."

A dark, black mass is foaming over the edge of the western horizon. Within minutes the sky is split. Half is brilliant blue, a glorious June day. The other half is dense, airless black, like a curfew curtain, blocking all light and racing toward us. Day switches to dusk as the face of the cloud hits with an explosion. Flats leap off the wagon, spew soil in our faces, and disappear on the wind. The greenhouse plastic snaps violently.

Racing toward us across the neighbor's field is . . . I don't know what it is. It looks like a vertical black wall. We duck behind the wagon as it slams us, a barrage of spinning, pelting, cutting soil. As quick as it hits, it's past, a narrow wall of dirt, racing across the fields.

But the wind doesn't leave with it. It's screaming, a howling tempest. I fix my eyes on the Oak and pray. Please don't take the Oak.

Anything but. We can buy another house, sheds, and tools. We can't buy a three-hundred-year-old oak. Please.

Sarah shouts, "God! It's a twister coming!"

I grab the wagon tongue to steer while Meagan pushes. Sarah throws the pack shed door open, then shuts it as soon as the wagon of transplants is in. We are being battered with sticks and grit; the wind is whipping our hair in our faces. It takes all our focus to stay on our feet. We have no caution for ourselves. There is only the immediate task, the plants and farm to be protected.

We push the last wagon in, and the wind drops to dead still. The cloud blows off, and the light returns. Not a drop of rain. The whole thing didn't last more than five, six minutes. Beyond a few things flying off, I don't think anything is even damaged.

We each go off in different directions to recover alone. I don't know which end is up, if my roots are down, or even in.

All spring I have been showing the crew roots in the greenhouse. "Lush, verdant tops are pretty, but it is the roots that count. If you have outstanding roots, you'll have healthy plants and high yields." Now these roots are being tested. They are the only thing that can pull these crops through, and it's not just the plants.

I think about my own roots. A line of women sprout in a garden row: my mother squatting between vegetables, weeding; behind her my grandmother, forking hay to draft horses; then great-grandma on a wooden kitchen chair, her misshapen feet soaking in a basin of hot water. They continue in a chain, this generational sequence of strong women who gave birth in succession. Women who nurtured and fed life. Women who grew and prepared food.

Not only their lives but also their losses are evident. The challenges they endured. It is an endlessly long row to hoe. I recognize square shoulders on some, muscular thighs on others, a certain stubborn set of jaw, short, sturdy bodies, and wide hips. Some have brown hair and brown eyes, others are blonde and blue, many are gray and stooped. But all of them are familiar. All of them I appreciate as parts of myself.

It is in their hands that they are every one and all the same. Their hands are my hands, small, experienced, strong. The old ones are heavily veined and marked with spots. A few are missing fingertips. There are scars. The young have smooth skin but calloused palms. They reach out with no hesitation. They know what they are looking for, and they know what they are doing. I look at my own hands. I grew up, and they didn't. They are surprisingly sturdy for as delicate as they look.

It doesn't take long before it comes to me. Lots of bad things have happened in my life, and I've always recovered, always come back even stronger. My roots are deep in fertile soil. It won't be the first time they'll pull me through. Somehow I just have to remember this.

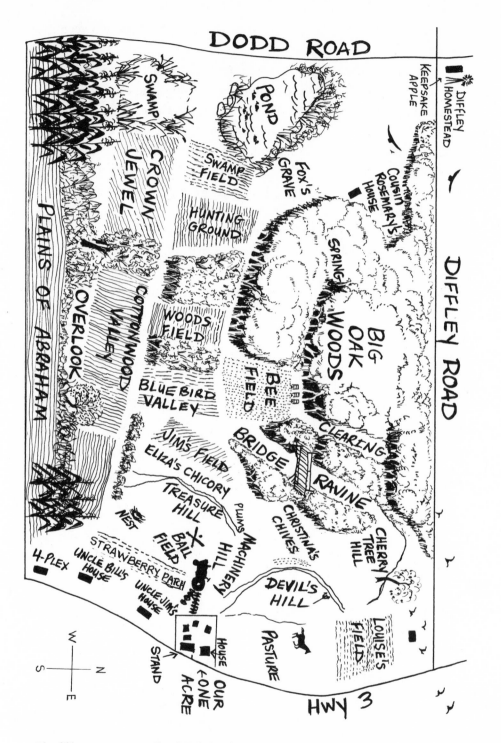

The fifth-generation Diffley family land in Eagan, Minnesota, circa 1985.

My Name Is Tina

My earliest memories are in the garden. Some people say the kitchen is the hearth of their family, and ours is important, but it is between the lettuce and carrots that my mother is most free.

Our spring ritual is following Dad, our feet bare, stepping into his big prints as he steers the rototiller. Birds hop around us pulling worms. Fresh earth spills the first smells of life. He is whistling, happy in his temporary role as family yeoman. Even Mom takes her shoes off and drops her winter cloak of serious. I assume this is how the world works, how people live. Everyone grows plants to eat.

My name is Tina. Not Christina as some people think. My brothers call me Tienie Wienie, and when my mom is mad, she shouts Tinamarie—in one fast word. But really, it's just four letters—tiny, like I feel—Tina. I'm the fourth child of six and in the first grade. We live in a Wisconsin hamlet with a lilac hedge, pear trees, and a catalpa with honey-tipped, orchidlike blossoms. The kitchen garden is out back. Just down the road, across from the church, my parents have a bigger garden where we grow sweet corn and winter squash.

I love elderberries. They grow wild under the trees next to the fields. When I wake up in spring, I smell the flowers before I even open my eyes. When they come ripe, my little sister and I snap them off the bushes and help Mom make jam. I can put one berry in my cheek and keep it there, giving taste, all the way from lunch until supper.

My favorite thing in the whole wide world is rain. When I sense it coming, I go out to the field behind the lilacs, lie faceup on the open ground, close my eyes, and hum. Then it's like god just reaches down and touches my skin. When the rain hits the dirt, it's god's perfume sprayed all over me.

When I look at my heritage, where I come from and who I am, my father's people and family land contain no mystery. Their history is laid out as straight and long as the rows of peas and sweet corn they grow for the cannery, as honest as the robins in the apple orchard beside their house, as wholesome as the cows that call their barn home. That doesn't mean there is no tragedy, no loss. But the stories are open. No one ever whispers. Their history is told with the same breath that speaks of the barn roof taken by a tornado and the cat scratch fever and sulfa shot that put Dad's mom into a coma. The family land is still a Schoofs farm, now in the hands of Dad's youngest brother. The lineage is secure. The only unknown is which of my boy cousins will take it over from their father. I know it won't be one of the girls.

I carry the last name, the Schoofs broad forehead and high hairline, my father's math intelligence. People recognize him in me. They say, "You're Ralph's girl, aren't you?" This is security and an external part of me, but it's an aside of sorts. It's not my rawness. It's not where I am going. And it won't be my name when I grow up.

It is through the maternal that my land lineage and emotional force comes—through my mother, her mother, and before. And here there are loss and secrets, mystery and shame with their opaque cataracts clouding over the family memory.

I watch my mother slip carbon between two sheets of thin airmail paper. Our family's rule of frugality is all-pervasive. "Waste not, want not" isn't just an adage for us—it is our lives, down to the cost of the stamp to send the letter. I am only six years old, but already I want to bust all these rules open, use regular-weight paper, and waste pennies on postage.

My mother is the dutiful daughter, trapped between two angry parents, striving to create an impossible peace. This is where she is least free. At our kitchen table, she is writing a letter to Grandma on the typewriter she received for her high school graduation. It was a big moment when Mom received her diploma. Grandma was lucky to make it to the eighth grade. Many girls in her rural community only got as far as fourth before they were sent out to help on other farms and to send the money home. Grandma loved learning, and she wanted her daughter, her Patsy, to have more.

I look over Mom's shoulder, and my name jumps off the page. "Tina is doing real well in school and is in the best reading group. On one end of the garden the kids have built a farm with hills and ditches and stone fences and grass clippings for hay. They sure play in that a lot. The only trouble is they get so groundy. The kids brought home lots of wild grapes and elderberries this year. I think that one week all I did besides the usual stuff was make jelly. Those fruits are slow to work with. Write once. Are you still so busy? I'm guessing that you're feeling pretty low. With all the ups and downs there are, you're bound to be 'up' pretty soon, hmm?"

These letters are my chief communication with this woman, my grandmother, who ties me back to who I am from. She doesn't have a telephone in her truck camper where she lives in Palm Springs, California, cleaning and serving parties for wealthy people. In our letters we ask her to call us. We just want to hear her voice. She writes back, "I work until 10:00 P.M. That's midnight for you. Three minutes cost one dollar. It is best to write."

The story leaks out between the lines. Grandpa didn't want to be a dirty farmer, lowly slave to the earth. He dreamed of breaking the family bond to physical drudgery through the freedom of the sky. He was going to be a pilot. His first attempt at escape failed when he had to leave high school in tenth grade after his father's death. He was needed on the farm.

His second break came when he married Grandma. They bought a Sears home kit and built a simple bungalow on a lake lot. Grandpa took flying lessons. Then the Depression hit, he lost his job driving a bakery delivery truck, and the flying lessons ended when the money ran out. He was forced back to the land, this time to Grandma's family farm. After that he returned to "just a dirt farmer," and a poor one.

No electricity in their house or barn, farming with horses on eroded clay outside of Kewaskum, Wisconsin. His dreams were grounded. He developed the habit of disappearing for months on end, often during harvest. No one says what the fighting was like. Mom only flinches when I ask. No one knows where he went or what he did. Mom, the eldest of two children, grew up doing the work that he should have. I'm just a kid, but everyone knows it's all hands on board, disputes aside, during harvest.

Divorce wasn't an option my Catholic grandmother would ever choose, and she was a hard-working farmer. The land was where she belonged. Instead my grandparents fought until the day Grandpa left and didn't come back, finally settling across the country in sunny California, land of 1950s dreams and postwar second chances. Grandma went after him in hope of reconciliation. When that wasn't possible, she couldn't come back and face the tongues of the neighbors.

I don't know if Grandma wrote or called. Maybe it was Grandpa, but I can't imagine that. There were still cows, animals that were left behind. I've been told that Uncle Gus, Mom's only sibling, requested a hardship discharge from the air force, where he was following his dream, and came home to care for them. That was before I was born. I picture the cows mooing to be milked, hungry and thirsty, and Uncle wearing flying goggles and a cloth helmet, running like an arrow, as fast as he can, from an airplane to get there. This scene is blurry with shame for me. Everyone knows the animals come first.

When I tell my best friend in first grade that my grandma is divorced and lives in California, I am speaking proud of palm trees and the ocean. I am seeing her packages that smell of coconut candy, filled with dates and citrus, toy puppets, and magic tricks. I am remembering our family trip driving across the country, sleeping in the hotel with a pool where Grandma works nights after her day cleaning job, the feel of saltwater when it dries on my skin, and shrubs pruned into mystical animals at Disneyland. But Karen says, "What is divorced?" I don't know the answer. I don't know anyone else who is divorced, and I don't know what it means. I do know it feels bad.

The word is dirty-gritty, like my mouth is full of ground. We don't say it out loud, and Mom's tears fall and smear the ink that forms the letters on the paper.

The animals are gone now—sold. Uncle lives in Minnesota. Mom manages the books, rents out the farmhouse and fields, keeping it together for when Grandma returns. There is never talk of the farm as Grandpa's. When we go there, we help Mom carry household items to the car, like sheets and towels so mice and bugs won't get in them. She places them, along with the good silver, on a shelf in her bedroom closet to keep safe. We don't use them. They are for Grandma—when she returns.

When people say I am like her, I picture a strong, pragmatic Wisconsin farm woman, like my sturdy aunts, hands gentle with the cows but tough like a mule and strong in the fields. Her clothes are worn and patched, because I know she doesn't have extra money. But she is happy. I claim her as mine in a special way. Really, it's that I proclaim myself as hers.

But the farm Grandma doesn't match with the woman who is maid to wealthy people in hot California and reduced to living in a truck camper. When she finally drives across the country to visit us in August, she is a closed, intimidating woman. She works even harder than my mother. The only time her hands stop moving is in church. They rest quiet on the back of the pew. I can see her veins blue and thick pushed up beneath the skin. They look like roots. They are so beautiful. Mine don't have any veins.

Then one day, while we're pegging wet clothes to the line—my favorite job because I like squeezing the pins—she floats me the highest praise in her repertoire, "You're a hard worker, Tina." I go to bed elated and connected to her warmth, which is the only thing I really want from her. In the morning I run outside to bring breakfast to her camper. The yard is empty. Tire tracks crush the grass and lead to the road. She didn't even say good-bye.

A few weeks later a letter arrives: "Dear Pat and all, Thanks so much for everything, the flowers and apples and vegetables. Every time I wanted to say something I would just break up that last day. I wish I was better at good-byes. A few days ago I watched a grandmother my age leave her family, grandchildren and all, and it was such a rewarding experience for everybody. Why can't I be like that? It seems the only way I can express myself is with money, and that isn't the real thing. I know I'm missing the best part of my life by not seeing the kids growing up. What to do?"

It takes almost a decade, but eventually the divorce is settled. Grandma is sole owner of the land now. On March 3, 1967, she writes: "There is a man from San Francisco staying at the hotel. He said if he could have had children, and would have land, he would never sell it. I felt that way too once, but now that I can't see so good, it's different. At least I can type and think. Sometimes I wish I could stop thinking."

Now the letters are about selling the land. The renter wants to buy. Price and terms are negotiated. Grandma doesn't even come to say good-bye to the farm. We don't go either. After the closing Mom brings home the aerial photograph of the homestead and hangs it on the wall of the den where we play. There's the house and barn in just the right place, and the trees in front, but a fake stack of hay is painted into the pasture, bright sunshine yellow. I want to scratch the lie off the photo with my fingernail, but there is glass in front. I can't get at it. I feel the photo always above me, pulsing, like an open wound, this line to family land severed, this land that witnessed so much pain.

We stand behind Mom while she is typing, "Tell her we miss her. Tell her to come." Mom writes, "Wish you could be up home once for Christmas."

Instead of writing back that she is coming, Grandma encourages Mom and Dad to buy land and a bigger home. "The Scheuers said I should make a gift of the money. That way it stays in the family, and the courts won't get it when I die. When you can save $600 in a month during the peak months, that runs up fast. The other night I added up, and now it's over $50,000. Money that is ready to go. Would you do things different if you knew money was available?"

My parents are hard working and frugal. I lie in bed and hear them discussing. They think they are whispering, but their voices are ringing bells. It has been their dream all along to buy their own land. We all talk about what we want, woods to roam in, fruit trees and acres of gardens, a pond, space for a dog, but Mom wants to borrow from the bank. Family money causes problems. Grandma writes again, "Don't be afraid of losing your soul over money. I feel a trillion times closer to God with $51,000 than when I didn't have any, because he took me every step of the way. I imagine that he is smiling when he looks down on your wonderful project. Amen. I really am not being facetious."

This is a woman with an eighth-grade education who lived her life in poverty. She saved this money working sixteen-hour days with failing eyesight and aching legs, cleaning beautiful homes while she lived frugally in a camper far from the people who love her. I'm a kid; my parents don't tell me about money. I have no idea what happens about that, only that they do buy land and build Mom's dream house with endless closets and a family recreation room in the basement.

Be careful what you wish for. I am thirteen by the time Grandma comes to live with us. We are settled on the new land; our beautiful home sits proudly on a hundred acres in the Kettle Moraine, a jumbled array of ridges and mounds, kettle holes, lakes, and enclosed valleys. My parents have given us the best of both worlds: the economic security of Dad's managerial job, and the space, the connection to nature, and the food security of a farm.

It is summer, and Grandma and I have our chance at mythical connection as we work in my garden patch. She teaches me little tricks, like pruning onions to make them stout. She drives me to the county fair to enter vegetables. I win blue ribbons and prize money.

We sit side by side on the piano bench playing duets. She doesn't read music, just listens to a song and then plays it by ear, thumping giant chords the breadth of the keyboard. My favorite is "When the Saints Go Marching In." I leap around the room waving a handkerchief in the air like a flitting butterfly the way she says they dance in

New Orleans. Mom stands in the doorway looking puzzled. Grandma didn't play piano as a farmer in Wisconsin. When we ask her where she learned, she tells us she dated Liberace in Palm Springs. How cool! Then when she makes the best fried chicken in the entire world, she says Colonel Sanders was her boyfriend and he gave her his secret recipe of eleven herbs and spices. Only three people in the world know it—the Colonel, his mother, and my grandma.

One day we are in the garden, and it starts to rain. Instead of telling me to run to the house, like Mom does, she takes off her shoes. We stand, faces to the sky, tasting the rain on our lips and bodies. Her eyes are closed, and she's breathing deep with the most beautiful smile. She doesn't say it, but I know she's talking with God, just like I do in the rain.

She is still here when the snow comes, but this isn't as we imagined when we stood behind our typing mother pleading, "Tell her to come for Christmas."

Grandma is dying. Of breast cancer. She no longer has any use for her linens and silver, the good dishes we saved. We were able to keep them safe, but not her. When I give her a sponge bath, there are lumps in odd places, under her armpit, on the side of her stomach, growing like a mean fungus, purple and festering. At the end she is wild, screaming about spiders on the wall and demanding scissors. Mom says, "It's not her. It's the pain and the morphine."

In the murky chasm between Christmas and the New Year we fall into silence. Mom doesn't come out of Grandma's room. Outside is thick and overcast. The day barely lifts out of dusk. We kids sit in the living room with books open on our laps, though no one is reading. Halfway through the afternoon I realize someone has to prepare the food, feed the family. I can't think of what to make except orange Jell-O with bananas.

Finally Mom comes out and says, "She's passed." We go in and stand in a half circle around her lying motionless on the bed, her heavy quilt tucked up under her chin. My sisters cry. Mom too. But not the boys. I just feel tiny and quiet. Like I'm watching from the safe inside of somewhere else. I want to reach out of where I am and trace the veins on the back of her hand, just one last time. I'm about to when the ring of Mom's voice stops me. She says, "She found her peace, right at the end."

Dad goes out to the kitchen and makes a phone call. Then men in white suits come clomping up the stairs, leaving a trail of melting snow. They zip her body inside an airless canvas bag and carry it on a stretcher out the front door of our house, the door that only visitors use. We huddle around the living room window and watch as they push her into the back of the ambulance. Big flakes of snow land on the warm hood and become wet spots against the black paint. The men slam the doors closed. The blue, green, and red Christmas lights illuminate our faces. We stand without talking, listening to the engine get quieter as it moves away, until finally it is just a whisper that won't ever stop. Everyone sits at the kitchen table, and I serve the Jell-O in Grandma's good china bowls. No one says, That's dinner? That's all?

But I'm saying it. That's all? That's all I get of her?

I move into her room, ignoring Mom's insistence that I can't. I wear her clothes and sleep in her bed under her quilt. I keep the door locked. Mom is angry, but she doesn't do anything about it except cry.

It's Not Here

I am sixteen now. The Catholic shrine, Holy Hill, is a walk of a mile, a
castle perched on the highest spot, ruling over not only our physical
domain but also our spiritual lives. Our land is a patchwork. We have
planted forty acres of pines and cedars on the low land, have dug a
pond, and have acres of vegetables, grapes, berries, even fruit trees.
There are woods. I am immersed in finding me.

More than five hundred thousand people from all over the world
pilgrimage to the basilica each year, but I can't feel God confined
inside the gilt-decorated walls. On Sundays, I tell my mother I will
walk to Mass. Then I run to the woods, which is where I find spirit,
there in the force of nature. For me, it seems God has to be bigger
than religion.

I am miserable in high school. It is a thick facade I have to pierce
before life will happen. I take an animal science class and am surprised to find it is feed formulas, vaccinations, and artificial in-
semination. I was expecting grass—the green uneven pasture with
rocks poking through where I fetch the cows for milking at Auntie's
farm—fresh air, and the bull that chased me over the fence. When I
imagine farming, I see my mother in the garden, hands in soil, seeds
and compost, plants that end in food.

There is only one thing I think about. Freedom. Which means
many things. It's about thinking outside the box, spirituality not
based on the church, growing food, and owning land. I can't make
sense of any of it, but I know I have to start my own life as soon as
possible. I don't know where my future is. I just know it's not here. I

take extra credits with the goal of graduating early. Finally it's January, and everyone else is riding the school bus but me. I run around screaming until it hits me: without the structure of high school, my life is completely empty. I say to Dad, "Can I study music at the community college?"

He says, "You'd never last."

"Can I get a job?"

"Not until you're eighteen."

That's eleven months away. Am I going to just stay in the house helping my mother with cooking and cleaning? Running away is the survival strategy I learned young from my grandparents. One month after my seventeenth birthday I'm waitressing at Red Lobster with a forged birth certificate and living in Milwaukee.

The food is terrible, both at work and store-bought. It has no life to it. No vitality. Just flat. I have no place to garden where I live. For now, I fill flowerpots and grow what I can. It's not forever, and right now just being free is good enough. But even though I'm the one who left and I'm the one who stays away, I feel like I am in exile. I miss the woods and garden and try to make them up in a park. It's not the same though. Maybe this is how Grandma felt.

All I think about is playing piano and what it will take to buy land and become a farmer. I fantasize myself as some kind of white Thelonious Monk of the fields. I find Anita Koenen through an advertisement for a caregiver position. Born in 1883, she's ninety-six now. On her way out. I'm on my way coming in. We need each other. Her home at the end of Auer Avenue is hidden in a wild oasis of land along the Milwaukee River just a mile from Lake Michigan. This is not a park but an intact ecosystem. Not only native trees and woodland plants, it is full of wildlife—owls, eagles, foxes, turtles. The yard is planted with medicinal herbs. There is a vegetable garden. Anita has an agreement with the Quakers to establish a nature preserve here after her death. For now, it is my sanctuary.

The house and everything in it is of a different era. Her beaded flapper dresses and cloche hats fit as if they were tailored for me. An old canopy is my bed. My writing is done with a bone-handled dip pen and inkwell at a drop-front secretary desk. I listen to big-band swing and jazz music on a hand-crank Edison phonograph. There is only one volume. I crank for fifteen seconds, set the thick shellac disk on the pad, move the needle arm in place, release the brake, and then listen and dance. One side takes a minute and a half. Late at night my favorite is "Tain't Nobody's Business If I Do."

In the attic there are photos of Anita marching in a line of women carrying banners and flags. In their elegant long skirts and wide-brim hats they look like they are headed out for a picnic, but their faces are set. Clearly they will not stop until they succeed. Anita looks determined, but she is always smiling in the photos, like she can already see the results of their effort. My real education is here now. I didn't learn any of this in school. A woman who signs as Ella writes, "We will make a nuisance of ourselves until we win the right to self-representation." The suffrage position is easy for me to understand. "Give the vote to the women of every state in the union by federal constitutional amendment." "Women are capable of understanding politics." "Self-governance is a democratic right."

I never thought about the process before. Suffrage could be accomplished only by a change of the Constitution, and this could only be obtained by the consent of the voters. Women couldn't cast their ballots for the right to vote and run for office. They had to convince the men who could take part in an election.

But the tyranny of the opposition startles me. There are flyers with lists of reasons why woman should not be allowed self-representation: "If women become involved in politics, they will stop marrying, having children, and the human race will die out." "Women are emotional creatures and incapable of making a sound political decision." "Men and women have separate spheres." "Past legislation in Parliament shows that the interests of women are perfectly safe in the hands of men."

I shouldn't be so surprised. I grew up with the message of women's inferiority, only it was masked with religion. I never saw it so openly, and I never thought about the effort it takes to battle it. The flyer that most shocks me into understanding this is "The system works—why change it?"

Works for whom? Women didn't get the vote because it was the right thing to do. Things changed because people worked hard, dedicated their lives. I wonder what Grandma would have said about all this. In the mid-1970s my mom told me she opposed the Equal Rights Amendment: "Women and men are not the same. God did not made them equal."

I was washing dishes. I whipped the washcloth into the sink and stomped off, locking myself in Grandma's bedroom.

Anita is a change maker. She has lived her beliefs and principles, even when it wasn't simple or convenient to do so. This is an entirely new model for me of what it means to be a strong woman. She holds on to who she is and sees herself as valuable, regardless of what other people or society say. She is not an extension of someone or something else. She takes command of her own destiny. Grandma was strong in the field and a hard worker; she made a life for herself in another place when her marriage collapsed. But she let others set her parameters. What I'm learning from Anita is that feminism and environmentalism are about respect and relationship.

There is no pattern here of running away. She knows that her involvement will effect change. I want to be like her. My name becomes Anita backwards: as if moving in reverse from her life ending will shift me into my future, as if carrying her name will infuse me with her self-determination.

She's old now and just wants peace. First thing every morning she drinks a glass of warm water with lemon and eats one fresh comfrey leaf. She claims it is the secret to her age and good health. She isn't interested in talking much. When I ply her with questions about life, she just says, "You'll figure it out." But this morning I am discouraged. I can't see how I will ever create my future. She says, "You have personal power. It's your choice. Use it or give it away."

My time is split between her care, the vegetable garden, and studying jazz piano at the Conservatory of Music. I don't make much money, but it's fine. I follow a simple rule. When I want something, I wait ten days before I buy it, and then if I still want it, I consider the purchase. Usually I don't even remember, and in five months I've got a start at saving.

I love music theory and composition class with its tidy structures to create emotional intensity, but I'm seeing that I relate to music from a mathematical perspective. It's not coming from my soul. Playing music is good, but it doesn't express my spirituality. I am no white-girl Monk. Music is not my mission.

I find a link to a future world I can believe in when I visit a store called Outpost Natural Foods Co-operative on East Locust Street. The display window is hand painted, a mural of rolling hills and a brilliant sun; stalks of wheat flow across the foreground. The front door is locked though the sign says *Open*. Around the corner I find a frizzy-haired guy carrying a stack of produce three cartons high. He shouts over the boxes, "I won't open until this truck is empty." I hop in, hauling cases into a jammed-full back room. When we are finished, he hands me a strawberry and says, "My name is Eddie."

The store is tiny, but it holds everything I want. There's a wall of plywood bins and ceramic crocks full of whole grains and beans. The sign overhead says *Bring your own bags and jars*. A very used produce case holds organic vegetables and fresh, locally made tofu in five-gallon buckets. Eddie is a blur stocking the produce, and he answers my questions without slowing down. He explains that Outpost Co-op started in 1970 with the goal of providing affordable, organic food for the community and economic and ideological independence from supermarket chain stores and the monopolies of giant food conglomerates. Now eight years later, he is speaking from his heart as he says the food co-op is member owned and controlled, adding that volunteers built the bins and shelves and do most of the work. I can join, be a working member, and receive a discount on what I buy.

I had no idea places like this existed. The food tastes real. I thought good food only came from gardens, fields, pastures, and barns.

We meet again when I am hired to play zither for the Milwaukee Area Co-op board meeting. I sit alone on the vast stage of the school gymnasium and play German polkas and waltzes. It's the strangest audience I've ever soothed. Seven men and one woman, seated around a long folding table, set plunk in the middle of a basketball court, eating tofu, brown rice, and vegetables, and arguing. He is the loudest, slamming his fist on the table to force his point. I jump and lose my rhythm every time. Days later he's at my door, shouldering a case of mangoes. He lays avocados, papayas, and plantain on my kitchen table. As a child I knew food as fresh and good and clean. Now I am introduced to exotic and zeal and delight.

We share the same dreams. We want land. We want to feed people organic food. We love co-ops. It all happens so fast. My life moves from I to we. I don't know if it's even an option.

It just is. We pick apples in Wisconsin all fall. The ladder work is a perfect fit for me, up in the trees; this is stretch labor, my arms reaching, the entire world expanding. Sometimes it seems like I am harvesting the clear blue sky gleaming between the branches. I feel like I am on vacation, some kind of interlude between where I came from and where I'm going. The owner puts us in his best trees. We are his most gentle pickers. In the evenings I work the cider room, running the day's ground-fall apples through the press.

When the season is finished, we hitchhike to Florida, where we pick organic oranges as migrants. The pay is piecework, sixty cents a bushel. It's not vacation anymore. We sleep in the warehouse, on the floor of a loft where the packing cartons are stored. Nothing is private. In the day we pack our bedding and clothing out of the way in a corner and cover them with a plastic garbage bag. Everything is always dirty, including me. There is no shower. I don't know where we will be until the boss gives us our pick sheet at sunrise. We drive all over the state working abandoned orchards. Often they haven't been mowed, and we are moving ladders in grass taller then my head. There are snakes. And spiders. Neither of which I minded in Wisconsin, but here I don't know them, which are poisonous and which are not. The rain isn't the same either. It's moldy and sticky, clammy, not fresh and pure. I can't feel God in it.

The honeymoon is over too. I didn't know it would feel like this. Like it's a one-person relationship. Like the me in we doesn't exist. At first I thought we just had to talk and we'd be able to fix it. But talk only turns ugly.

The first time it happens I don't even see it coming. I tell him to leave, and he goes but returns the next morning crying and saying he will never do it again. By the third time something in me shifts, and I believe him when he says it is my fault. Grandma's model is no help. I know what Anita would have done, but she had a strength that I don't, and she stayed single her entire life. Is that where I went wrong? I don't know.

Create your own destiny? I'm just a nobody migrant. I go where I'm sent. Pick and pack what I'm told. I don't really live anywhere. Don't even stay in one place long enough to grow a pot of lettuce. The best part of my life is the other pickers. When Eddie and I fight, they move in around me and erect a shield of humor and presence until the tension de-escalates. I don't know why it is safer to be with big, strong men who have worked hard all their lives and have nothing, but it is.

Spring comes, and the citrus is finished. I thought winter in Florida was humid. April is unbearably heavy and sticky. It's time to head north. Eddie and I rent a one-room cabin surrounded by hay fields and woods outside Polonia, Wisconsin. It's not much, but it's home. There is fresh water from a well right out the front door. I luck out, becoming the produce manager at the Stevens Point Area Food Co-op. The job is the perfect training for someday in the future when I'll be farming and need to know how to meet a produce buyer's needs. I have a garden again.

Actually, it's more of a mini-farm—there is no way we can eat it all. I spend my savings on hundreds of heirloom cultivars, and I experiment with different ways to trellis peas and with heat-catching cloches made from gallon glass pickle jars collected at the college.

I read *The One-Straw Revolution.* Trained as a scientist, Masanobu Fukuoka teaches that the best forms of cultivation mirror nature's own laws. I dig small circles out of the hay field and set three squash seeds in each mound. The land between is left covered, like a living mulch. I feel like I've found my church again.

By fall there are mountains of produce. I market some at the food co-op and give it to friends.

The fighting is still there, and I can't find me in the relationship, but I have a life here outside of us. My own job, a place to call home, friends, and, best of all, my hands in the soil growing food, even feeding others. I think about Grandma. She never expected more than this. Sometimes I feel I am following her path, only making it better. I have a hammer dulcimer, an Irish harp, and musicians to play with. So marriage isn't the happiness I expected. Other things are good. I'm finally putting my roots in. I remember a letter my mother wrote in 1965 to Grandma: "Farming is changing so much these last few years, that I doubt if people will start with small farms anymore. Either they have to work in town too, or they rent land to get enough acres to farm full-time."

Now it's 1982, and my mother's words seem prophetic. It seems impossible to get started. Land prices keep going up; interest on loans is over 15 percent. I have no clue how I will make the leap from gardening to farming, but I'm finding a hold on a start at life.

Then in spring, just when the fall-planted garlic is busting through the winter's crust, Eddie starts to talk about moving to Minneapolis for a produce job at a food co-op. He tells me it's just for a year or two, and we'll build equity. I refuse. I've had enough. He can move but I am not. He and the city are not my future. Freedom is so close I can taste the promise on my lips. But a day comes when I set a glass of water and a sharp knife on the table. He bumps the glass while we are arguing. The water goes flying through the air like light itself, and I hear the glass shatter into a gazillion jagged pieces as it hits the floor.

Suddenly everything is my fault. I am flat on my back, pinned down with his knee pressed into my chest. The shards glitter like jewels all around me. But they are fool's gold, and I've been duped, daring to think I have a right and a voice. From here I should be staring up at the cracks in the ceiling. Instead, I can see the veins on the back of his neck pulsing red and hard with anger, and the empty, ripped hole in his back jean pocket.

I might have Anita's name, but Grandma's blood is coursing in my veins, and she's my childhood model. This is reality. Before long we're driving our old Chevy Apache pickup west, up and down the hills, through the small towns that line rural Highway 10, leaving Wisconsin.

The back is loaded with our homemade banana box furniture. My hammer dulcimer and harp are on the front seat. I'm squeezed in the crack between them and the door, pregnant and barefoot, this crevice a fracture between who I want to be and how I'm going to get there. Right now the only ground I own is sticking to my feet. Two hundred miles takes nine hours. The truck goes into violent speed shimmies if we go over thirty. Maybe this is an omen.

The truck, like me, is moving but not willingly. Every mile the fissure widens, until finally we're crossing the bridge at Prescott, Wisconsin, going over to Hastings, Minnesota.

Under the span the clear waters of the Saint Croix River disappear as they mix with the muddy Mississippi. That's how I feel, holding on to the dulcimer, no longer clear, my dreams lost, drowning in the water that has run off the land and is now draining, full of fertile soil, to the Gulf, where it will be part of a dead zone. This marriage is the rushing current draining my dreams and self. It hits me how it must have broken Grandma to leave her farm and never come back. It seems the longer I live, the better I understand her.

In Minneapolis I have a garden out back. But it's so tiny. I'm barely out there and the work is done. I try not to think about my mini-farm abandoned, the experiments left unfinished. Grandma used to say, "What to do?" That's how I feel now. No wild blackberries to harvest. No hay fields to fill with squash. I miss the open air of the outhouse and the simplicity of one-room living. On warm days I take my hammer dulcimer on the bus to Nicollet Mall and play the lunch crowd for tips. I go for walks, but the sun has a film over it, and the trees don't seem real. I don't belong in the city or this marriage, but I don't know how to get out of either, especially now with a child coming.

This feels like Grandma's story all over again. She was married to a man who didn't respect and honor her as a person. They fought. Then they collapsed. My marriage looks so similar. What's going to happen next? I don't want a child to grow up with this, but I don't want to get divorced either. I thought I was on the right path. How and when did I steer wrong?

I feel like I've been weeded, yanked out, my roots dying in the sun.

The Other Has My Heart

Roots are one thing to recognize—with their hold on the soil, the way they channel life and ancestral lessons, knit communities together. It is harder to find a beginning. Where is that point, that magic line called start? Is it when the seed goes in the ground? When the field is first worked? Way back before there was soil, when boulders weathered into the fine particles of parent material?

Is it when two lines meet?

I had been to the Gardens of Eagan before. Bill, the driver from Roots and Fruits Warehouse, drove Eddie and me out in the new cab-over delivery truck. Before we even pulled in, I knew we had arrived. The sign by the road got my attention. TURN HERE → SWEET CORN. Right away I thought about selling corn on the side of the road with my siblings when I was a kid. How we'd wave at the cars to get their attention. How excited we were when one stopped.

We turned in, and there it was. Bushel baskets of tomatoes flashing red. A table flowing over with sweet corn, leeks, herbs, and greens, the aroma of onions and fresh basil, and everything fresh. I had the door open and had hopped out before the truck even stopped rolling.

I was disappointed the farmer wasn't there. Eddie and Bill stood talking with the roadside-stand clerk, so I went for a walk alone. The farm was real pretty; wild hills with vegetables nestled in the fertile valleys. I smelled a field of rosemary, chives, tarragon, and eggplants before I saw it. Berry brambles, crab apples, plums, flowers, and chokecherries filled any niche. Something about it made me reflect on how long the land had been there. Maybe it was that the fields were small and slipped in, part of the landscape, instead of taking over and dominating like most midwestern farms do. When I got back, I saw the dusty cider press sitting lonely next to an old tractor. My first thought when I saw it was, that press is just waiting for me to give it another chance at life. Then, maybe it's me that will start breathing deep again.

The farmer was named Martin Diffley. I'd imagined him as an old-timer, weathered and grizzly. When I called to ask if I could come out and use the apple press, his voice on the phone was friendly, but it gave no indication of his age.

Meeting him is a different take altogether. Some kind of new breed, he's nothing like the tobacco-spitting farmers I grew up with. I hadn't realized that the clerk was Martin, the farmer. I look at him and think of bluesman Bo Diddley's lyrics, "I may look like a farmer, baby, but I'm really a lover." Only this man is the opposite. It might be more accurate to sing, "He may look like a lover, baby, but he's a farmer." My opinion changes though when our conversation begins.

"Where did you get the apples?" he asks.

"I picked them in yards on the way here."

"We had an orchard across the road, and city people were always driving out to steal them."

"Well just because you had problems with apple thieves doesn't mean I am one. I ask before I pick. And just because I live in a city right now does not make me 'city people.'"

He looks surprised. Maybe I was a little overreactive. "You can back your truck up to the press," he says. He's all business now. "All the parts you need are there on the picnic table. Do you know how to use it?"

It is a simple affair. I can see instantly how the setup works, but he takes the time to explain the process. Pour the apples into the hopper and turn the crank. Apples go through the crusher into the press, cheesecloth on top of the pulp. I am distracted watching his hands as he gestures to the parts, touches the crank, and lifts the wooden plate. They are square and strong. Yet the way his hands curve and communicate with the objects he touches, it's like he's actually feeling them.

I can't tell the difference between a maple and an elm—even standing next to them. But I can spot the form of an apple tree from a speeding vehicle. In the seventeen-mile drive from University Avenue in Southeast Minneapolis to Gardens of Eagan, I've picked twenty-three bushels. Just after I crossed the Mendota Bridge, I found a Wolf River Red. I've never seen one outside of central Wisconsin before, where they were first discovered in 1875, but I'm positive that's what it is. The fruit is five to six inches across in diameter, huge and dark crimson. One apple will make a pie. The flavor has an edge to it, sweet but a bitter hop essence. Makes for real zip. Not just sugar, a piquant impression, stimulating to the mind. The tree was mammoth. I'm guessing close to fifty feet tall, and wide, like a century tree. Only one branch was still alive, but it yielded close to three bushels of fruit.

There is also a heaping basket of what I am quite certain are Keepsakes, my all-time favorite. Developed in the University of Minnesota's apple-breeding program, they are perfectly adapted to this northern state, getting sweeter in storage and staying crisp through to spring. I memorized the location of that tree. A farmstead on the corner of Dodd and Diffley, though from all the suburban development I saw in the area, I don't imagine it has much time left. I tuck the Keepsakes and the Wolf River Reds into the truck cab to keep for winter eating.

The rest are long-forgotten cultivars or the fruit from wild crabs. I pour the first bushel into the hopper, grab the handle, and start to crank. Right away I get hot and take off my bulky sweater. For just a little while I completely forget my life is on hold. While I am pressing apples outside in the sun and wind, I am living true to myself.

Martin comes around the corner, and I see him noticing my belly. "I'm sorry I jumped on you," he says.

"I do live in the city now, but I grew up with an orchard and garden. It was a sin in my family to buy food that could be grown and preserved at home. Besides, I picked fruit as a migrant." Then I stop. "I'm sorry too. I was a little overreactive."

"You did? Where?"

"Apples in Wisconsin, and you are looking at the 1979 Florida Organic Tangerine Queen."

He grins and then goes off to help a customer at the stand. The press is full of ground apples. I slip in the cheesecloth and cover, turn the wheel, and fresh, sweet juice pours out of the spout. It doesn't take long before the crates are empty and the back of the truck is loaded with five-gallon water jugs full of cider. After I clean everything up, I find him sitting on the porch steps playing a weathered Martin Dreadnought guitar. He is singing quietly to himself, "One Has My Name, the Other Has My Heart." The song barely has a melody, more of a drone. When I studied jazz piano at the conservatory, country music was referred to simply as "déclassé." I want to say, "You are what you sing." Instead I hold out a gallon of fresh cider.

"Thanks, but I don't drink juice, too much sugar. It makes me tired."

I sit down next to him on the step, "How long have you been farming?"

"I'm a gardener, not a farmer."

I saw a bunch of tractors out back, far more vegetables than one man could eat, and he runs a roadside stand. Doesn't that make him a farmer? "What's the difference?"

"The level of passion. My relationship with the land, plants, and customers."

"Oh. I guess then I'm not an apple picker but an amateur pomologist." I don't know why, but I feel defiant around him, like I have to challenge him or fend something off. I don't like how cocky I sound.

While we're talking, his hands keep playing, just softer, like they are able to live independent from the rest of him yet harmonize with his spirit. His voice catches the chord change and modulates when he says "land." His hands aren't just playing the guitar. They have a private relationship with it. I grew up around farmers. Their hands were rough, broken mauls. His are smooth and well cared for, full of sensitivity and precision.

"Do you garden?" he asks me. Again his voice resonates with the chord change, this time when he says "garden." It's like he is the chord progression.

"I do, but my yard is so tiny. I want to farm. I want to feed a lot of people." I notice then how he smells of fresh air, corn pollen, tomato leaves, and earth, like he's a compilation of all things vegetable, air, and soil. And there's a faint tinge of engine oil, but it's not repugnant. I'm thinking back to music school. The word *chord* derives from *accord*, in the sense of "in tune with one another." Is that what he is with himself? Me, I'm all about melody. The "idea of the music."

"How did you get to be an organic tangerine queen?" he asks.

He keeps bringing me back to this conversation, like he's responsible for holding the rhythm. "I was joking. Most of the other migrants were big men who had worked citrus their entire lives. They could easily outpick me on grapefruit and juice oranges. When the fruit is hanging, it picks quickly, and the hardest part of the job is running down the ladder with fifty pounds in a sack around your neck. But tangerines have to be cut with a nipper, and they are fragile. My hands were more dexterous. What I lost in ladder time I more than gained in harvest. That's how I earned their respect, and they called me Tina Tangerina, or the Tangerine Queen."

"That's a great story," he says. "In 1973, my first year at the Minneapolis Farmers Market, I was known as Mr. Organatic. When I went in to the market master to sign up, I told him I wanted my sign to read *Gardens of Eagan, Organic.* When I came in mid-July to sell, the sign over my stall said *Gardens of Eagan, Organatic.* The market master had never seen the word before and didn't know how to spell it. I left it up because it started good conversations. People would say, 'Are you crazy about organic?' "

"Are you?"

"Crazy? No. I'm real serious. We don't need to contaminate our children's earth with chemicals. When is it time?"

"Huh?" Is he talking about tangerine season?

"The baby. When are you due?"

"Oh, when the apple trees are bare of fruit and leaves and winter is knocking on the door."

I don't know what to think about this serious-crazy man, an artistic organic farmer-gardener and country musician, with a cider press and chord sensibility, an attitude about city people and apple thieves, food awareness, and sensitive, powerful hands, who smells whole.

And what about me? A well-written melody does not wander aimlessly. Why am I? Why can't I get my life on track?

The next time we meet, I am playing Irish jigs on the hammer dulcimer for tips at the Riverside Café. He comes up in the middle of "Banish Misfortune" and puts a two-dollar bill in my case. Most people give a few coins, a dollar if I'm lucky. I flash him a smile. When I look for him at the end of the tune, he is gone.

Eddie and I go out to buy the cider press. We argue while we are loading. I say it is top-heavy and needs to be tied down. He says I'm making a big deal out of nothing. I sit in the passenger seat staring out of the truck window in a huff. On the way back to Minneapolis it flips out on a corner and barely misses hitting a Jaguar convertible. I burst into tears. Not just the apple press is broken but all our dreams. I think the press can be fixed, as it's just the wooden frame that is cracked, but the marriage is shattered beyond repair.

It is a harsh, windy day in February. I am focused on weighing a sleeping Eliza on the digital scale in the North Country Co-op bulk department when I hear, "Looks like it all came out OK. How old is he/she?"

I turn around and recognize Martin Diffley. "She. Eliza. Chicory is her middle name. Nine weeks, 14.73 pounds, counting her clothes—a little off the charts."

"Chicory. I like that."

"The first thing I sensed about her, before she was even born, was that she has great tenacity and will be strong through life's challenges. I love the bottomless periwinkle blue of the flower. And how sparse and unshowy the plant is. But really, I picked it because chicory thrives in rough soil."

He reaches over, takes the diaper bag off my arm, and asks, "How long was your labor? What will you always remember?"

No man has ever asked me about birth before, and no man has ever noticed my arms were full and took a diaper bag. When most people hear I had a home birth, they say, "You are so brave." He acts like it just makes sense. He follows me through the checkout line talking about the garlic he planted last fall. "On a day like today, I like thinking about the cloves deep in the ground with their little roots set down, safe from the wind, snow, and cold. When the soil thaws, they'll come shooting up. Eager to be alive."

I remember when I used to wake up in the morning and hop out of bed. Eager to be alive. I slip Eliza into a front baby carrier and close my wool coat around her. He picks up my groceries. "Where's your car?"

I point to the baby buggy parked outside the door. It is a beautiful old carriage with a velvet basket and big wheels. I put the groceries and diaper bag in the buggy and wrap a thick, wool blanket around them. I'll keep Eliza warm against my body for the walk home.

"Can I give you a ride? It's a raw day."

On the way he tells me about his Martin guitar. "I first met Jake Monroe and his D28 guitar when I was ten years old. He played blue-grass on the Grand Ole Opry. Then I was able to buy his guitar years later from his widow."

I tell him how I found my hammer dulcimer in Miami from a business card beneath a stranger's couch. I didn't question that I was meant to buy that instrument. This feels just as right. Like we've always known each other and the conversation comes natural. I don't feel defiant like I did when we talked at his farm, just easy and relaxed.

He parks in front of my house. We both reach for the handle of the diaper bag. His fingertips brush the back of my hand. A jolt of electricity tears through my body. My breath goes with it. Eliza wakes up and starts to laugh. It sounds far away, not connected to anything real. I look down at her. For a short moment I don't know where she came from or who she is. I look over at Martin. He is slumped, flaccid against the door. His face is flushed. I smell his sweat.

It's like the whole world just spun, landed in a new place, and my life has been rewritten. Our eyes meet. I thought his were brown, but now they're green, and they have no bottom. Suddenly everything is calm. Like something bigger and stronger than us has everything under control. I can just let go and trust it. It's very short. Confusion crashes down, and I'm on the other side trying to find it again.

He carries the groceries in for me and starts to put them away. We don't talk or look at each other. I'm caught between marveling that he just seems to know where everything belongs, and feeling like I have to say something, anything, just to have sound and dissolve the electricity. Get us back to normal and before. But I don't know that anything can do that. I say, "When I was a kid, I always said I was going to be a hobo or a farmer."

He breathes out, like the sound of words is a relief. "That's funny," he says. "I always said bum or gardener." His voice is high, and he's still avoiding my eyes.

"Actually, I said farmer's wife. I didn't understand then that a woman could be a farmer in her own right." He smiles. I notice my shoulders relaxing.

"Of course they can," he says. "The way I saw it, bum or gardener, they both spent all their time outside and it didn't matter if they got dirty."

My breath comes a little deeper. "And they both had independence and ate out of gardens." I sound so eager. I just want this to be an ordinary conversation between two people with common interests. Life is too complicated. "Do you really think of yourself as a gardener? You seem like a farmer to me."

"Gardeners have relationships with nature, land, and people. Farmers get so caught up in making a profit and maintaining their image that they lose the connection."

"Gardening is putzy," I say. "I want to feed others, and I want to stay in relationship with the natural world. Isn't that what organic farming is? But what do I know? You've done it. It's just a fantasy for me. I know how to garden, not farm, and now that I'm a mom, getting started seems impossible."

"Gardeners feed people too. When I was growing up, Eagan was full of market gardeners who delivered food to the Twin Cities."

"I believe organic farming can work, but I want to know it beyond a doubt," I say. It's like everything important to me is just spilling out.

"I just sold my equipment."

My heart stops. Who is this man if he's not a musician-farmer? For a sound configuration to be a chord, it must have duration. "Why?"

"I've been running the Gardens of Eagan for ten years and where did I get? I'm burnt out and in debt. I know organic works. It's making a living that I haven't been able to accomplish. I can sell everything I grow, but it's cutthroat. In the winter I teach barbering and cut hair, in the summer I do construction, and year-round I'm up until three A.M. playing gigs in smoky bars on the weekends. I fit gardening in between. I'm not making a living, and I don't get much sleep. I'm going to take a year off or more, be a bum for a while, and have more time for music. I don't know if I'll farm again. I've rented some of the fields out to Faye Jones, and she's bought my Super A tractor. She has worked for me and other farmers for two years now and wants to start her own business. The rest of the land I'll plant to hay and give it a rest."

"I can't believe you just quit. Five months ago you were the proprietor of a roadside stand. How can you just stop? Hey, just now, you called yourself a farmer."

"Well it's the farmer that quit, the gardener lives on, and I'm not a blood farmer."

The way he defines it, blood farmers go through disasters, family tragedies, economic upheavals, whatever hits them, all to maintain their farming vocation. His family believed in preserving the land not just as a farm but also as a community. They stayed out of chemical agriculture because they could see it becoming corporate. They saw the death that it spreads, not just because pesticides are toxic to life but because they saw how the commodity monoculture system

decimates a community. If they couldn't market direct and have relationships with people and the land, they weren't interested in farming.
"A blood farmer loves farming more than the land. I love the land more
than I love farming. It's more important to preserve it than farm it."

"Maybe growing food on it is one way to preserve it. You are living on one of the last farms left in Eagan, aren't you?"

By the time we say good-bye our conversation sounds natural
again. It doesn't feel that way though. His last words are, "Good luck
with your garden next summer."

After he's gone, I put Eliza to sleep then go down to the basement
and scream. I don't want to feel this when I'm not free. I know my
marriage with Eddie won't ever be healthy no matter how hard I try.
We got together because we both love organic produce. I believed
we were meant to work together, and that might still be true, but I've
known for a long time it isn't as a family. I go to bed sick with confusion. It's day three before I hear Grandma's voice repeating in my
head, "Don't follow my path."

But it's not easy to get out, especially with an infant. The word
is still dirty-gritty. Good women don't get divorced. I'm starting to
understand what it means to be codependent. I'm sure everything is
my fault, and I need Eddie's permission to live my own life. Everything is confusing and complicated. He comes home with a sky blue
1967 Ford Custom 500 that he bought from Martin. I keep saying,
"This marriage is not working. It isn't healthy for Eliza or us. It never
will be."

He says, "We have the perfect relationship; we just need time
away," and insists we go to a cabin for the weekend. We try talking
for two days. Now it is Sunday night, twelve degrees below zero
with a hard wind. We are driving back to the Cities, silent, watching
the ditches for deer, when the fuel pump goes out. It is almost ten
o'clock. There is no place open to buy a new one. This is how my life
feels, cold and stranded. I can't see a way to fix anything anymore.
We walk to a convenience store to keep Eliza warm, and Eddie calls
Martin for advice. "I have a spare pump here," Martin says. "I'll come
up and put it in for you."

I don't know how he gets here so quickly. He has tools and the part. He installs it as quickly as changing a battery, won't even let us pay him, just says, "The car came with a guarantee. I just want you to be safe."

We don't look at each other. He follows us south on the freeway until we come to the split of I-35E and I-35W. Eddie and I fork west toward Minneapolis, and Martin goes east to Eagan. All I can think is, I am in the wrong car, going the wrong direction, but it's too late now to do anything about it. The license is signed. The cars are moving. I'm just a passenger, not the driver of my own life.

I am sitting at the edge of a folk dance in the upstairs hall of the People's Center. Eliza is an active one-year-old, wiggling on my lap, excited by the fiddle music and the bright, twirling couples. I'm trying to work her arms and legs out of a thick snowsuit, but she isn't holding still. I love dancing.

After a good night of music and spinning, I am happy for days. And I have the right outfit for it. A handmade bright-turquoise square dance dress with the perfect whirling skirt—comes with a good story too. I was in St. Louis visiting the Heart of the Beast River Tour crew. We were spending the night in a host woman's home, and she said to me, "You look just like I did when I was your age. I have a dress I want to give you."

Eliza loves to fly on the music as much as I do. I turn to set her snowsuit on the chair next to me, but it's not empty. Martin is there, wearing black slacks and a shirt that's the couple's match to my dress, handmade also and the same bright-turquoise fabric. Eliza reaches over and traces the braiding on the Western lapel. She beams at him and babbles. He grins back and rubs her cheek with the tip of his fingers. She is in the not-so-sure-about-strangers stage, but she acts like she's always known him. I'm so surprised to see him that I don't know what to say. "Where did you get that shirt?"

"In Babb, Montana, from a lonely widow trying to buy a bit of company with her deceased husband's clothes," he says. Maybe I look confused. "I got the shirt and got away. She didn't get her night with me."

He doesn't ask about my dress or even seem to be surprised that we just happen to be at the same folk dance in outfits that make us the best-matched and most visible couple in the building. He waits patiently while I give Eliza her spin to the music and then nurse her. When she's asleep, I tuck her into the buggy. He takes my hand and moves me out to waltz. The floor is ours. Couples part when we are near and leave a lane always open. The electricity isn't a jolt but a steady voltage with a strong beating pulse.

I think about Anita and what the suffragists faced. *The system works— why change it?* Is that what this is about? It is working for Eddie but not for me? Which means if I want something to change, I'm the one who has to make it happen. What about Anita's lesson on respect and personal power? Here I am unhappy that I'm not being respected, but the bottom line is that by staying in the relationship, I'm not respecting Eliza or myself. I've been giving up my personal power so long now I don't know what it will look like to take charge of my own life. But staying in this marriage isn't going to make it clear. I have to take the step.

Those letters: November 30, 1968. "Dear Grandma, We got two inches of snow on Thanksgiving. I made a snowman and named it Eddie, but it collapsed. The snow did not melt yet."—Tina Schoofs

My siblings just wrote their first name on the letters. But I wrote both, first and last. Right now I don't know who I am, and I don't understand how the world works, but this is too uncanny. Eliza was born on November 30, fourteen years after I wrote this letter to the grandmother who collapsed. So the marriage with Eddie broke, but I made the snowman, and I named him. I'm in charge here. I'm not going to break, and if Eliza is the snow, she won't ever melt.

As soon as the divorce paperwork is clear, I buy a four-month round-trip ticket to Ireland. My life is so off track. I have to go away and start all over, the span of an ocean between my past and me. I need to climb to the top of a mountain and sit in the fire of loneliness until it doesn't burn anymore. Take all the false dreams and ideals that Eddie and I used to cushion our lives and our marriage, tear them into tiny shreds, and throw them into the wind. I need to be completely finished before starting anything new. If I ever get married again, it is going to be healthy, and I won't give myself up.

But right now, I don't even know who I am, much less where I'm going.

Martin and I meet to talk at McDonald's on University and Snelling. We figure that nobody either of us knows would go there. Eliza is happy in the playground. When she's older, she'll likely claim deprivation because her parents never took her to the Golden Arches. I'll be able to say, "Your parents took you there, just not to eat."

He says, "I knew we were going to be something the first time I saw you, hopping out of the Roots and Fruits truck while it was still moving."

"But I was married."

"Not really. And not for long."

"I was pregnant."

"I like children."

"I didn't even know you were you yet."

"You just weren't looking." He chuckles, "I knew for absolute when I saw you flying on the cider press crank."

"I'll be back in four months."

"I waited thirty-five years for you. I can wait a little longer."

"I don't imagine a fellow as charming as you has been any too lonely while you waited."

He just smiles. I'm trying to take this real slow, but it's something way beyond my control, something even more determined and full of life than spring.

Forward through Fire

I must look a complete pauper at Shannon Airport, or maybe they are thinking the ships have reversed and the immigrants are returning. It's me, pushing the hammer dulcimer in a giant plywood box on rollers, with Eliza sleeping in a baby carrier on my back, our clothes in a home-sewn duffle beneath her seat. We are taken into a tiny windowless room. There are two customs agents. I am told to seat myself at a small table; one sits across and questions me, the other leans against the wall and watches my face from the side.

Mr. Customs 1 says, "Open the case," then looks surprised when he sees eighty-one strings. What was he expecting? Drugs? If he only knew! "Show me your money." His eyebrows scrunch when I lay 125 U.S. dollars on the table. "Where are you going to sleep?" he asks. I point to the tent tied to the back of the baby carrier. "What are you going to eat?"

"The child nurses. I know how to eat well without a lot of money." He makes a sour face when I say my ex-husband is going to mail a check for $137 each month. What I don't say is I have seeds tucked in my socks. I just need a little soil. In a month we'll have lettuce greens, beets, even first radishes. In fifty-one days we'll have peas. Wrapped in a cotton skirt and hidden under the dulcimer are kohlrabi and broccoli transplants. I say, "Oatmeal and potatoes are cheap."

He scoffs, "And what if the check isn't sent, missy?"

I show the divorce decree and point at the child support listed. "He'll send it." I can't go back. Only forward. "I grew up in a frugal family. I'll eat seaweed and periwinkles if I have to."

Now they add nuts to pauper. Frugal is spelled p-o-o-r here, and seaweed is linked to famine. Periwinkles have some credibility if you live on a beach, but even so, they are "poor man's escargot." Mr. Customs looks at the paper again. I hear him say, "periwinkles," low and quiet like—to himself. They sound delicious rolling off his Gaelic tongue. His cheeks have blushed, and I realize he's not here but somewhere on the Irish coast, barefoot in the sea breeze with someone he liked very much, long ago.

I know we're in now. Eliza wakes, lifts her head, and stares at him. She is a beautiful child, big eyes, irresistible smile, round pink cheeks, and blond hair. She starts to cry—her hungry voice—but I don't want to nurse with these two staring. We come to terms. I agree to report each month to a police station and show I have enough money. I sign a paper saying I won't collect the Irish dole or work illegally. They open the gate. We're in.

The first night the tent rips in a heavy, blowing rain. I set Eliza on the mat under my curved body to keep her dry. She never even wakes up. The dulcimer is safe in the case—it's OK. I locate an empty Irish cottage, dangling over Dingle Bay, on the side of Mount Eagle, surrounded by thousand-year-old stone beehive huts. It's almost all the way out to Slea Head on the coast at Glen Fahen, meaning Fairy Glen, a small curve in the road where a stream crosses over surrounded by ferns and brambles. The owner says, "No." But I don't go away. I just stand there, eyes asking, Eliza in my arms. Finally he says, "OK."

I immediately reply, "I can afford $40 a month."

It's been empty for years, since the old bachelor who spent his entire life here died. There's a fireplace on the west end that doesn't draw well. I keep the door open in all weather for air and light. His things are still here, a couple of teacups and a cracked Belleek china bowl, three mismatched plates, and an aluminum pot large enough to boil two eggs or one cup of tea. In the loft is a box of old papers, letters, and photographs from America. His tweed suit stands stiff in the corner. I tell Eliza not to play with it.

For drinking, keeping food cold, and wash water, there is a lovely, fast-moving stream just down the hill. There are no trees. Collecting dead berry brambles, dried donkey dung, and weeds for heat and cooking is a daily chore. The yard is rocks and tough grass. Eliza and I carry soil in from anywhere we can scratch dig it. My scarf serves as portable bucket. We pile a raised bed on the south side of the shed against the rock wall. The rocks hold the heat. The wall keeps the wind off. I lay old windows over the seeds to germinate, and by the end of the week we have new sprouts sending down their roots.

Mostly we are just here—hanging on to the side of this mountain. Every few weeks I walk or hitch the ten miles to Dingle for oatmeal and eggs from Fitzgerald's, carrots and potatoes at the green grocer, and fresh mackerel for a quarter each off the fishing boats in the bay. Picking wild blackberries in every hedge fills the months July and August. Our one luxury is Irish wool yarn, flecked with color like sunshine. The coast is right there, but it's a treat when we go, as it's hard to reach, there's a cliff, and I have to walk a long way with Eliza on my back. At low tide we gather dulse and carrageen. Eliza loves collecting periwinkles in a little basket woven from the tall grass that grows next to the stream. She looks real sweet, piddling about, seaweed caught between her toes and seagulls screaming around her. All the way home she licks salt off her arm.

Sometimes it feels like there are three of us here—Eliza, me, and the hammer dulcimer.

Other times I feel completely alone. Stark. Cutting. Loneness. I want to hike to the top of Mount Eagle and soar into the Irish sky. I put Eliza into the backpack carrier, load food and water, and set off for the summit. Halfway up I'm sitting light-headed on a rock. I don't understand it. The peak is not that high, only seventeen hundred feet, nor is it steep. I am a strong woman. But I have nothing now—just this weight on my shoulders. I try again when it is cool and overcast. High up the flank the fog closes in. I can't see a foot in front of me, but there is a stone wall. I edge forward slowly, my hand tracing the rocks—suddenly it is gone. Just ends. Life has no guide.

Maybe I'm at the peak, maybe not. There is no way to know. I don't dare go farther. I'll lose our way. The fairies will nab us. We'll never get out of here.

No soaring for me. I sit with Eliza in front of the cottage, knit wool socks for her little feet, and watch the green hills kissing the blue water. What I love the most is the black slate roof, especially when it is glistening wet. It is the most God-beautiful place on earth, which makes me even lonelier than one. There isn't even a full me here.

I know I have to do this. It's only after I've faced myself that I'll be able to start again, but it is the hardest thing I've ever done. There is nothing now between me and I, no one else to blame, no fighting to distract. It's just my patterns and me and loneliness. I sit in the fire of emotion for what feels like forever, until gradually the heat diminishes. By the time the four months pass, I have a start at seeing myself as good again.

When I step off the plane onto American soil in Baltimore, I have one uncashed check and a quarter in my pocket. I use the coin to call Martin from an airport phone booth. I just want to hear his voice.

Past in the Present

Martin says, "It was at my father's wake in 1972. My Uncle Aubrey said, 'You should move home now and help your mother with your father's businesses. While you're there, you could grow pumpkins and Indian corn, like back when you were a kid.'"

We are lying on the side of the hill behind his house, soaking in the late fall sunshine. It was a simple question I asked, "How did you get started farming?" I knew that his great-grandparents settled this land in 1855. But I didn't realize the answer to my question would go back to them. He says, "Being close to the cities, my ancestors had a vendor's route in Saint Paul, selling vegetables and eggs, firewood, and hay. It was a day's work for them to drive a horse and wagon in—sell and deliver."

Now with cars and the freeway, it is a twenty-minute drive, but I'm starting to learn that a conversation with Martin is more like a horse and wagon than a motorized vehicle.

Tom, Bill, Jim, and Mary were the third generation of Diffleys who lived with their families on the land when Martin was a boy in the 1950s. But his father was a barber and a carpenter, not a farmer. Known as "Tom the Barber," he ran a shop from the front room of the house he built for his French Canadian city bride, Corinne. As their family grew and needed more space, Tom moved his barbering to an art deco room off the garage. Then for a while, he cut hair in a converted city bus that he moved daily on a rotating circuit. Later, he ran his business out of the four-unit apartment building that he built on the land, and sold gas in the front.

Martin is laughing as he tells me family stories of his dad running out to pump gas, straightedge razor in hand, leaving a customer in the chair half-lathered. I ask, "What does that have to do with you becoming a farmer?"

"The barbershop, the rural equivalent of the local men's club, was my day care. Sweeping up hair, I learned the history of most every farm in the community, how the families were related, what crops were grown, and how they were marketed."

Then he tells me that as a carpenter, his dad built houses on the family land along the road and rented or sold them. Like the barbershop, it was Martin's true education. Helping his dad build, he learned carpentry and tools. He learned to read by searching the want ads to furnish the apartments. He learned to negotiate listening to his dad buy and sell. "Our home was a roadside distraction. Not just the barbershop but also the energy of the place. There was always something for sale out front, usually vehicles or things on wheels."

Finally he tells me how his dad's brothers, uncles Bill and Jim, were responsible for the farmland. They had dairy cows, hay, grain, and market vegetables. In the mid-1950s they sold the cows and put the land into an Eisenhower-era soil-bank program for set-aside. As a boy, he had free run on family land that was resting. He grew up in the oak woods, on glacially deposited kame hills, in fields thick with bromegrass. He absorbed the stories of the land and the family, their values, beliefs, and the ancestral lessons. Eagan and Inver Grove were still full of truck gardeners who produced on the urban edge and sold their produce to Twin Cities' grocery stores and farmers markets. He worked for them in the summer, weeding and harvesting.

"It was the best of all worlds. I grew up in relationship with the land, and each relative, neighbor, and plant had a different thing to teach me. I was the family gardener as a child. There was nothing I loved more then digging in the soil. Some kids had animals in 4-H, I raised vegetables. My mother canned, and I sold the surplus from the side of the road and at my aunt and uncle's grocery store."

What would I be like if I had grown up on my grandmother's land, surrounded by relatives? In contrast to Martin, I feel like an orphan, until he tells me Aunt Mary's story.

Born in 1900, she was the self-appointed keeper of the family's history. She taught Martin how to grub a tree and how to store root crops in a dugout so they'd make it through the winter. She showed him where the fresh springs were, and the wild apples and berries, the mushrooms, herbs, and nuts. She was also a lieutenant colonel, serving in World War II as head nurse in General Patton's army.

Her life changed forever the day she walked into Dachau concentration camp with the liberating forces. It was her job to do a health assessment of the survivors and find food from what local farms still remained. She told Martin that most wars were fought over soil. While walking the family land with Martin, she challenged him, "Feel what this land gives to us? Imagine what it would mean to be landless, to be denied a homeland, a right to your family and culture, and all dignity as a human." She showed him pictures she took those first days in Dachau. Anytime Martin complained about something, she put it in perspective. She told him about people without shoes, without a home, parents, or freedom. People who were segregated and degraded, disenfranchised not only as citizens but as human beings, and murdered.

While he's telling me this, I am not picturing the Jewish people whom Aunt Mary was describing, but the Dakota people who lived on this land before—people who were denied their homeland, their rights to their family, spirituality, language, culture, and all dignity as humans.

He comes back to the start, telling me how he moved home after his father's death to help his mother. He was there on the land that he knew. The historic Russian grain deal was happening. U.S. Secretary of Agriculture Earl Butz was saying that high grain prices were here to stay. American farmers were "feeding the world." Land values doubled in one year. "Get big or get out" was the driving mantra. Everybody came around asking to rent the land. Uncle Jim told him, "The last time we rented this land out, the tenant plowed through the ravines and waterways, and we had major erosion. That's why we put it into soil bank. I'm kind of leery of opening it up again. It's your turn to take care of it."

Martin had always wanted to be a market gardener. Now he had the chance and the teachers. Uncle Jim taught him how to lay fields across the hills so they wouldn't erode and how to make a fine, moist seedbed with a digger and drag. Aunt Mary showed him where to avoid the rocks, which fields grew the best potatoes, which made it through the drought in the 1930s. Uncle Bill taught him how to weld and helped him repair his first tractor, an International Harvester Farmall H. "Through them, I gained one hundred years of experience," Martin says. "How each part of the land will react in different weather conditions. It's like folk wisdom passed down."

Then he tells me about the day that Uncle Bill took him to visit Great-Grandfather William's grave and told him, "You're going to be dead a lot longer than you'll be alive, so make your life count for something."

We're soaking in the warm sun, but when he says this, a chill runs down my backbone. It's like his Great-Grandpa Will just sat up in his grave and handed Martin the responsibility for the land's legacy. It feels like a burden as well as a gift. "That's how I got my start," he says. "Agriculturally I was in the right place at the right time, different track. Instead of scorched earth, I was looking to nurture life. While everyone else was ramping up, pouring on the fertilizer, I was asking my relatives and neighbors how they did it before the chemicals, figuring out how to do it organically."

"In 1973, when I started selling at the Minneapolis Farmers Market, mainstream grocers were still backing trucks up to the market loading docks and buying produce. The food wasn't marked local in the supermarkets. It just was. The natural food co-ops were getting started, and they were coming to the farmers market to buy. Organic wasn't a universal ideal in the early food co-op days. A fair return for farmers and whole foods grown with ecological principles smashed head-on with the ideal of cheap food for the working class. I had the opportunity to educate them about organic and develop a delivery route. I bought my parents' one acre and the family home. My relatives own the farmland. I take care of it. I can't say how long it'll last."

He pauses and takes a deep breath before he continues. "Eagan has no land left zoned for agriculture. This land has survived droughts and storms and nurtured four generations of Diffleys, but when the sewer and water assessments come through, it will force them to sell." Then he pops the question, "Do you want to garden with me?"

"Garden or farm?"

"Don't get caught up in semantics."

"Well, there is a difference. Garden, yes, but I wouldn't be able to make a commitment to farming. Eliza comes first."

This is a huge conflict for me because I know he means growing for market, which is exactly what I want for myself and the childhood I want to give Eliza. But I haven't figured out how to do it and support her financially. I want nothing more than to say yes, let's go farming, but then I ask him, "Do you want to farm together?"

He says, "No, there's no money in it. I've enjoyed this time as a hobo. I played a lot of music, and I want to go to Montana in August."

We have this conversation like a repeating chorus. The only chord change is variations on the excuse. I don't know if we are both afraid of commitment, playing hard to get, or just confused, but we are doing the dance that two lovers do when their step is out of time. As strong as the pull is between us, I feel like the woman his father cursed him with when he was a wild teenager. "Someday you'll marry a German woman, and she'll whop you into shape."

I know how to work hard and live on nothing. But I'm not willing to be this man's whip, and all he talks about is history—agricultural, musical, his family's legacy, the land's, and the community's. I'm all about the future and where I'm going. Could we ever meet in the middle and work in the present?

Spring's Fault, 1985

It's spring's doing that people jump into farming and gardening. Every time I am in the field or garden, there is one plant or insect, one leaf or flower, one line or shape that jumps out from the rest and catches all my senses with the profound beauty of its lovely self. It might be a simple cabbage plant—round leaves, plump from an evening's rain, red veins transparently glowing—or a long stalk of dill aslant in its garden slot like the leaning tower of Pisa, leaves, ferny sprays of lacy greenness, yellow flowers buzzing with pollinators.

Sometimes it's not the individual but the balance of the group and the symmetry of the whole. The plants and insects creating a microcosmic bio-network of green lines and curves, accented by color shades and seeds, each with a unique purpose and nutrient system. It can be a full minute of deeply breathing the essence of nature. Other times it's a subtle flash that carries on inside me, soaking into my cells and tissue. These moments are the food of my soul.

Here I am, standing in the garden, the tough skin of a kohlrabi falling to the ground as my knife cuts around it. I'm thinking, it's wonderful that I feel so hungry and I can enjoy this simple nourishment. My hunger is the sauce that heightens the purity of this simple vegetable. My hunger is now, and this kohlrabi is the gift.

I call Eliza from her game of "pioneer," gathering twigs for kindling, which she piles next to her "log cabin," a brown scarf spread on the ground. "C'mon, Eliza, hop in. We're going to dig some chives."

You know—happy day. Everything is right. The birds are screaming with spring joy. The trees are covered with catkins and buds, that almost here, ready-to-erupt tension. Bright yellow dandelions are polka dots of sun, beaming their light, color canceling the long gray winter with yellow essence, a nutrient for wellness as essential as any food.

We drive out to the herb patch. The chives have gone to seed, and the entire bed is germinated thick with two-inch seedlings. Eliza hops right to work filling the flats with empty peat pots. She's only two and a half, but she's an eager and focused worker. Using a spoon, I dig circles of baby chives and tuck them into the pots. Gardening? Farming? I don't care. My hands are dirty. I'm outside. Eliza's happy and healthy. Roots and Fruits, the co-op produce warehouse in Minneapolis, has ordered twenty flats at $10 each.

It is my first sale. I had the idea, made the call and the deal. Won't Martin be surprised when I show him the check! I had no idea it would be so easy, already an order for $200. It doesn't take long with Eliza helping. We have the flats loaded in the trunk and backseat of the '66 Ford, drive to town, drop them off, and are back before 10:00 A.M.

Martin comes home with truckloads of goat compost from Bobbie Mueller, who grew up next door in a house Martin's father built. As boys, Martin and Bobbie rode horses all over the Diffley land together. Now Bob and his wife raise goats two miles away. We string wires across the field and drive the truck straddling the center, shoveling in lines five rows at a time. My arms are strong, my body a machine. I feel as if I was made specifically for this work and the act of growing food. Martin laughs at me when I babble like this. "You are waxing eloquent," he says.

"Your prayers have been answered; all your problems have been solved. You don't need a tractor, you have me." When he chuckles at that, I say, "Don't laugh, I am the best thing that ever happened to you."

He stops teasing and says, "That's true."

After it's spread, I go over it with the only motorized tillage equipment he didn't sell, a Montgomery Ward garden tiller that his parents gave him for his twelfth birthday. When it's time to plant, we set two wires, twelve inches apart.

Martin calls this a European double row. He learned it in 1977 on a tour of organic farms in France, Germany, Austria, Switzerland, and Holland led by Eliot Coleman. There wasn't much happening yet in the United States, but Europe was decades ahead, and many of his organic systems are based on that trip. When I ask him to tell me the most important thing he learned there, he says, "Soil conservation in Europe is a century ahead of us. In the United States we still think of land as an endless resource, as if there is still more west of California."

With a six-prong dibble, he moves next to the wire, making holes. I move behind, bent at ninety degrees, slipping onion transplants into the slots just as fast as he makes them. I can feel the roots, crisp and alive against my forefinger as I push them down into the loose earth, then squeeze soil close around the bulb. I test one with a gentle tug. This onion is home, where it belongs. It will be growing in no time. I'm starting to feel the same way.

My feet are bare; dust coats the soles. There is the wind on my sun-warmed legs. It caresses the hair and dries the sweat. At the end of each day, the work is laid out behind us. We can see what we've done and what is left.

It is eleven days now since I sold the chives. Eliza and I are at the kitchen table feasting on beans and rice, smothered with olive oil and fresh chopped chives, when the phone rings. It is Lori, from Roots and Fruits.

"Hi, thanks for calling." I hope my voice doesn't show how excited I am. "Are you ready for more?"

"No, there is a problem. They are dead."

"They looked great when they left here."

"I pulled some out of the pots, and they had very little for roots. I'm sorry, but we can't pay for them."

All air leaves me. I am just a single mom with her daughter sitting

ns and rice, not the successful farmer expecting
id I do wrong? Will she ever buy from us again?
ing career on the first sale?

can't remember if I even said, "Thanks for calling."

get up at sunrise and load the pickup—a spool of
takes and hoes, watering cans and seeds.

n to emerge out of the community. A neighbor
s and peppers. Martin comes home with a trunk
plants, and lettuce. He says he sold his equipment,
lling some interesting and useful device out of a
mes attached to a long story about where it came
ost or who made it, though I can't keep track. Every
object are somehow related to each other, either by
ighbors, or all three. I think all he really sold is his
spect it won't be long before he brings one home.
tly pulling into the yard with machinery borrowed
eighbors, or is sort of buying—sort of, because every
cated relationship that seems to span decades, mul-
l repeat equipment transfers. Money is not necessar-
could be labor or a spare part, future produce or an
I learn it is the second or third time the piece is in his
etimes it was his uncles' or grandfather's.

k him about this, he tells me his grandfather had a
p on the farm and held two patents for a check valve
pumping windmills. That sounds like the end of the
goes on, saying that Uncle Bill and Uncle Jim bought
r and acetylene torch in Eagan; then the war broke out,
ouldn't buy new equipment. There was so much need
l fabrication that Bill and Jim couldn't get their own
d would trade fieldwork for welding. They thought the
slow after the war ended, when farmers could obtain
ent again, but then they were busy converting horse-
ment to hydraulic systems for tractors. Jim would work

out repair deals where his payment would be the right to use
equipment, and some of the use seems to have passed down to N
tin as an inheritance. Most of these families are gone now.

Their land is developed into housing tracts. Their children liv
the suburbs and cities. Some of the old-timers hang on with a
time right to remain in the farmhouse until they die. The house
on land trimmed down to a suburban lot, with the barn and
buildings, the animals, garden, and fruit trees cut off like ex
waste. When they are lucky, there are enough trees left around
house to block the view of what is happening. One old veget
grower said to me, "When they started to bulldoze, I just felt li
would vomit. Now with the leaves, I can't see what they are do
which makes it OK."

I can imagine I'd feel the same way, wanting to vomit, but I d
think I'll ever say it is OK. When the time comes for this land to
destroyed, I don't plan to stick around and watch.

Today, when Martin pulled into the yard with an onion so
from Otto Holz, I wondered if he is gathering up the last pieces
way of life before it is gone. He talks about the coming day when
land will be sold for development like it's inevitable and he's po
less to stop it, yet he doesn't seem to connect that to leaving him
to moving. When I suggest he look at land elsewhere so he is re
when it happens, he just brings home more. Perhaps the equipm
is his defense fortification.

But he also brings home symbols, and new life, and welcon
inclusion into his world. Today it is in the form of a chicory pl
carefully wrapped in an old burlap sack and tucked safely out of
wind in the back of the pickup. He lifts Eliza up to see. She recogn
it right away even though it doesn't have flowers. When I sho
them to her on my parents' land in Wisconsin, I pointed out
tough, grooved, and hairy stem, and how the leaves are drawn-
lobes. She knows without being told that it is hers. She and Ma
plant it on the west slope of Treasure Hill above Jim's Field whe
overlooks Bluebird Valley.

In the evening—when we run out of plants—none of us wants to go inside. We take off walking the farm, which is a history lesson and a geology tutorial of glacial impact. Each place has a name, like it's a member of the Diffley family.

The Ball Field behind the house is one of Martin's favorites. I don't know if it's the memory of the baseball diamond he and his siblings had here, or the rich, fertile loam washed down from the hill and trapped in the valley, but he claims it has never failed him. As we cut across, leaping sideways over the rows, he tells me, "One year I grew Lady Godiva naked-seeded pumpkins here. I hauled the pumpkins in a dump truck down to Stanton, where the Northrup King seed research center separated them for me. Then I dried the seed on racks. My timing was perfect; there was a shortage of pumpkin seed that year, and I was able to sell them directly to the food co-ops."

"Why didn't you keep growing them?"

He says, "It would have turned the farm into a monoculture."

We climb up the steep east slope of Treasure Hill. Reaching the top, we walk the spine of the kame deposit. The vegetation is thin here; rocks and sand show between the grass clumps. Shallow impressions reveal where the boy Martin dug for agates, arrowheads, and rusty horseshoes. He still has the collection in his closet. He tells me, "When I was a kid, I so much wanted to be a part of this hill, I would drink the snowmelt running off in spring. I could taste the plants in the water—the acid of the fallen sumac berries, the stored chlorophyll from the dried grass, the sugary sap of the cherry roots."

Long before we come to it, we can hear the cluster of wild plums that once defended his favorite fort. "That's the Noah's Ark of Birds," Martin says, and I realize the joke when he continues, "It's a catbird, in the mockingbird family. I used to lie on the east side of the hill, there in the yarrow, watching the sun come up, while the catbird sang the new songs it had learned on its migration. It was almost like taking the trip myself."

Machinery Hill, with its four-generation collection of "crucial spare parts," is visible from here. He loves to recite where every piece of equipment on it came from and what it cost. We can see the herb patch too, in Christina's, long rows of thyme, oregano, and chives. Martin tells me how he sold fresh herbs to Bergin Nut Company in the 1970s. "They loved all the basils. I even grew rosemary for them. But I was ahead of the trend; there wasn't enough volume to make it work."

Eliza runs ahead to the field road. After it passes over the ridge, it splits into two around a gathering of hawthorn, cherry, elm, and red cedar. She takes one path while we take the other. I sing, "You take the low road, and I'll take the high road, and we'll meet at the bottom of the hill."

She can't see us, but she can hear me singing. She knows right where we are and that we'd come rushing through the brush if she needed us. She feels independent and competent, yet safe. The paths meet again next to Jim's Field, a terrace cut with the topography on the west slope of Treasure Hill. At the bottom is Bridge Ravine. We sit on a rock at the edge of the gully, and Martin tells us how he built a bridge across it when he was ten.

"I started chopping the cottonwood down in late September. The days were short, so I only had an hour after school, and my camp-fire ax was small. I cut about four inches a day, and the tree was at least two feet across. When it was close, I had to wait for a calm day. I wanted it to fall on the south side of the stump. It went down in just the right spot. After that, it was pretty simple to finish. I had to tack two smaller logs together for the other cross support. I cut the tree's crown into short sections and lashed them to the cross logs for the flooring. No one knew I was building it. After it was finished, I showed it to Aunt Mary. She had seen a lot of bridges built in her life, and she thought mine would hold up all the relatives. It gave us a shortcut."

The bridge is long gone now. We walk alongside the Bee Field to the Clearing, a sheltered homesite, slipped into the Big Oak Woods. Martin finds the square-shaped hollow where the cabin once stood. We lie on our backs in the thick grass.

From there, it is a tromp through the Big Oak Woods and past the Spring before we emerge in front of Fox's Grave. Martin tells how Grandpa Tom and Aunt Mary dug a hole right next to where Fox, the draft horse, died. They rolled him in with Great-Grandpa Will's crowbar and buried him there beside the Hunting Ground. A stand of sumac now grows over his bones. We're standing in the path listening to Fox's story when Peaches, the cat, pounces out from the sumac. He patrols the entire farm, all the way to the back, a half mile from the house. Eliza tries to pick him up, but he's already learned she is rough. He follows us past the Crown Jewel, the richest soil on the farm, and up to the Plains of Abraham, a fertile expanse, flat and high.

We sit on the edge, like a great bench overlooking Cottonwood and Bluebird Valleys. The slope is a waterfall of spring color, first violets and dandelions. Wild strawberries add their delicate scent to the evening perfume. From this rise, we can see the IDS tower in Minneapolis, the tallest building in Minnesota. For Martin, it marks the land's urban-edge relationship and Eagan's long history as a secure food source for the city's population. To the south, Rosemount's twin towers of success, the blast furnaces of the Brockway Glass Plant, can be seen above the tree line. Running twenty-four hours a day, seven days a week, it transformed Rosemount from a farm community to a factory town. Martin says, "The land it is built on was once my great-uncle's home place. My dad always said, 'We can finally see his land—vertically.'"

Peaches curls up on Martin's lap, and Eliza on mine. She says, "Tell your story, Marty."

"Well my great-grandfather William Diffley left Ireland in the 1840s, during the potato famine. All the potatoes had blight, and they rotted, so he had nothing to eat but the grass in the ditches—here, taste it, you wouldn't want to live on grass either."

He hands her a blade; she puts it right into her mouth, chews, then spits it out and says, "Yuck, that's all he had to eat?"

"Yep, that was it, so Will thought he'd come see what was for dinner over here. It took him awhile; it was a long, long way. First he had a rough trip across the Atlantic Ocean in a big boat. Then he worked in Providence, Rhode Island, making ax heads for the Kelly Ax Works foundry. That's where he met my great-grandmother Catherine Corcoran, who was from Galway. They got married and had the opportunity to come to Minnesota Territory with their two children and a third on the way. At first they lived in a cabin of Catherine's brother along Dodd Road—which followed an Indian trade route between Mendota and the Pipestone quarries—and pre-empted land for themselves one section over. *Pre-empt* means they were able to purchase the land at a low price before it was offered to the public."

Every time he tells it, he adds something new; another leaf of the story unfurls. "They had eighty acres and few neighbors, the opposite of Ireland. One day a family came down Dodd Road in an oxcart, headed to an area then known as Lebanon, now called Apple Valley. It was November, and an early winter storm blew in. William and Catherine sheltered the family, and they enjoyed each other's company so well that they gave them their land. Land was more plentiful than neighbors. Then they claimed land on the corner of Diffley and Dodd Road—except there was no Diffley Road yet back then. They had a beautiful pond and spring, loam soil, and more oak trees than in all of Roscommon County. They said, 'This is like old Ireland before it was denuded by the British.' So they stayed, built their homestead, and now here I am."

"And now here I am," Eliza says.

"That's right, and now here you are," he kisses her hair, "and your mom. Will and Catherine are glad you came."

Listening to this story, I finally understand why Martin is always talking about everyone's history. I had always thought the expression "good connections" meant knowing people in high places, but it's the clerk in the grocery store, the farmer down the road with manure, the teller at the bank. This is what creates a secure community. Being rooted on land taught his family relationship, and food is the oldest connection and strongest bond of all.

I'm constantly aware that impending development is like a noose around his neck, and he never knows when it will tighten. But times like this, the rope seems to be completely dissolved. We start walking along the ridge. The light is long and low now. Our shadows fall a hundred feet into Cottonwood Valley below. Our shadow hands reach out and pick blooming violets—scented essence of yellow and purple in the falling light. We bring them to our shadow mouths to nourish our spirit selves with the flower-sugar shadow of dusk.

Our spirits touch things our bodies cannot. They stretch and expand—fly up to meet the sky.

Songbirds Nesting

On the kitchen table is a little, brown, square box with an antenna—the Great Oz.

First thing in the morning, while we are preparing breakfast, we invite Oz to speak, and again at lunch, and before bed. It is a major offense to make noise while Oz is pontificating. Fortunately, since Eliza lacks the patience or respect to worship Oz with silence, he is a grand repeater. He has a great deal of power over Martin. If he says the "r" word, Martin is likely to go into a complete panic. He doesn't hear the percent chance, the time, or the location—just the word. Rain.

While Oz is speaking, I make a four-day graph on scrap paper. I fill in expected high and low temperatures, percent chance of rain, sun, and clouds. I then play the voice of reason—something that Martin doesn't seem to have when it comes to the weather—and the paper gives me hard-copy backing. I point at it when I want to emphasize my words. I can tell when it's time to plant corn because he gets extra edgy about rain. He disappears with the corn planter—like it's a secret act of male seeding. When he reappears, he's happy and sassy. If I ask questions about the process, he gets standoffish. I guess I won't understand until someday when I have a crop of my own.

I hate dirt in my shoes. My feet feel hot, confined. The soil feels grimy. Martin lectures me when I take them off and says I need the protection. Usually I ignore him and plant barefoot.

I want to know the why of everything. Martin just wants to tell me what, where, and how, but for me, tradition is a lousy reason to do anything. He seems to take my constant why-ing as a questioning of his competence, and sometimes he's telling me the why and I can't see that it has anything to do with my question. I'm asking him why we're planting a winter squash I've never heard of, and he starts telling me about Dave Frattalone, King of the Saint Paul Farmers Market.

"Self-proclaimed or crowned?" I ask.

He doesn't answer, just keeps talking about the first time he met Frattalone. Initially the excited people swarming Dave's market stall attracted his attention. When he maneuvered his way through the crowd, he saw a pile of apple-sized striped squash, framed by braids of hanging garlic. Behind the squash were eyes that looked like variegated leaves, holding every color of the garden, shining out of a face that looked like a round full moon with a summer tan.

He brought home some of the squash, ate the best meal of his life, went back, and learned it was grown from open pollinated Sweet Dumpling seed that was smuggled in by Dave's family when they emigrated from Sicily. They have been growing it, marketing it, and saving the seeds for decades. The squash and the man pushed Martin far beyond the parameters of Acorn and Buttercup and illuminated new concepts about the future of food in America. And that is the why we are now walking alongside this wire that is stretched the length of the Bee Field, dipping our hands into a brown lunch bag, and dropping four seeds per hill—seeds that Martin saved from squash that he bought from Davie and grew out isolated from any other.

I am excited to meet this King of the Market, but I am not prepared for Dave's personality when he pulls into the yard hauling an Allis G tractor. "Marty, you lucky dog you. How do you get any work done in the fields?" He's not even out of his truck yet, and his own tail is already flapping.

"Did you buy a tractor?" I ask Martin.

"No, Davie wants me to fix it and sell it for him." Martin then whispers in my ear: "But we'll have to try it out for the season before I sell it."

When Dave gets out, he walks straight up to me, grabs me by the shoulders, and pulls me hard into his chest. He presses against my breasts, shaking with his full body, while pulling my butt against himself with one broad hand. His other hand is on my upper back, just as firm and intent. He nuzzles his cheek and head into my neck and moans, "Oh bambino."

I feel everything—his perfect little mustache as his lips burrow up my neck, all the way down to my feet, which are wrapped between his, held tight, unable to move. It is a sense of complete engulfment. And it feels completely safe. Anyone else I would instantly knee, but there's something about Davie. I feel like I am being blessed as a holy carrier of life. I surprise myself when I squeeze him back, just as hard. It's like hugging a round barrel of garlic, basil and . . . he smells like White Castle hamburgers?

He pushes back against my shoulders still holding with his body. His eyes dart over my face. I can't tell where his head, neck, and shoulders meet; there is no delineation, just a round tube of skin and flesh. He pinches my cheek and finishes by kissing the back of my hand, then turns to Martin. "Keep this gal, she's got it." Then he pulls four flats of plants out of the truck cab and says, "I brought you Italian Saladettes and Cubanella frying peppers." Next he's in the middle of a recipe, telling me to "slice the peppers as thin as the knife blade, sauté them in cold-pressed virgin olive oil, add the tomatoes, garlic, and basil *after* the peppers are well roasted—just a minute— sprinkle the salt, and it must be sea salt from Corsica, aromatized with myrtle." He moans when the dish is done, "Oh baby," just like he moaned when he hugged me. "What you going to be doing about broccoli and cabbage plants?"

We just switched from cooking to transplants? I shrug, "I don't know. Martin brings them home."

"That's no good. You gotta know how to grow them." He pulls seed packets out of his front bib overalls pocket and says, "Come on. Davie'll show you how. Give me some little piece of corner ground." He directs me to bring a rake, hoe, stakes, and wire, and we walk up to the Ball Field. "I'll show you how to make a good seedbed and grow the best bare-root transplants. When I was growing up, we didn't have fancy plastic houses like now. It's better this way. The plants are stronger, ready for the real world."

He demonstrates how to rake out a bed, how to stretch my fingers wide and mark the spacing, how to trench six rows with a hoe, how to plant the seeds twenty per foot. I take a turn, but everything I do he criticizes, "Not like that." He has plenty of patience while he is showing, but none while I am doing. He wraps his arms around me from the back and guides my arms on the hoe. We are the same height, but he's so round, his arms are stretched to reach the handle. Then he covers the seeds with soil and points out how shallow they are.

But no matter how close I listen and no matter how hard I try, when I take another go at it, he says, "Too deep, they won't ever push up through all that. These are cabbage you're planting, not potatoes."

Martin drives past in the truck. I roll my eyes. He winks and encourages me, "Stick with it."

"You need some soil as black as your Mamaluke's hair." Dave must be referring to Martin, but what is a Mamaluke?

I rake and level another section of bed, draw another set of rows with the hoe. "It's a rake, not a pickax. Hold it up. Straighter," he says as he draws the rake in one smooth sweep, sketching a perfect, even bed. He makes it look so easy. "And your rows—the depth must be even so all the seeds will emerge at the same time." I try seeding again. "Still too deep, and what are you packing the soil like that for, you think they can bust through concrete? This is a garden, not a basketball court. Feel the seed when you plant it. Feel the soil."

He bends down—which is challenging for him—picks up a handful of soil and rubs it across my cheek. "Feel it?" He takes my hand, flips the palm up, pours soil into the cup, and presses it with his squat, rough thumb. "Feel that?" His eyes are boring into mine. "That is where the seed lives. What it touches. What it eats. You wanna grow vegetables? You gotta feel what it's like to be a seed in the soil. And a root. And a plant." He takes a few seeds and pushes them into the soil in my palm, then folds my fingers, and holds the closed fist in the pouch of his two hands together. His hands are so . . . they match his body. They are short and thick and powerful. They are harsh and scratchy at the same time as they are soft and caressing. And his voice also, "Like that, feel here, how they come together." He coos rough gravel. He places his palm flat on my stomach, right over my womb, and says, "Women have to feel it here."

I go at it again. I don't think I'm doing any better, but Dave seems satisfied that he told me and showed me everything. When we run out of seed, he hugs me and says, "You just keep feeling it. You have the touch. You'll get it."

I stay under his arm, "Thanks for showing me, especially the feeling part."

"Nobody knows how to do this anymore—it's a lost art." He gives my back a paternal pat.

I don't know if he means the seedbed or the feeling is the lost art. I am guessing both. I have never before met a man who understands what it means to give birth and who feels and worships the life force in a seed. Or have I? Maybe my Mamaluke does.

We walk back to the house, and I water the plants that he brought. "No, no. That's all wrong." He grabs the hose out of my hand and waters, but I don't see what he's doing so special. I try again, and he turns redder. "No, no, no. You rub spaghet on your knee and expect to get full? Bless them." He waddles over to the spigot and turns the pressure down. "Look. Like this. Plants are holy. So is water."

He is holding the hose under the leaves and watering the roots, plus the water is flowing gently, not spraying hard. I try again, and he says, "There, you feel the water going in? You feel the roots drinking?"

After he's gone, I practice making even rows and covering mock seeds, but I'm not very good at it. Finally I dig up a cabbage seed. I lie on my back in the field, seed and soil in my closed hand resting on my womb. I close my eyes and just let myself feel. For a while there's nothing, just the itch of pigweed against my calf and some dirt inside my shirt. Then I get it. It's right there. I can feel the life inside the seed, real quiet, but there. Waiting for water, soil, and sun. Waiting to be cabbage. It's the same thing I was feeling when I was a kid lying in the rain listening to God. I felt the earth drinking as the water soaked in and the soil life expanded. I felt the swelling in the weed seeds and the shudder when they took their first deep breath. And it wasn't just what I felt, but all the things I knew about nature without having to ask.

Five weeks later, the seedlings have six true leaves. We pull the plants, and it's clear what is meant by bare-root transplant. There is a main taproot going down with a few laterals, but no root ball. I'm impressed with how simple it was to grow them and how stout and sturdy they are as we pack them into wooden boxes. It's easy to feel the life in them. But by the time we get to the field and are ready to start transplanting, the leaves are soft and sagging limp. When we are finished with the second row, the first plants are drooping almost flat on the ground, and I'm back to doubting. "Martin, you and Dave are both nuts. No way these plants are going to make it."

"Don't look for four days; then tell me we're nuts. It works. Just don't plant in the heat of the day."

Of course I look, and of course he is right. Each morning they are a little crisper and a little straighter. By the fourth day they are pointing straight to the sky.

We've moved all food and dishes to the outside summer kitchen. It is a simple lean-to roof, open on three sides, containing a stove, refrigerator, cupboards, and sink. It's great to have food preparation and dining outside in sunny and warm weather, and cleanup is a snap, but I've been wondering what it will be like when it is wet.

This morning it is dark and drizzling. I turn to Oz, and he is a voice of damp gloom. I put off going out as long as I can, but Eliza is hungry and getting whiny. We grab an umbrella—which she loves— and it is absolutely glorious. We whip up waffles and eat while watching a light mist kiss the trees. Then the sun busts through a crack in the clouds, and everything is glistening. Martin comes in looking for our help. He's set up to plant corn. The rain didn't amount to more than a wetting of the dust.

He drops me off on one end of the Plains of Abraham and drives himself to the other. It's the highest spot on the farm. From here I can see a bright-blue day pushing in strong from the west. He pounds a metal stake three feet from the field edge, then attaches the end of a check wire that is laid out the length of the field. He signals down to me. I draw my end of the wire taut and slip it through the metal clip of a stake. Then he pulls the corn planter into the field and slips the check wire through the seed-dropping mechanism.

The check wire has a knot every thirty-six inches. When the knot passes through the planter, it trips a lever to drop four to five seeds together in a hill fashion. The planted result is a field of corn with squares like a checkerboard. Each row is straight and lines up both lengthwise and crosswise with a cluster of corn stalks at the exact intersection of each line. It means we can cross-cultivate from both directions, making it relatively easy to boast a weed-free field.

It is a beautiful sight. Order and structure create a sense of stability, righteousness, and safety. In a rural culture, straight, weed-free rows dictate the community opinion of what type of farmer planted it, which reflects on the character of the man, and eventually rides back to the family's value and position in the community. Farmers associate crooked rows with sorry people. But setting the check wire exact is a time-consuming art form, and straight rows of one species are completely contrary to nature. The sense of stability, righteousness, and safety are a false human construct.

Martin says, "Planted this way, the sun shines evenly on all the plants, making for even maturity, and the multiple stalks growing together are like a tower of corn; the roots twine and support each other in a windstorm—just like you and me."

A few days ago I read a study in a 1944 plat book that revealed that laying out, moving, and picking up check wire consumes 50 percent of corn-planting time. "Martin, this is 1985. Check-planting corn was replaced by line-planting in the 1950s."

"Oftentimes I find songbirds nesting in the corn towers; they don't nest in line-planted corn. My uncles laid out their fields with wires and check-planted corn with handheld corn planters, stabbers. They planted four acres a day without having to bend over. We're modern with our two-row planter. The best part is the old-timers. When they drive past, they remember growing corn like this. They stop and talk to me if I'm in the field. What I learn from them alone is worth the extra work of setting the line, and they won't be around much longer. If they don't pass it to me, when they die, their knowledge will go with them."

I'm starting to understand that Martin will do mostly what he wants, and I confess, this is one of the things I love about him. He check-plants corn because it is his way of staying in touch with his heritage. Also, he respects who I am. I get to be me too, no matter what he thinks. He doesn't expect me to exist as an extension of him. Our personalities and how we think and make decisions are completely different, yet we are equals. I'm starting to learn what a two-person relationship is.

We sleep in an outside cabin now too. It is funny how we found it. I stopped at a garage sale and saw a small toolshed out back. I knew the property was going to be bulldozed to build the new UPS warehouse, so I asked about the building. The woman said, "That was a guardhouse at Fort Snelling; then it was sold to a floral business on Minnehaha Parkway in South Minneapolis, where it was used for a drive-up flower shop. We moved it here and sold sweet corn out of it."

"Would you consider selling it?" I asked.

"If you leave your number, I'll have my husband call you. He already has a bid from someone else."

When I got home and told Martin, he said, "Was that at Clark's, the vegetable growers, on Highway 149? What time were you there?"

"I left five minutes ago."

"Well, I beat you by half an hour. I'm the other bidder."

Martin brought it home on the back of a trailer and slid it off under the century-old cottonwood, then used his grandfather's long crowbar to place it exactly. I washed the inside walls and made it fresh with white paint. It is perfect for sleeping, with windows on three sides.

After the sun is down, we are just here, together, until the first rays of light at dawn. We don't keep a clock or a light. The rustling cottonwood leaves sound like water—sometimes I think it is rain when it is not. There is a pair of orioles nesting in the tree. They wake us in the morning with bright slurred whistles. Eliza points out at the sack nest. She wants to know if there are eggs in it. Martin says, "Yes. Soon there will be babies. They have nested there since my dad was a kid."

There is not much we go into the house for now. It is just a building where we store and wash clothes, take a shower, and keep books. Martin tells me when he was little, he was always breaking out of his playpen. Uncle Bill got so tired of repairing it that he finally welded the metal bars into the frame. Once Martin realized he couldn't escape anymore, he just sat in it screaming, which worked even better than breaking the bars. I don't think he's changed since. This man will not be penned in. I guess I'm not much different.

Ancient Need

Every inch of the roadside stand is being scrubbed, raked, or painted. Eliza is taking her job as stand assistant seriously—fetching baskets, straightening bags. We pull out the sign I remember from the first time I came, TURN HERE → SWEET CORN. I joke, "It should work on customers; it sure reeled me in."

Martin tacks a small metal plate over the tomato display, *Century Farm.* He says, "Uncle Bill and I got this in 1976 at the state fair."

A full sheet of plywood is painted, **GARDENS OF EAGAN—** *Certified Organic.* Eliza sprays it with a hose, and I scrub it. We hang it on wooden posts already set by the road. "How did you come up with the name?" I ask.

"When I was sixteen, I worked at Visitation Convent for my aunt, Sister Mary Angela. She was cloistered there. They didn't allow men in, but I was her nephew and a boy. I worked in the garden, did maintenance, and later helped them move from Crocus Hill to Mendota Heights. The sisters referred to me as Martin, the boy gardener from Eagan. Sis Ang would always say, 'How are things at the gardens of Eagan?' She meant, how was everyone in the family doing?"

He shows me his favorite display tricks, "Pile it high, kiss it goodbye," cascading displays of color and shape, putting produce together that cooks together. "They shop with their eyes. If it doesn't look good, they won't touch it. They're fussy, that's for sure."

He's just warming up. "When you make a display, think about mimicking natural bounty—only exaggerate it. When a fruit tree would be laden with a bushel, create a cascade of ten. Bring the majesty of a tasseled cornfield into the mass of green ears on the sales table. To show the lush fertility of watermelons vining in the sun, make a display of melon diversity and bounty. Immerse the eater in the scents, the colors, and feel of the food. Squash mountain is a winter full of security and warmth. This is an ancient need—to have good food. It is a primordial desire and driver. It starts wars and generational feuds between families. Above all, satisfy the human fear of not having enough. Send a visual message of plenty. Let them know through their senses that we will take care of them."

"Wow. Can you write that down for me?"

He pulls out a box of onions that have bad spots, crushes one with his fist, and then rubs it on the underside of the display table. He grabs a few more and stomps them into the ground in front of the stand. "You thought we picked too many," he says. "We'll be harvesting again before the day is over."

Maybe there were multiple reasons the market master called him Mr. Organatic. Then I smell it. Suddenly, all I want to do is eat a gigantic bowl of sautéed onions, or French onion soup, or fried onion rings. I don't care how they're prepared. I just want onions. He says, "The ones with a little rot are best. Extra pungent. I used to do this at the Minneapolis Farmers Market before they turned on the lights. No one could figure out where the smell was coming from."

He sprinkles crushed basil leaves around the tomatoes. I'm remembering the first time I pulled in and smelled the onions and basil. Then he puts the *OPEN* sign up, and cars start rolling in. The summer-kitchen oven is full of sweet corn. The roasting scent mixes with the onion juice and basil, like he's written a recipe for success. He grabs the grilled ears and hands one to each customer. The sweet corn passing from hand to hand looks like a handshake between them, like a commitment to a good meal and a satisfied stomach. Every client leaves with a Diffley Dozen—that's thirteen ears—a bag of tomatoes and basil, and a five-pound net of onions. He doesn't seem so crazy anymore.

But I'm still thinking about when we hung the sign over the stand.

Printed beneath **GARDENS OF EAGAN** in bold letters is *Martin Diffley.* He said, "We need to add your name."

This led to a conversation about our names and the future of our relationship. I was surprised to learn that it wasn't the idea of marriage that scared him. It was giving me his name. It took a while to get to the resistance, but when it came, it was like straight, weed-free rows and the community opinion. *Diffley* means "Black Lad," and they have been pillars of this community. "I'm afraid you'll get my name in the paper," he said.

"What's wrong with that?"

"It's not the paper. It's what you might do to get there."

Once he said it and we laughed about it, he said, "Oh, that's silly." But it has left me wondering, what does he think I might do that's crazier than smashing onions?

Every day now, a retired engineer comes into the roadside stand. He doesn't buy much—a few ears of corn, one tomato, a bunch of carrots. If Martin is there, he shops quickly and leaves. If I am alone, he stares at me and looks nervous. Today he tells me a long drama about doing reconstruction work after the Second World War and, of course, the most beautiful German girl. I should have seen this coming; he says, "You are just like her, pure and unmarred."

I want to tell him, my ancestry is not all German but also Dutch, and maybe he should just leave. But I check myself. Martin has taught me to tolerate ridiculous customers and conversations. He goes on. Instead of marrying him and living a life of luxury and care in America, she married a "boorish, half-wit of a German farmer." Within a few years her "rosy, glowing skin was rough-red and coarse, her hair was dull, her lively bounce was gone, and she was heavy with child." He scowls as he says, "She gave her youth and beauty to a dirt farmer. This will be your fate too if you don't get out now."

I tell him not to return—we don't want or need his business— but I am upset. Martin says, "Forget him. He is a lonely, bitter man. He could be singing 'Fraulein, Fraulein,' remembering her pretty face and the stars; instead it's 'The Bottle Let Me Down.' It has nothing to do with you."

But this is how Grandpa felt, that farmers are stupid and uneducated. Not salt of the earth but dung of the barn. How did he see Grandma? She was a real farmer. Customers come in, and I wonder how they see me. Despite pride in our produce, I feel shame. I look at my hands, and they are—as always—stained with whatever I last picked. Right now they are fragrant green from tomato leaves. I go into the bathroom and start scrubbing with hot water and Lava soap. After a few minutes the stain is still there, and I am getting bored. I want to get back outside.

When I was young, my parents partnered with a neighbor farmer to produce sweet corn for both his and our family. My dad bought the seed. The neighbor planted both fields and cultivated. When the crop came in, every meal was sweet corn, and we filled the freezers for winter. Both families sold their surplus on the side of the road. My parents were growing it for the food, but I thought we were in business. We charged forty-five cents a dozen, and I wanted to know "our competitor's" price. I put on a scratchy, black toy wig, walked over to their stand, and with a "city" accent said, "How much is your corn?"

They said, "Go home, Tina; we know it's you." I had no idea how they saw through my disguise, but I was proud to be a farmer then and I realize . . . I'm proud to be a farmer now.

I am leaning back against the kale field cottonwood, waiting for there to be enough light to pick. This time alone in the hush moment before dawn is the best part of my day. There is the tenseness of dawn building, as if the sun can't break through the horizon until the birds call it up. It starts with just one voice and quickly passes from branch to branch, a swelling excitement. I feel a vibration in my back through the skin of the tree trunk. Even the grass under my bare feet seems to be waking up—part of the morning ceremony—a language older than words.

The kale leaves are crisp now, fresh from the night. The dewdrops on the serrated edges run down my forearms as I group six leaves into a kale bouquet, twist the wire tie tight around the center, and pack them in rows in the waxed cartons. It doesn't take long to fill the boxes.

When I get back, Martin has the flatbed truck loaded with the rest of the order, picked yesterday. Cornstalks and tassels drag off of the bumper and undercarriage, snagged when we used the truck in the field for harvest. The Golden Jubilee sweet corn is in the front, packed sixty ears each in gunnysacks. Yellow Doll watermelons are heaped in a pile against the corn. There are leeks and Sweet Spanish onions, Early Cascade tomatoes, fresh green-top beets, cabbage, and Contender green beans, even the first Saticoy muskmelons.

We should have a box truck to protect from the sun and wind—but we don't—so we tie blankets and a tarp over the load. "Someday we'll have a refrigerated truck," Martin says. "We'll be able to pick everything and load it the night before."

I look forward to that someday, but right now I'm glad for today—and this morning. I carry Eliza up from the cabin and lay her on the seat of the truck. She is still wrapped in sleep and her cotton blanket. Martin started this delivery route serving the Twin Cities food co-ops in 1974. Driving it feels as right as the idea of sharing his name.

Our first stop is Linden Hills Co-op on Upton Avenue in the heart of the southwest neighborhood in Minneapolis. I like to arrive early, before the Roots and Fruits truck, so that I can drop my ramp right through the back door, straddling the foot-high concrete floodwall. The produce buyer, Pat, greets us with his usual, "Hey, man, everything cool?" He signs the invoice, slips half of a sticky cinnamon roll from the Great Harvest bakery next door into my apron pocket, and we're back on the road.

The next stop, East Calhoun Co-op on the corner of Bryant and Thirty-Third, is only two miles, but it takes eight minutes to wind past Lake Calhoun and Lakewood Cemetery. The early food co-op organizers envisioned stores in each local community run by volunteers. East Calhoun still fits this prototype, a small community store in the CARAG neighborhood dependent on worker-members.

Another mile and a half down Lyndale Avenue, and I'm parking under the massive cottonwood tree that shades the back door of the Wedge Community Co-op. Now operating out of a former 7-Eleven store, the Wedge got its start in 1974 in a basement on Franklin Avenue. One of Martin's first wholesale accounts, they feel like family.

Eliza runs off with Elizabeth to help fill gallon glass jars with herbs and tea. Eddie is a little put out. He was looking forward to a visit with her while I unloaded. He's the produce manager here now. I never could have guessed that this was the work we were meant to do together. Our mutual passion for organic farming and fresh produce is far larger than and overrides any conflict we've had. To Eliza, it seems natural that her dad works at a store we sell to. He and I have never discussed it, but if we want to talk about produce and about Eliza, we make two phone calls. They can be back-to-back and to the same number, but they're two separate calls.

Here in the heart of Minneapolis one is rarely more than a mile from a food co-op. The next two stops are Whole Foods Co-op on First Avenue, tucked into a basement near the Minneapolis Art Institute, and then over to Powderhorn Co-op on Bloomington Avenue. This just makes sense. Good food from local organic farms readily accessible to the people who need it.

Seward Co-op still operates out of the same building where it started in 1972 on the corner of Twenty-Second and Franklin Avenue. Backing up to their alley door is tough. It is a short space and requires a repeating series of a few feet back and a few feet forward while pulling hard on the wheel; the truck doesn't have power steering. Eliza is excited to be here. Mary in the deli gives her broken cookies. I've told Eliza—but she never remembers—Mary was at her birth. After I have the order in the cooler, I tuck sweet corn in all my pockets, a few more under my apron tie, and walk around the store handing them to the staff. "May the cob be with you."

Soon the store is filled with primordial moans. The way humans latch on to raw sweet corn, the sugar must be an imprinted memory of mother's milk. They seem to transfer the emotion to the people and the farm that grew it.

At North Country Co-op on Riverside Avenue I park at the side delivery entrance on Twenty-Second, throw a sack of corn over my shoulder, and set it next to the display cooler that lines the back wall. I am outside fetching a second bag when the produce coordinator runs out shrieking and dragging the sack behind her. She empties it onto the sidewalk. "There is a cricket in here. It's going to get loose in the store and drive me nuts."

We pack the corn back into the bag, searching for the cricket, but find nothing. It starts to chirp again. Eliza jumps around chirping herself. I say, "Eliza, help us look. You can bring it home and let it loose on the farm."

I empty the bag again and turn it inside out; maybe it's clinging to the burlap, but no. We resack. Chirp-chirp. Finally I pick a different sack that I think has been quiet all morning. Noisy corn isn't something I've noticed before. The coordinator eyes it suspiciously but signs the invoice. I'm back in the truck when the humor of the cricket hits me. Opening in 1971, North Country Co-op evolved from the People's Pantry, which started on a back porch on the West Bank in 1970. I imagine there might have been a few bugs or crickets on that porch. The beginning idea of People's Pantry was a stock of food in a place where people could come and get what they needed at cost. Martin still has a flyer advertising People's Pantry wares:

> Available NOW are stone-ground wheat and rye flour, honey, oil, molasses, old-fashioned oatmeal, raisins, raw Spanish peanuts, sesame seeds, and sunflower seeds. Short-grain brown rice is ordered and will be available around the end of August. Although the food is not organically grown, it is all non-processed with no preservatives. Organic food will be available as soon as possible. Please bring your own containers and any extra for those that forget.

I love seeing this side-by-side progression of the food co-ops and organic food. Organic was a dream then. Now it's reality with an expanding future.

Just a few blocks down, on the corner of Riverside and Cedar Avenues, our next stop is Eliza's favorite, the New Riverside Café. She knows the kitchen crew will give her a plate of butter-fried hash browns, ruffle her hair, and sing chick-chick-chick-a-dee. They love her middle name. I load up the two-wheeler, including the now-quiet sack of corn. If it starts singing here, the crew will just join in. As I stack produce in the backroom, I watch Eliza greeting homeless people who are eating at cloth-covered tables along the wall of southwest-facing windows. Their faces light up when they see her, a joyful spirit skipping through their morning. Many of them know her by name. The café not only serves hot oatmeal for a quarter anytime of day, but they set out leftovers to eat free after they close in the evening.

Organized in 1971 as a café and coffeehouse with the purpose of providing good music and healthy food at low cost, the Riverside Café is still operated by a worker collective. In its early days there were no menu prices; each customer decided what to pay. Salaries were based on the money available. This has since changed to set prices and wages, but their ideology still includes affordable good food, and live music is a nightly event. I played hammer dulcimer here myself before I started farming.

Next stop is a key component of the local organic food system in the Twin Cities, Roots and Fruits, a worker-owned produce warehouse on Twenty-Fourth Street and Kasota. Rick Christianson tells me the history of the warehouse, that it grew out of a number of food co-op produce buyers who were running into each other at the conventional produce wholesale houses and decided they should join forces. Rick laughs when he says, "It was an underground operation."

It sounds more like an "overnight" operation. When they started in 1978, they used the DANCe warehouse in the middle of the night while it was closed. From the warehouse phones, they called the food co-op buyers to take orders. Then with a rented truck they ran around town to pick everything up. They sorted it in the warehouse, reloaded the truck, and put the warehouse back together again before it opened in the morning. Any leftovers had to be sold to the stores because they didn't have a cooler. Rick worked at Whole Foods Co-op at the time. He would stay up all night getting the Roots and Fruits orders together, then take the truck and deliver. He'd end the route at Whole Foods Co-op, speedily stock the produce display with what was left, and then rush the truck back to the rental place.

Our last stop takes us to the corner of Saint Clair Avenue and Pascal Street in Saint Paul. Started in 1979, Mississippi Market is now six years old, a cozy grocery just a door away from the barbershop where Martin's father apprenticed in the 1930s.

Sunrise in the kale field feels like a former lifetime now. People think that we are called truck farmers because we deliver produce in a truck. But the word *truck* is originally from the Middle English word for barter, *trukken*, based on the Old French *troquer*. It means to exchange, to barter, dealings, business—hence the adage "we'll have no further truck with him." *Truck* became a colloquialism in 1784, meaning "vegetables raised for market," and maybe we really are "gardeners," which was preserved in *truck farm* in 1866.

I'm proud again when Martin shows me how to plant rye and clover. He says, "This is how we preserve and fertilize the soil—with plants, atmospheric nitrogen, and the energy of the sun. It is the only fertility system that is completely renewable."

He goes on to explain that legume cover crops can supply most of the nitrogen our crops need. Seventy-eight percent of the air we breathe is nitrogen gas but in a form unusable by most organisms. Legume plants, through a relationship with rhizobium bacteria, "fix" atmospheric nitrogen in their roots, stalks, leaves, and seeds. When the plants die, they become food for microbes, worms, insects, and other decomposers. The nutrients cycle through the soil food web and become available for the next plants to use.

When he digs up a yellow clover plant and shows me the heavy white nitrogen nodules on the roots, it hits me how elegant organic systems are. There is nothing stupid or uneducated about this. It moves agriculture from the industrial age to the information age. But it's when our organic certificate arrives that I'm absolutely busting with pride. Martin has had the farm certified since 1974. The certification process provides third-party legitimacy and authenticity. It is a formal confirmation that our practices are true, accurate, and genuinely in compliance with organic standards. It is a seal of credibility for the farm and the organic movement.

I am proud that everything we grow is sold within thirty miles of the farm, but local on its own is not enough. The question for me is, how does the production affect the environment in which it is produced? What is its local impact? Buying local must include choosing products that do not damage the regions they affect. If synthetic fertilizers and chemical inputs are used, the effect is not only in the region where the farm is using them but also where the inputs are produced, transported, and sold. Purchasing organic products from another area can be more supportive of the local concept than purchasing from our home territory. Fortunately, anything that can be grown in our bioregion can also be grown organically.

Martin loves to say, "Early, late, or ornate. That's where the money is." I saw the early and late following the local season through the roadside stand and selling to the food co-ops; now I'm gaining an understanding of ornate. The very same people who complained about paying a fair price for quality sweet corn think nothing of dropping a hundred dollar bill on jack-o'-lanterns, cornstalks, Indian corn, and straw bales. It seems the more expensive their shoes and cars are, the more they are willing to spend on decorations.

Eliza and I spend most days now in the pumpkin patch. I snip the vines, leaving a long artistic handle, and line them up in windrows. Some kids have imaginary playmates. She has talking pumpkins.

After the cutting is complete, we drive between the rows with a tractor and hay wagon, loading from each side, taking care not to snap the handles. When it is full, Martin drives back with Eliza riding in the wagon surrounded by the jacks, and I run. We unload at the stand, filling every corner with color. Then I run back, Martin and Eliza drive, and we do it all over again. By dusk we have hauled an ocean of orange—a car-stopping roadside attraction.

I really don't care if farming might wreck my skin or make my hair dull, and I can't imagine it will ever threaten my bounce.

It's November now—the cycle of annual life, from birth to death— is finished. The corn stands brown with bent and tattered tassels. Brittle husks rattle against the stalks, a loose scratching in the wind. The field is side-lit with streaks of evening sun. Pencil-long shadows define space. The trees in the hedgerows are still holding the last autumn hue; the color blends with the falling light and tints the air a blush of maize gold. As I walk between the rows, dry leaves break under my feet, sending up the loose-dust scent of seasons changing.

I am drawn to this corn and the rich fullness of the seed. With the side of my thumb, I break kernels into the cup of my hand. I rub them between my fingers and dribble them behind me—an eatable trail. I'm not sure what I am marking, or if I even want a way back to the woman I was. Farming this summer wasn't planned. It just happened—one seed and one plant at a time. I'm not sure where we're going next. I'm just here. In the present and right now that's a good thing. I break another handful into my palm, roll them like dice, shake and toss them on the ground.

They fall in patterns and groups—tips down, up, or sideways— my fortune waiting to be read. A white egret swoops low, flying a cut in front of me, its call a low, hoarse croak—kuk-kuk-kuk. It hits me full on, a knowing without doubt.

I stop walking, and the corn slips from my hand.

There is a seed planted and growing within me. No matter how well marked, no trail will take me back to who I was.

I am with life myself. I am sure it is a boy. He is golden and as full of energy as this corn seed. Already I know his name.

Rock and Bird

Martin's winter job in a barbershop connects him with a customer named Spud from Prince Edward Island. The economy of the rural community is based on small-scale agriculture, hence its nickname Garden of the Gulf. Spud is a professional hockey player with the Minnesota North Stars, but he grew up working with vegetables. Today he brings in an article about a new potato variety bred by Gary Johnston, a researcher at the Ontario Agricultural College in Guelph, Canada. The sentence that gets Martin's attention is, "The local Dutch and Belgian farmers in the region were asking for a yellow-fleshed variety like they had 'over home.'"

Mr. Johnston became inspired to breed a yellow-fleshed potato after eating a small yellow potato given to him by a graduate student from Cuzco, Peru. He made the first cross in 1966, between a North American white potato, Norgleam, and a wild South American yellow-fleshed variety. The family he selected was from the sixty-sixth cross that year, hence G6666 was "born." In the first field tests, sibling number four was retained for further testing and multiplication. The new potato cultivar is called G6666-4y and is described as "a large, yellow-fleshed potato, with excellent shape and appearance."

Martin calls the college; the potato is not available in the Midwest. He calls Lyle, our regular supplier, who drives to Winnipeg to pick up seed potatoes. Five minutes later, Lyle calls back. G6666-4y is twice the price, but he can get it. We go for the gamble, ordering a thousand pounds. They arrive in mid-April, just in time to prepare them for planting. The first step is to bake up an oven full. Eliza eats four servings just because it's so much fun to say, "Please pass the G6666-4y."

As far as we know, we are the only Minnesota growers with them, but they need a more descriptive name. They are big and flaky with flavor like creamy buttered milk. We sit around the kitchen table twining their characteristics into a cultivar name: Big Gold, Butter Spud, Pie Crust Potato, Pie Gold, Flakes of Gold, Peruvian Gold? Yes, Peruvian Gold.

They are A-size; we need to cut them up for planting. It is important that each piece has at least two strong eyes and is large enough to feed the plant until the roots are ready to take over. The eyes fascinate Eliza. While we are cutting, she "helps" by drawing circles around them with a marker. Over and over she asks, "Why shouldn't you go naked in a potato field?" Then she throws her head back, roaring at her own joke. Martin asks her, "Why shouldn't you tell a secret in a cornfield?" She laughs even harder.

It takes us almost a week to plant them all. Eliza carries an ice-cream bucket full of seed and carefully drops one piece per hole. She falls asleep over supper every night but insists on planting all day. Once we are finished, we start on the lettuce.

Keeping my body low as I move along takes the effort out. I am skimming across the surface of the soil, a water bug sailing without a care, popping plants into the holes Martin makes with a hoe. I feel like a trained athlete at the peak of skill and strength. When I want to look at the sky instead of the soil, I switch to a squat, moving along the row like a crab on its haunches. The baby isn't in the way at all. It doesn't affect my balance. I don't get sore or tired. When it is time to stake the next row, I run back and forth. I must look funny, or perhaps it's just that seeing a woman bent in half planting at eight months pregnant is not a common sight. Visitors take Martin aside and say, "She shouldn't be working so hard. She'll hurt herself."

He shrugs. He can barely stay ahead of me. But nonetheless, he believes we need to mechanize planting, and he takes me to meet Mr. and Mrs. Peach, retired market gardeners. We go out back to the toolshed, where he slides a wooden door open with ceremony and says, "One owner. They bought it new in the 1920s."

I'm always saying, "Can't we farm without machines?" But this is an unveiling; it still has the original factory-orange paint, no rust to speak of, and rides on steel wheels. "What is it?" I ask.

"A New Idea one-row transplanter. You'll be riding in complete comfort with your feet up, planting in the trench made by this shoe." He points to a V-shaped plow in the center of the transplanter, then at a pair of angled metal wheels. "After you put the plant in, these wheels close the soil around the roots and stem. It's almost impossible to find these in good condition."

I see it now. It's truly a piece of art. The handles to lift the trenching shoe have sprung handgrips. The seats are pressed steel. The footrests are adjustable. There is a fifty-gallon water tank with a hose running to the trenching shoe and a shutoff handle to control the flow.

"It was originally horse drawn," Martin says. "See how they converted it with this tongue for tractor hookup? They sold everything else fifteen years ago but couldn't let go of this. I stop once a year and let them know I'm interested in buying it. They finally said yes."

"What can we plant with it?"

"Everything. Seeds, plants, potatoes."

"But I won't be touching the soil, and I won't get any exercise."

"Believe me, you'll still get plenty dirty, and I think we'll manage to tire you out eventually."

It is June 15, 1986, Sunday, Father's Day, and Aunt Mary's birthday. I wake up knowing—today this child will be born. When I tell Martin, he bolts off saying, "I have to get the mowing done."

Eliza and I go out to pick the last of the strawberries. The small cramps are a minor sensation. Hours later we are sitting in the yard, cleaning off the stems for freezing, when a white egret circles my head, "Kuk-kuk-kuk." My uterus clamps hard. My vision goes cloudy. The songbirds stop singing. Eating strawberries in winter suddenly seems completely frivolous. I am, however, the most practical person I know. I put the berries into the freezer before I call the midwife. Then I take Eliza to be cared for by Evelyn, who works here, and finally I go out to get Martin.

I find him mowing thistles in Bluebird Valley. He is leaning against the steering wheel, driving much faster than his normal conservative cautious. His straw hat is bouncing behind his back, held by a string about his neck, and he is wearing ripped, oily overalls and dirty gloves. Quite different from the lover-not-a-farmer I first met. I signal him to stop by holding my arm up and closing my hand into a fist, then clamber up onto the tractor and shout above the noise of the engine. "This is it. You need to come in now."

"You said it was time before," he says. "This is my last chance to mow."

He looks like a complete state of panic. Suddenly I see it. He's been saying he's committed to Eliza and me, but it's more like he's been practicing. Deep in his heart, he's still a bachelor. Romantic relationships fade and end, but father-son is forever, even if the relationship is broken or distant. I've been a mother all along, but he's on the emotional cusp of moving from bachelor of one to family of four. I leave him alone to spend his last moments as a childless man. I have more urgent things to do right now than to counsel him through this transition.

The midwife is waiting in the yard. We go into the house, and everything is prepared and routine—as planned and expected. Contractions are strong. This is so different from when Eliza was born and I couldn't see any future. Now I have no fear or hesitation, just this labor before me, this natural process that will make our family one person stronger. I am in full labor when Martin finally comes in. His face is flushed. He is sticky with sweat and cut grass. He showers and then goes into the kitchen and sautés onions, beans, and rice. The cooking smell turns my laboring stomach. I go to the bathroom and vomit. Finally he comes in and lies next to me, but immediately he falls asleep. Through the cloudy veil of my irritation with him and the labor pain, I can see how frightened he is, and really, he is doing the best that he can right now—which I forget as soon as another contraction starts.

The midwife wakes him, and he's a different man. He's here, like a rock, and I can be a bird. She starts yelling, "Push," but I don't hear her until Martin looks me in the eye and brings me back with a whisper, "Come on, Atina. Push. Now."

The world is moving in darkness. There is singing in my ears. It is my body, not my mind, that knows what to do. Instinct passed down a succession of women. Martin's hands are on top of my womb as the crown of the head shows. My body moves again.

Martin is crying or laughing. I am not sure which. It must be both. Out the window I see a cloudless blue sky. There is no such thing as time. I reach down and feel the baby's head with the pads of my fingertips. It is wet and fuzzy and warm, damp warm, like a puppy pulled out of the center of its litter, and cozy warm, like bodies under a deep pile of down comforters in winter. The warmth has a rhythmical current. I can see that Martin is feeling it through his hands on my skin. His eyes are locked with mine, and suddenly he looks ancient. Not old, but like all of his ancestors are present and watching through his eyes for this new coming.

Then—a first sound from our child. A tiny expulsion from his chest, coupled with a resonance more like a hello than a cry. Ten short seconds of hard rain hit the window, a water greeting from a cloudless sky.

He is here now, lying facedown on my chest. I am here. Martin is here. There is nothing beyond this circle of now and us. His breath. His skin touching mine. Martin's face full of light. My hands move over his limbs and torso, as if they are shaping his energy into the substance of a body. Martin is holding his feet and hands. We don't need words; sensing and silence are wholeness in this moment.

His limbs and head are covered with fine hair of golden red. He was in me before, and now he is out, but reentering in a new way that is intimate and permanent. I hold him up and we gaze at his perfect, holy face.

"There are a few moments in life when a person's entire purpose shifts," Martin says. "This is the second time for me. The first time was when our hands touched."

I see the baby has entered Martin also, and the flowing is moving both ways. Martin and his heritage are pouring into the presence of this child, becoming his history. "His hair is the color of ripening corn silk," I say. "He is Maize."

"Camille," Martin says. "Camille Pissarro painted Parisian urban-edge market gardens before they were developed into suburbs. He is the last Diffley who will be born on this land. The fifth generation."

"Camille Maize Diffley," I say. But he will always be Maize to me.

Eliza bursts in skipping and giggling. Her hands are immediately pulled to Maize's body, and her little fingers flicker tickles on his tummy. She picks up his feet and plays with each of his toes, then his hands, tugging on each tiny finger. "The bird came back," she says. "Just like before. I heard the baby cry, and then I heard the bird, and it flew around the house. It went three times."

"His name is Maize," Martin says. "Camille Maize Diffley."

"Can we call him Angel or Salio?" Eliza asks.

"Sure. You can have a special name for him," Martin smiles.

With my hands around his chest, I hold Maize upright. He opens his eyes and pushes his legs up and down. The motion excites Eliza—he is just born and already a playmate. She jumps around the room singing. "I'm the big sister."

In the evening we make our first visit to the outside world under the welcome banner of an orange-red sunset. As I step out the door with Maize in my arms, the sky breaks into a double rainbow. But there are no clouds and not a drop of rain.

Maize is happy for hours under leafy trees watching birds flitting and singing. Under the open sky with far-off blue and passing clouds he cries.

He lies content on a blanket between plants. I line bushel baskets in a wide circle around him—baby zone. He cries in the confinement of the baby buggy.

Martin sorts tomatoes one-handed with Maize resting on his left arm. Maize's eyes follow the tomatoes from box to box.

He laughs when bugs or ants walk on his skin.

When he hears a tractor, he cries until Martin picks him up.

He likes to be held facedown over an engine. His eyes follow hoses, study shapes and connections, stare at the dipstick. His hanging arms move as if drawing a schematic. When we close the hood, he cries and wiggles as if he could crawl.

If he is in the house, he throws his arms and body toward the door and screams. He flips to happy when we take him outside.

On Sundays the egret returns at 2:14 P.M.—the time of Maize's birth—and circles the house three times. "Kuk-kuk-kuk."

We have silk and tassel and pollen. We have cob and stalk, leaf and root. We have rain. We have heat. We have sun. Everything is just right—the sweet corn is gorgeous. I make a nest on the corn sales table to prop Maize in a half-sitting position. He is surrounded by texture, shape, and scent. Customers come up, smile and coo at him, play with his fingers. They say, "He's beautiful. What's his name?" Then, "Maize?"

"Look at his hair. Look at his color. Doesn't he look like Maize to you?"

He can hear my voice as I move around working the stand, and I can see him from wherever I am. Not only do I know he is safe, but he is right there in the center of our business, surrounded by produce and customers, learning sales and relationship on an intuitive level. He will know what his parents do, how we earn money, and what our values are. He will know where he is from and who he is.

Dorothy and Pat Sell, third-generation vegetable farmers just two miles west on Diffley Road, are having their auction. Their land was sold years ago to an investor, and they were allowed to stay living and growing on it until it was time to develop, which will now be next spring. A way of life and a source of food are ending. Once they are gone, the only two vegetable farms left in Eagan will be ours on the east border, and the Adelmans' on the west.

They are selling everything, farm equipment and tools, even the household goods. The equipment makes sense to me—they are old enough; it's time to quit—but I don't understand why they are selling the furniture and dishes. I think when it's our turn, we'll want to take it with us, to carry our history and reseed our future.

The old-timers and relatives have come like it's a reunion or family picnic. Most of them quit years ago; their land is long since bulldozed and turned into housing tracts. They have no fields to plant, no use for tractors, diggers, or transplanters. They are not here to bid but to reminisce about storms and crops and people now dead. It's kind of a death too, an auction. If a farmer doesn't buy it, the scrap-iron man will, and then it's gone historically. Martin says, "It's truly a funeral when it's sold for scrap or parts, never to run again. If I can breathe life into it—give it another go—it's worth it. Use it here or forever gone, melted into eternity."

Is this how he feels about his heritage? That it will disappear forever once the land is gone? And what of his place as a gardener/farmer in the world, does it die when the tools go? I'm not sure if he's keeping the equipment going, or it him. The bidding comes to Dorothy's good china. The auctioneer holds up a plate. "Lovely rose pattern. More then twelve dinner plates, cups and saucers, soup bowls, platters, even a gravy dish. Good condition. No chips. Who will start it off? Give me ten. Ten. Ten."

No one even looks interested. Mrs. Sell pushes her way through the crowd. People hold her arm and help her climb onto the porch. She takes the serving platter from the cardboard box and holds it up for everyone to see. Her hands are shaking. "These are good china," her voice wavers. "We always took care of them."

Her worn voice can barely be heard against the auctioneer's. I look at her hands and see a lifetime of work—growing, washing, and selling vegetables. The china is lovely. She must have saved it for special occasions only. "Sold," the auctioneer shouts. "Number forty-six."

The dishes sell but not for much. One less farm in Eagan. It's only a matter of time before the houses are at our door. The land, no matter how well cared for, isn't being valued any more than the china. Martin comes home with a greenhouse. Putting it up calms the feeling that we are being pushed out. We are increasing our stake on this land, claiming our permanence with a structure. But how much time do we have? Will it be long enough for Maize to absorb the family lessons?

Health Is True Wealth

Maize is fourteen months old, but he's not a toddler. He rarely falls, though he climbs everything and runs barefoot through mud and rocks.

It's a typical Saturday morning in August. I'm whipping through a stand setup. Maize is entertaining himself by dumping driveway gravel onto just washed potatoes. I move him to the sandbox and hand him a bucket and shovel, but he doesn't stay there. Soon he is on top of the tomato display making sauce. I cut a muskmelon in half and stick a spoon in it. That will keep him occupied—for a little while.

Martin is in the house with Carmen Fernholz and Ray Yokiel reviewing organic certification inspectors' reports. Together they serve as the certification committee of the Organic Growers and Buyers Association (OGBA), a nonprofit membership organization made up of farmers, gardeners, buyers, and consumers.

The original goal of OGBA was to provide a link between organic growers and buyers. In the early 1970s, the supply of organically grown food was limited or largely unobtainable. Organic farmers were working out systems on their own farms; often they were isolated and faced harassment and ridicule in their own communities. Two of the greatest challenges at the time were lack of growing information and confusion about what organic meant. OGBA quickly saw the necessity of consistent organic standards and a third-party certification process.

Martin was part of the participatory group of growers and buyers from throughout the Upper Midwest who studied organic standards used elsewhere and created OGBAs to fit this bioregion. Criteria based on the principle that "organic farming will do no harm" were used, and the impacts of conventional farming on biological diversity, birds and other wildlife, erosion, and the land itself were critical considerations. By bringing the growers and buyers together, commonality, consistency, and a fundamental certification system and methodology were created.

Then in the early 1980s, the State of Minnesota worked with OGBA to draft state organic rules and regulations, which passed two years ago, in 1985. Having state standards has increased the uniformity, credibility, and visibility of organic farming in Minnesota, and the organic community is thrilled to be able to say, "These are our standards, written by organic farmers and buyers."

All around the country, other organizations have been doing similar work. The next step now will be to come together and create federal standards to solve reciprocity issues and confusion in the marketplace.

The certification process itself hasn't changed much over the years. Every organic operation must create an Organic System Plan (OSP) that details how their individual farm is managed organically in accordance with the standards. The OSP must show how they support the organic principle of continuous improvement of soil and ecological health. In season, if farmers want to do something other than outlined in their OSP, they are required to contact their certifier, even if the practice is allowable.

A third-party certifier assigns an organic inspector to scrutinize all relevant aspects of the operation. A thorough inspection is made of the fields, equipment, and buildings, including borders and adjoining land use. Contamination and commingling risks are assessed. All management records are reviewed: seed sources, compost production, inputs used, and records of harvest, storage, sales, and transportation. Finally, the inspector submits a detailed report to the certifier. Inspectors only record and report observations; they don't make decisions. But observe and record they do, and thoroughly. Hedgerows and weeds are checked for signs of herbicide use or drift. In the office sales records are matched with planting records to verify the farm did not sell more products than the acreage planted could have produced. Sometimes the inspection is a surprise.

A certification committee with expertise in organic farming and certification standards then reviews the Organic System Plan and inspection report. This can result in several outcomes: approval for organic certification, request for additional information, notification of noncompliance, or denial of certification.

From point of purchase all the way back to the seed, certified organic products have a reliable paper audit trail that allows back-tracing to the specific field where the crops were grown. Certification provides a huge contribution to the integrity of the movement. I'm grateful that Martin does this work, but I wish it happened during a less busy time of the season, and in some ways certifying organic farms seems backward.

We know that chemical pesticides and fertilizers have a negative effect on human health and the environment. It seems that farms that use toxic inputs should have to be labeled, not organic farms. Chemical farms should be required to maintain buffer zones, prove that they are not polluting the air and water, and go through a third-party inspection process. But conventional farming is the status quo. People believe that agricultural chemicals are a necessary evil. They're not.

Martin's sixteen-year-old cousin, Colleen, arrives to clerk the stand, and I run out to harvest sweet corn before the day heats up. Maize is always easy in the field, where he plays with plants, insects, rocks, and soil. When I return, Colleen is frantically restocking. She says, "There were a bunch of potheads here while you were gone. They bought everything!"

I realize I never explained chemical sensitivity to her. "Did they have difficulty thinking? Did they buy in large quantities? Were they wearing face masks?"

"Yes, all that."

"That's not marijuana."

Our clients with multiple chemical sensitivity tell me that they are hypersensitive to levels of chemical exposure far lower than those considered toxic. Some report difficulty breathing, thinking, and remembering; hives and headaches are common problems. Others talk of neurological symptoms, dizziness, and seizures. They all struggle with weakened immune systems and food and perfume sensitivity. They often tell me stories of violent reactions from eating food raised with pesticides. Many say they had no symptoms before a single large exposure to a toxic chemical. For sufferers with chemical sensitivity, the avoidance of pollutants and toxicants is key.

Today's world is a challenging place for them to live, and help can be hard to find. The American Medical Association does not recognize multiple chemical sensitivity. The question of whether it is becoming more or less common is unanswered, and there is not scientific consensus on the cause or the diagnosis. Avoiding chemical exposure is difficult, and they often become isolated in the attempt. For them, organic food—and the Gardens of Eagan—is a lifeline.

Our regulars know what certified organic means, but people who haven't been here before need education. I'm learning to let the vegetables reel them in. Usually it's around the third visit when a customer says, "This is the best food I've ever eaten. What do you do?"

I explain: soil-building, rotation, biological diversity, beneficial insects, no chemical pesticides or synthetic fertilizers, thirty-six months in compliance with Minnesota organic standards, certification. By the time I'm finished, they are converts. About two visits later they realize this is a seasonal business. They come in panicked, "What am I going to do when you close?" I hand them a list of Twin Cities natural food co-ops. This opens up a conversation on diet.

I avoid overwhelming them with a long list of denials and scare stories. Keep it positive—after all, we are in the midst of vibrant organic vegetables. With the already initiated I say, "It's fun and delicious. Eat lots of organic fruits and vegetables; focus on whole foods and good oils." For people who are completely new to food awareness and the connection between diet, human health, and the environment, I say, "It's simple, just four things to remember: avoid white flour, white sugar, refined oil, and preservatives. Eat organic if you can." Cutting out processed food is a big enough step for beginners. They say, "Oh, that's easy." It's not until they get to the grocery store that they realize that includes most everything on the shelves.

It is a process, learning how to live healthy and reduce impact. There are many different entry points, and understanding develops with time and exposure. Some people enter because of illness or food allergies. Others realize their cleaning supplies are toxic, or their lawn care is running nitrates and toxins into a wetland. From whatever point they enter—food, water, health problems, cleaning supplies, lawn care—they usually come to the others. They are all related.

We have the entire season to go through this conversation. By thinking about white flour, they start to think about how the flour came to be white. They see the entire process of how the grain was grown: Was it in a monoculture and with what inputs? What was the impact of the growing system? How was the grain processed? What was lost? They can see the simple truth in keeping it whole and minimizing the steps from field to stomach.

This simple truth applies to everything. Confining cattle in feedlots and hauling their food to them result in their fertile feces becoming a concentrated toxic-waste product. Put them on pasture, and the animals harvest their own food and spread their own rich manure; the nutrients recycle into the plants, which use the renewable energy of the sun to grow. Why use valuable and precious fossil fuels to grow and haul feed and manure when the cattle are healthier doing it themselves? Suddenly chemical and industrial agriculture doesn't make any sense. Food is supposed to bring us health.

The most important thing that I tell our customers is, "Eat as close to the source as possible." Buy direct from the farmer or grow your own, and eat unprocessed foods. The source is also about the life force. Don't kill it with chemicals. It is just common sense that food should not be sprayed with poison.

Some people have preconceived notions that organic food will be insect ridden, small, and low quality. I just say, "We grow food to support life. Why would it be necessary to use chemicals toxic to life to do so?" I go on to explain the process, how a balanced soil and ecosystem create healthy plants and resist pests and disease.

But sometimes they insist pesticides are necessary. Then I pull out a picture I keep in the corn table drawer of a farmer spraying a field of broccoli, wearing chemical protection, a face mask, and a body suit. "Pesticides are designed to kill. All forms of life are affected. That includes people." I rarely have to say, "If it is so toxic that the applicator needs to protect their health with a face mask and body suit, do you want to eat it, put it inside your body?"

Once in a while a person comes in a little hot about the price of corn. If there is a regular customer present, I don't have to say anything. They snap, "This is the best corn in Minnesota. If you don't appreciate it, you should just leave."

I'm continuously surprised by the strength of their indignation; they want us to be the best-kept secret in town. "There's enough for everyone," I say. Once they eat it, the food speaks for itself.

Today I had what Martin calls "a striped whistler." An old-timer farmer, dressed in blue-and-white striped overalls, he came up to the corn table and whistled, "Whew, that's expensive."

"Is it just you and the missus?" I asked.

"Yup, just me and the missus now."

"Here, try three on the house." They'll both want the extra ear, and the tension of wanting will imprint the memory of how good it is. I remind myself of Martin's advice, think of customers as a long-term asset. It's not today's sale that is important, but all the future sales that will be generated from this one person. Think really long term—generations.

A middle-aged man comes in. I say, "Check out the broccoli. It's gorgeous today."

"It does look great," he says, "but it's not on the list." He sounds disappointed but switches to proud. "Every Saturday we write our menu for the week; one meal's leftovers become the base of the next. It's very economical, and there is no waste."

"Skip the menu. You can't go wrong with broccoli this good. Eat in season. Shop with your senses. Ask your body what it's hungry for. Are tomatoes on your list?"

"Nope."

"You can't pass on these; they're at their peak. Lynne Rossetto Kasper told me they are the best tomatoes she's eaten outside of Italy." I wave an Italian Saladette and crush a leaf of basil under his nose. It quivers, and his tongue juts out.

Maize walks past eating a slice of yellow watermelon like it's a golden smile. I say, "The Yellow Dolls are dreamy right now. Just look how happy that kid is."

"Not on the list," he says.

"Well what is for dinner at your house?" I ask.

"Zucchini and green beans."

"Dang, the zucchini is OK, but it's nothing spectacular, and we are out of beans. Forget the menu. Minnesota summer is too short."

He looks at the paper, then at the zucchini. His eyes scan the display tables, taking in the tomatoes, broccoli, and melon. He holds the list up as his defense—but weakly. Then he crushes it into his pocket. Slow at first, he picks up speed as he gets the hang of listening to the produce, and before long he has a heap at the checkout. I pull a French Charentais muskmelon out from under the table, hold it under his nose, and say, "Smell this." He moans. "Wait till you taste it. Share it with your family, and forever you'll be the candy man."

We don't have many of these. I save them for people who appreciate their intense aroma and flavor. "Here, a gift to welcome you to the Eat What Calls You Club. If I'm not around next time you come in, tell Colleen I said you have the produce passion. She'll make sure you get the best we have."

I shout over to Colleen, "Remember this face." I point to him. "He's in the club."

He leaves glowing. A week later his wife comes in and glares at me. For the rest of the season she does all the shopping. I don't see him again until pumpkin season when he comes with his family. His wife tells the two perfectly groomed children to choose a pumpkin and then disapproves of each one they pick. He stands next to the checkout with his eyes on the ground until it is time to take out his wallet and pay.

Dave Toombs, on the other hand, has a fully developed zeal for produce. He calls ahead and asks, "What's good today?" Then orders by the case. President of our small-town farm bank, he and Martin have a third-generation relationship. Their fathers, uncles, and grand-fathers fed and financed each other. Tom the Barber cut their hair since the 1930s. Martin cuts it now. Everyone in the bank knows us; on the phone they recognize our voices. They know what land we farm, that we grow the best sweet corn in the state, and that no Diffley has ever missed a payment. When I go in with a deposit, Valerie, the teller, says, "Your money always feels different. I can feel the soil on it."

This must be what Martin means by long term. I can't believe how fast my life has changed. I never knew I could be this happy.

Drought of '88

Every morning I look at the horizon, sniff the air, and listen to the train whistle; then I write down my take on the weather and the forecast from Oz. He keeps offering chances of rain. I provide none. At the end of the day, I check who was right.

If this is a contest, I am winning. Does this mean I am smarter? Perhaps it is just easier to forecast the weather when you live outside instead of in a little brown box. Or maybe it means we are doomed.

We are working in loose clothes and straw hats, but still we are too hot. It felt absolutely glorious to have sunny heat in late March. But now it's early May. It wasn't just a nice day or two—all spring has been dry with hot southern winds scorching April's freshness. At first I thought it was great to get the work done early. The compost is spread. Planting is ahead of schedule. But this is spring. We're supposed to be complaining about wet fields and wishing we could get into them. We should be charging the water table, not worrying about sunburn and heatstroke.

"It's up!" Martin says. "I planted four inches deep to place the corn in moisture. I didn't know if it would make it through, but I knew it didn't have a chance if it dried out, and there is no rain in sight. It was gamble or nothing."

I dig through the powder-dry soil but find only a pale flush of damp. I don't know how the seed found enough water to swell. "Damn, this feels like the '76 drought," Martin says. "I had gorgeous Crenshaws and Honeydews, and the Crown Jewel had enough moisture, but not much else."

May and June are no different. It stays unseasonably hot, sunny, and windy. Occasionally a cloud passes through, but it never amounts to more than a wetting of the dust. Martin shallow-cultivates the fields to create a loose layer of dry earth that will prevent surface evaporation. "Uncle Jim called this a 'dust mulch,'" he says. "The soil grains in the surface layer are so far apart that the moisture cannot pass from one to the other and is preserved."

"Too late. There isn't any moisture left anymore," I say.

We go through the motions, planting like we expect a good soaker, but it is too dry even for weeds to germinate. The first corn sets tassels on two-feet-tall stalks. We keep plants alive with water from a tank, but only the watermelons and tomatoes grow—nothing else thrives. Irrigation is a meager substitute for the real thing. I offer deals to the rain gods: "Just give us enough to sprout weeds and I'll never complain again about hoeing." But nothing changes.

Martin tells me that weather tends to stay in patterns. This one has only two characteristics, hot and dry. The variations are limited to wind speed and hot or hotter. Eliza carries a yellow umbrella everywhere she goes. Maize refuses to wear any clothes at all. He is as brown as the world is becoming.

It is July. The soil is dusty talcum; the intense solar radiation has burned up much of the organic matter. I've lost count of the days since rain. I tie a tarp between sumac bushes to shade the kids and stock it with water to drink and a bowl for splashing. Eliza keeps her umbrella up under the tarp. We're in Bluebird Valley, planting. Martin drives over the row with a tractor pulling a water tank. Sunny, our dedicated staff of one, walks behind with the hose and soaks a hole every fourteen inches. We've been waiting weeks to plant this broccoli, hoping it would cool down. Finally we decide to just plant. We have the plants, and we have the field. Martin says, "The weather could change."

"It is better to fail than never to try," I say.

But this is ridiculous. As I come to each hole, the water is already absorbed, and the soil is barely damp. It's like we are planting in desert sand. We stop and talk about what we should do. We agree to continue. Martin keeps driving. Sunny keeps flooding the holes. I keep planting. The broccoli keeps wilting. Martin says, "It could rain, you never know."

I change my reply, "Trying is just the first step to failure."

There is a six-feet-tall rain barrel under the downspout of the roadside stand. It is empty now, completely evaporated. We fill it with water from the well. I climb up the ladder with my clothes on and slip into the cool wetness. I drop down under the calm water and sink to the bottom, then rise slowly to the surface. For as long as I can hold my breath, I am no longer hot. I am not dusty or sweaty or sticky or dizzy. As long as I stay under the water, I am free. I am not thinking about bolted broccoli or shriveled lettuce. The water is mindless. As long as I am floating, I have no identity.

I break the surface and gasp for air. Sunny is on top of the ladder waiting to get in. I climb out of the tank into the oven of the world, and reality crashes down. I am back to getting the truck ready with sacks and gloves to harvest corn, back to greeting customers at the stand, back to keeping the kids cool and engaged.

It is noon. We go out to pick corn in Jim's Field. Eliza brings a jug of water for her chicory. Normally we wouldn't pick in the heat of the day, but now, it really doesn't matter. It's just as hot in the morning and evening as it is at noon. My clothes are already dry. The corn plants are half the height of normal. Most of it is ruined. I run my hand down from the silk tip until I feel the kernels. If they start within an inch or two, we pick them. Sometimes I find nothing. It is slow. At the stand we show each customer. They say, "It's not any better anywhere else."

We work down a double row and loop back. I have close to a full sack. It is light though. The ears are half the size of normal, and there is no weight to them. Eliza is sitting on the hillside next to her chicory, singing "Over the Rainbow." Her umbrella shades her and the plant.

"We need eighteen sacks to get through the day," I say.

"We are gardeners, not magicians," Martin says. "Set a limit of four ears per customer."

Maybe Eliza takes her umbrella everywhere because it feels like the world is ending. Or maybe she believes if she is prepared, she can cause rain. Or maybe she is just pragmatic, like I used to be, and doesn't want to see the sun and feel its relentless beating. I don't know. I buy mint chocolate chip Rice Dream by the case and eat it for breakfast, lunch, dinner, and in between. The strange thing is, in the morning there is always heavy dew. I think it is the only water the plants are surviving on. When I complain to Martin, he puts his hands on my cheeks and says, "In gardening you see all sides of life, and that includes death. Focus on what you want to see. It's the farmer's prerogative."

It's good advice, and diversity is key to success in farming. Watermelon evolved in the Sahara desert with roots capable of sourcing groundwater in dry conditions. Tomatoes also grow deep and do well in drought; with the low humidity there is no disease. Both are thriving, and the fruit is extra sweet. But we're not in this drought alone. The wildlife is struggling to find food. The crows move down the row pecking holes and then leave the fruit to rot. The deer are eating tomatoes and melons too. They've never touched them before, but there really isn't much else now.

We make elaborate scarecrows out of old clothes and hats; long strips of shiny ribbon flutter from the arms. It works for a day, then the animals move back in. So far the most successful scare method is a truck tuned to a righteous AM radio minister at full volume. Crows seem to have a fear of hellfire and damnation—like they know eventually they'll have to pay for the theft. Even the deer don't challenge a preacher.

George, an old-timer neighbor, pulls up in his early 1960s Ford Galaxie. His daily outfit is a long-sleeve cotton shirt worn over a union suit, with a brown chewing tobacco stain down the front. "Do you ever take that suit off?" I ask.

"In winter it keeps me warm; in summer it keeps me cool."

Warm I get, but cool? "Have you ever farmed through anything like this?"

"Don't do no good to whine," George says. "It don't fix nothing. Some years are bad; others are worser. Just don't spend no money and you'll be fine. It's still nothing like the dirty '30s."

"There's nothing to eat, and everything is brown."

"I do just fine on day-old doughnuts and Spam," he says as he opens his trunk. "I got some beast here in my live trap looks like the picture of a devil we had in our Sunday school catechism book."

We all swarm around. "Gross," says Eliza. But she adjusts her umbrella to shade the animal.

Maize shoves a dandelion leaf between the bars. It's the only green left. "It's hungry," he says.

"That's a Minnesota marsupial," Martin says.

"A what you call it?" George asks.

"An opossum—remember the *Beverly Hillbillies* and Granny's possum stew? I've seen them in Louisiana hanging upside down in the live oak trees. I just read in the paper they're hiding in the hay that's coming out of the South for drought relief—to help the farmers."

"Help the farmers? He's the one been eating my zucchini. Sure hope he don't move his whole damn family up here."

The film crew comes out for *Turn Here, Sweet Corn*, Helen De Michiel's video about suburban development changing a rural community. Helen first stopped at the roadside stand last summer, when we were in the midst of plenty. She was just driving past, and the TURN HERE → SWEET CORN sign caught her attention. But there is not much to be proud of now. Most everything is brown and dried out, the grass, the corn—me. I never imagined someday I would feel ashamed of not having weeds. There is something terribly wrong when land doesn't have what it takes to germinate and grow its own soil protection, which is what a weed is.

The stand is an embarrassment. The space is just a roof with plywood display tables. It is the vegetables that make it beautiful, and this season there aren't many. The potatoes got to be the size of an egg, then the vines just quit. The cabbage grew a head the size of a softball; the flavor is mustard hot—it is not edible. The leeks and onions died back in July. The broccoli is still alive, but it's just leaves; it's not making heads. Even if it rains now, it's too late to save most of the crops.

Martin takes the crew out to film watermelon harvest—at least we can show some bounty here. Maize squats at his feet eating a melon that is cracked in half. He brings the melon and his face together and eats as an animal would, taking deep bites of the red flesh. There is nothing for him beyond the sky and sun, the field of vines, the wind, and the scare cloth snapping and cracking. Nothing but the cool, moist flesh against his sun-dry cheeks and tongue, the sugar wetness in his mouth sliding down his throat and filling his stomach.

He makes sounds of moaning that are the essence of pleasure distilled.

The film crew captures Martin tapping each melon to check its maturity. He's always got a smart saying. "This one'll eat. This one's a little green. This one is near perfect." But he can't make it rain.

While we are still in bed, Martin pushes Oz's button. I don't know why he turns him on anymore. Today Oz gives a 15 percent chance for rain—which is what he usually says—and the summer's current tally, forty-three days over ninety degrees, evaporation 40 percent above average, and 20 percent more solar radiation. I feel like screaming, "I know that already. I'm a farmer." But I have the power. I don't need to yell. I turn him off.

First thing in the morning, before it gets too hot, we are on the Plains of Abraham picking watermelons. This is Minnesota; melons always get fungal disease from the humidity. But this year with the drought, the plants are still green and lush, no disease to be found. They have flowered and set a second crop of fruit, which is what we are now picking. At the farmers market everyone with melons said the same thing. "Our farm too. We're picking a second crop," and "No, never happened before; I didn't even know it was possible for melons to set twice."

I'm head down, focused on picking, when Martin says in a voice that is low and full of amazement, "Would you look at that." Like he's seeing something for the first time in his life that's impossible to believe. I glance up and then stare at a low pouf of cloud in the west. I can't remember the last time we saw a cloud, even a wisp of one. And the last time it rained? I don't know. I stopped keeping records. It was too depressing, and there was no challenge in always being right. I even threw the rain gauge in the trash.

It's moving really slow, but it is moving, and in our direction. Martin says, "We better get these melons out. They are so used to drought, if they get hit by a soaker, they'll explode."

It takes the morning. The field is running dead-on ripe, and we pick it clear. Martin is running through every rain song in his repertoire. By the time we're finished, the mushroom cloud has spawned up the horizon and flattened out to cover a quarter of the sky. Martin is on the Dee Clark tune "It Must Be Rain Drops." He stops singing long enough to say, "This is good, coming in slow like this. It might not just blow through. It might just sit over us as slowly as it's coming in. We might get a long soaker."

"That's a mighty lot of mights, Martin."

He doesn't care. "It feels like raindrops," he's back to singing.

The cloud sets the parameters of the day. We unload the melons at the stand and go out to pick every ripening tomato we can find. Martin is convinced they'll crack from the "impending downpour." He's crazy. Tomorrow will be an easy day, with all the harvest done and no rain. It will be hot and sunny. Just like every other day.

By late afternoon the sky is a densely woven blanket—not a drop of blue. Eliza shoves her umbrella to the bottom of the trash and says, "I won't need it anymore."

Martin is rushing around closing windows and shed doors. When customers leave, he shouts over, "See you after the rain."

It's perfectly calm out. I don't know how he can stand to allow hope, and he is going to feel awful when it doesn't amount to anything. I'll be just fine because I have no expectations. Eliza sets her little lawn chair in front of the stand, and another for Maize. She takes his hand and tells him to sit down, then moves her own seat a half inch to the north, looks up at the cloud, and adjusts it a split hair more. Maize copies her. Minutes later she shouts, "First one. Landed on my nose." Maize laughs and sticks out his tongue.

Martin is singing, "I can see clearly now the rain has come."

"Stop leading them on," I say. "The kids are going to be heartbroken when this blows over."

"No drought lasts forever," he says.

The first drops are big, the width of a pencil, and spaced far apart. I feel one hit my shoulder and run the length of my arm. They hit the ground and send poufs of powder up against my legs and into the lining of my nose. Soon miniature craters are marked out like night stars in the driveway dust. They grow smaller and closer together, filling in the sand with pebbles of light. The leaves of the crab apple drop dust-filled gray water.

Instead of stopping, it runs through stages, every kind of rain that should have happened this summer and didn't. We stand in the driveway together, faces up to the sky. Rain fills the hollows of my eyes. I taste it against my lips and in the back of my throat. Clean ribbons of liquid stream through my hair and wash down my body. I start to dance, finally willing to feel disappointment if that is how this ends. Once I stop fighting it, an explosion of fresh scent hits me. It feels like a baptism. Martin grins at me and runs his hand across my cheek. I suddenly notice the rain soaking through my skin and rehydrating my spirit. "It just went through the dust."

The star craters are long gone, replaced by moon puddles and Milky Way rivers. We stomp in them, sending sprays of water flying. Eliza shouts, "Look. The trees are drinking. It's already in the roots."

We run out of energy long before the rain does. When we can't dance another step, we head to the Acropol Inn to celebrate. Martin drives, humming at the wheel. Eliza joins him, rocking in her seat; she knows exactly what song it is. When I ask them to clue me in, Martin says, "The tires, rolling on the wet pavement."

There is a family at the table next to us. The woman says, "Isn't this awful, we were planning to cook out. We had everything all ready when the rain started."

Eliza pats my arm. "Ignore her, Mom; she doesn't know any better."

Our favorite waiter, Dionysus, is giddy. For years we've been trying to get the secret of their avgolemono, chicken-lemon soup, and he's never leaked even a tablespoon's worth of information. Tonight it spills out of him without us even asking. Not just the ingredients but also the secret to the process, when to add the lemon, and how to pour the hot broth into the eggs while beating, rather than the other way around.

When we go back out, the rain has settled into a steady rhythm that feels like it could last all night. We sit at the stoplight, marveling at the reflections half a block long. Each time the light changes—green to yellow to red—we say, "That's the best color." When it changes again, we say, "That's even better than the last one."

Martin says, "I not only forgot how rain smells and how wet tires sound, I forgot how stoplights reflecting up from wet pavement make me feel."

"How did you know for sure?" I ask him. "You didn't have any doubt."

"Didn't you hear the coyotes this morning, yammering from Devil's Hill? While we were picking melons?"

"I did, but . . . ?"

"My Aunt Mary always told me, 'In times of drought, the coyote is the announcer of rain returning. If they howl after the sun has risen—the later in the morning the better—and it must be from a high spot, then it will rain. You can bet on it.'" He's not finished. "And didn't you see Peaches eating grass during lunch? And the ants, while we were picking tomatoes, they were swarming, all in a rush to build mounds around their holes, and the poplar leaves were turned upside down, and the sparrows were making a racket. Everyone and everything saw the rain coming except you."

"I saw it," I say. "I smelled it. I was just afraid to trust. I was protecting myself from what I'd feel if I allowed hope and then was wrong." After I say that, I feel awful. What has happened to me? I never doubted when I was a kid. I smelled it coming and went out to meet God.

There is no need to shield. It is a night of pure serenity. The scent is a mist filling my lungs, entering my pores. The gentle drizzle rinses pure my blackest fears. The morning comes in cleared out and screaming fresh. In the melons I find thick green vines covered with a third set of tight blossoms—a testimony to the importance of crop diversity. Before the day is over, it rains again. A few days later every field has a flush of weeds. Spring flowers in the desert, glorious sight—weeds.

The world is green again—just like that. The magic of a good shower sprinkles life through its drops. It is too late to save the rest of the crops. But at least it can rain.

It sometimes happens that one dry spell is replaced by another.

I come in from admiring the weeds and find Martin with his head under a truck hood studying the engine like something is really wrong. I know that look. The something wrong is not with the engine. I stand behind him and wait. "Cousin Rosemary was here," he says. He doesn't turn around, just talks under the hood like the engine is a counselor. "The school district wants twenty acres from the back of the farm, including the Crown Jewel. It's the best land— the only land that made it through this drought."

Martin often says, "In death there is life," and as a farmer I'm familiar with the opposite, life is full of death. So where is the life I am supposed to focus on now? "At least it is only twenty acres," I encourage him. I've only been here four years, and this feels like the end of all joy. What does it feel like to him? "We still have the rest of the land. And now that it rains again, we're back in the green."

"Rosemary and her sisters can't say no to a school. If they don't sell, the school district will condemn it. The school will bring in development assessments—road, sewer, and water. It will be too expensive. They'll sell it all." He's still under the truck hood. "The road and the services will provide access to the rest of the land. That's how this works; the land loses. This is the beginning of the end. I expect the rest will go within a few years. Uncle Bill always said the government giveth and the government taketh. This land was preempted, but that was just a loan. Now they want it back."

"When?" It's the only question that matters anymore. I thought we would be more ready when it came, and part of me never really believed him. The land was here so long; how will it just cease to be? I can see us on this ground, farming and raising our family, but I can't see around to the other side, after the land is covered with houses instead of this farm. I'm not in that picture. But I'm not in any other image either.

I remember when I thought I would just leave when it was time. It seems like a lifetime ago. I had no attachments beyond Eliza. What Martin and I've got now won't ever be over. We might move and do something other than farming, and sometimes we quarrel, but we'll always be a family. That's just the way it is, and nothing in the world can change it.

"They are working on the terms now. They plan to break ground in spring. I'm just glad it waited as long as it did."

In spring? But we just got out of the drought. Don't we even get a chance to get back on our feet? He's all calm and logical, but his head is still under the hood; he's still talking to the engine. This is a much bigger brown spot than the drought was. "The rest will go very soon now," he says. "Appreciate each moment as the last."

Endangered Species

Martin truly believes that if he sings the right song, it will solve any problem. Since his other cure-all is repairing engines, he is now singing Woody Guthrie's version of "Going Down the Road Feeling Bad" as we drive to Joe's Junkyard to buy a Ford carburetor.

We come up on a rusty grain truck parked on the side of Rich Valley Boulevard. "It's a '66 International," Martin says, as he slows to pass it. I hear pigs squealing and glimpse moving pink flesh. Hog stink simmers in the heat. He's back to the second verse, "I'm a-goin' where the water taste like wine, Lord, An' I ain't a-gonna be treated this way." We come upon a guy walking down the centerline, swaggering like he owns the county. Dressed in a green Pioneer seed company coat and MoorMan's Feed hat, with square husky shoulders, he looks like a typical farmer from the 1940s. Martin stops and shouts out the window, "What's wrong?"

"I'm out of gas. The gauge don't work, and I didn't check the tank."

"I had an International, and I could bet on the gauge not working. How'd they screw that up?" Martin says. "Hop in, we'll get you some."

I slide over to the middle. The truck leans to the passenger's side as he settles his weight in. Suddenly the cab seems very small. "What could be worse than running out of gas with a load of fat hogs and the price is high?" he yells, as if he's on an adventure seeing the world.

Martin replies just as cheerily, "Well, I just got the news that my best field is being sold."

"God. I can always raise another load of hogs, but I can't raise another piece of land." All of a sudden I like this guy. He gets it. Since I don't know his name, I start thinking of him as Mr. MoorMan.

He and Martin dive into meeting each other farmer-style, finding their common ground in equipment from International Harvester. "What tractors do you have? What trucks?" IH takes a beating as they discuss every chronic problem the company's equipment has. They come to, "What do you grow?" before sharing their names. His list is diverse, "Hogs, chickens, used to dairy, now pasture some long-horns." His row crops move beyond corn and soybeans, with "barley, rye, wheat, and oats." He gets excited when he talks about how fertile soil is after a hay crop.

"Look around here," Mr. MoorMan says. "When the animals left these farms, you might as well say the soil left those fields. They had oats, undersown hay crop, three- or four-year rotations. They had pasture. You know the plow always pulled easier in land that you ro-tated with hay and grain than in land that you just kept cropping and cropping on. What do you grow?"

"Organic vegetables," Martin says.

"Does that really mean that your soil is in better condition when you leave it than when you start?"

"That's our goal. Annual crops like vegetables are inherently hard on soil. We make a practice of reversing the damage they do by grow-ing soil-building crops."

"Well, I'm a lime spreader, and the guys who have taken care of their soil, they have nice farms and outbuildings and good dental work. These other scratch farmers are just pulling that anhydrous, putting the chemicals on. Between the bank and the elevator, I don't think they have any money left. Who got your land?"

"It's been coming a long time. Developers, school district, people wanting to get out of the city, come to the country and turn it into another city."

"Don't that make sense."

It's not until after we've driven to the Cenex station on High-way 55 to borrow a gas can, filled it, driven back, and are pouring it into his truck that they get to names, "Hey, name's Charlie. Charlie Schaefer."

"Martin Diffley. This is my wife, Atina. We're from just up the road on Highway 3. Where's your farm?"

"Hampton, east of Little Oscars. Hey, I got a piece of hay, grandmother's farm, twenty acres of high ground, never had chemicals on it. If you want to rent it, I have a big shed full of cow manure. You can drive the spreader. I'll drive the loader, and we can get it covered."

They say good-bye like the oldest of neighbors.

"See, honey, everything is going to be fine," Martin sings. "One man's crisis is another man's opportunity. If we hadn't had the news about the land, we wouldn't have come for the part and been here to help him. If he hadn't run out of gas, we wouldn't have met him and found the land."

"Eighteen miles is a long way to drive to a field," I say. "We have to buy our own."

"Even if he has hills, that's highly productive land between Hampton and New Trier," Martin says. "If it qualifies for organic certification, it will be just what we need."

The sewer and water lines to serve the school will cross the rest of the farm. This means that the land will have access to the services, so it must pay for them. There is now a sewer and water assessment lien against the land.

I don't understand why a landowner has to pay for something they don't even want, especially when they are the party experiencing damage. The city's perception is that access to sewer and water makes the land more "valuable" because it is "improved" and can be "developed." I keep saying it already is developed—as an organic, fresh vegetable farm and market. But the city planners have left no land in Eagan zoned for agriculture; they already see it covered with houses. They don't value what is here. Martin's relatives own the land, but they can't say no to sewer and water easements, just like they can't say no to eminent domain for a school. The lien has to be paid when the land is sold, and with 11 percent interest. The assessment is a weight pulling the noose tighter around the neck of the land. Cousin Rose-mary is talking with developers about selling the rest.

People say the land is too valuable to farm. I say it is too pre-cious to put houses on. It is only twenty-two minutes from down-town Minneapolis and Saint Paul—over three million people—and all of them eat. No matter what it is worth in development value, as long as it is farmland, it has the ability to support a family and feed thousands of people.

The Diffley family land is a clear illustration of this. When the three brothers inherited, Martin's father, Tom, as carpenter and barber, in-herited the land along Diffley Road and Highway 3. He built houses on his land and sold them. He fed his family, and the land and the money are long gone now. Uncle Jim and Uncle Bill, farmers, received the agricultural land. The land fed Diffley families through farming, is still feeding a Diffley family, and if it was preserved, could feed fami-lies for perpetuity. When I look at the value with a long-term view—a multiple-generation perspective—it *does* work to farm urban-edge land.

If they never, ever sold, the lien wouldn't matter. It could just be a number on paper at the county office and would never have to be paid. But never ever is a very long time and a fairy tale, and 11 percent interest means that every seven years the assessment doubles—a ticking time bomb. I feel completely powerless. I know our custom-ers would back us, would stand up and say the loss of Gardens of Eagan is too great; this land should be preserved. I know we could fight this. But Martin and I don't own it, and it's not my family. Martin says, "We always knew it was coming. It was just a matter of when."

But when I say to him, "We have to move. We have to buy our own land," he reaches into his never-ending file of ancestral sayings and fortifies his barrier, defends his stuck position. "Great idea, but we don't have the money. My dad always said, 'Don't let your yearn-ings get above your earnings.'"

I call the Nature Conservancy. They ask if there are rare or endan-gered species on the land. I reply, farmers. They say, we understand.

I can't see a way. Does he really think I'm going to stay living here on one acre in his parents' house after it is surrounded by suburbia, farming rented land farther out in the county? Like the old-timers who sell their land and stay in the house, waiting to die? Is reattaching to new land a betrayal of family history and his male duties as the family farmer? Can't he see a life beyond this familial fortress?

Eliza is only six, but she remembers the history of the entire farm. Our formal tour guide, she stops at each field and tells its story, proud to be in charge of crop memory and serve as farm hostess.

She tells about the sparrow's nest—with three speckled eggs—tucked in the cluster of corn plants, and the nonvenomous redbelly snake living beneath the squash leaves, eating slugs and insects and guarding the fruit. In front of the red potatoes, growing lush and green on the Plains of Abraham, she remembers how last year in this same field, during the drought, the watermelons set fruit on the same vines three times in one season. She recounts losses too: the beets that Martin disked because he didn't know I'd planted them, the sack of corn forgotten in the field, the squash that rotted because the fall was too wet.

She tells how we planted and when, based on her observations of nature. Potatoes when the nettles are ready to eat, carrots and beets when the lilacs are at first leaf, muskmelons—never before the oaks are leafed out. She talks about the work that she does, picking and washing, helping customers, carrying empty sacks in the field. Then she picks edible weeds, lamb's-quarters and purslane, and passes them around for everyone to taste. She digs up clover with her little shovel and points at the lumpy-white nodules on the roots while explaining nitrogen fixation. "The clover is friends with bacteria, and together they make food out of the air to feed the soil that feeds the vegetables."

It is easy to see the natural system of order through her child's perspective. School starts when the pumpkins show their first tinge of orange, early cucumbers signal fireworks day, Maize's birthday will always be linked to strawberries. When the plums bloom on the side of Treasure Hill, she runs out to pick the asparagus. She knows the sequence of seasonal bloom and crop maturity from earliest to latest, from first spring blossom to last kale leaf picked. If one plant were to bloom or mature out of order, she would notice, and she is the one who reminds us that we can't farm by the calendar.

All over the farm, next to every field, she and Maize have special forts. In some there is not much evidence of the preferred place, maybe some grass bent from their sitting, or a circle of rocks. In others they pile and arrange, draw borders and territories, collect and treasure—milkweed pods, fallen bird nests and broken eggshells, weed seeds, and dried-up salamanders. Once they are drawn to a spot and claim it as their own, they never abandon its location. Martin and I see this placing and arranging as a claim on this land for their own relationship.

Each fort has a name reflecting the attributes of the surrounding area, the natural topography, the species that live there, the crops we cultivate. Magic Hole, Fairy Spot, Circle, Bush House, Grassy Nest. Corn Fort is a living museum of ancient maize culture. A small handful of seed buried and sprouted in a corner is living testimony to man's relationship with corn. At the foot of the plants they have laid an offering of tassels. There are rooms sectioned off with dividers of dried corncobs, and husk dolls sleep between corn-silk comforters.

Sometimes they play make-believe games of family or farming. In spring they pick violets and dandelion flowers to "cook" snacks. During harvest they pick produce and "make a picnic." They lie on their backs, look up at the clouds, and Eliza recounts Diffley folklore for Maize. Eliza's Chicory is now a sea of periwinkle flowers. It is Eliza's most sacred spot. It is here that she lies quiet when she seeks counsel from a voice larger than us.

Their play here is their way of praying, as they accompany, step-by-step, nature's cycle of death and rebirth. The farm is the space that contains their day-to-day experience of the miracle of life. For them, nature is their church, the woods a sanctuary, the fields a classroom. The cycle of natural life and death they memorialize in art form. The connection to nature that happens here brings them into the holiness of being. It is here they see creation in the making. This is the space where devotion models the earth.

I believe they can hear the world speak. The moon sings lullabies, the trees call to play, the stones tell basic truths from long before people, and the stars listen and hold their secrets.

Martin makes holes with a round post alongside a wire that is stretched the width of the Woods Field. I follow and slip in tomatoes. Eliza trails behind, jabbering nonstop. I'm not really listening to her but to the birds, and noticing how the roots feel as the soil moves in to hold them. Maize is running around with a jar collecting beetles.

Martin says to Eliza, "Your Great-Grandfather Tom and Great-Aunt Mary cleared this field with Fox the horse. They cut down the trees and sawed the good ones into lumber, which they used to build the barn that is still standing on the home place. They trimmed the small trees for fence posts, and the broken or rotten ones they used for firewood. Fox hauled the wood out and then pulled the stumps, roots and all. Now here we are planting."

Eliza has heard Fox's story many times, but she never runs out of questions. Now it's, "Who led Fox? Aunt Mary or Grandpa Tom? What was the first thing they planted? What was Fox's favorite treat?" I get irritated when Martin tells these tales—the kids love them—but where's Fox now? And Aunt Mary and Grandpa Tom? I want to scream at Martin: That is so long ago, a different world. Get in the present; look what's coming.

We hear bulldozers start up, back where the school will be built. Martin and I meet eyes, but we don't say anything. He glances sideways at Eliza, then back to me. I tip my head toward the wire, and we keep planting. The idling engine changes to the crushing and falling of trees and the beep-beep of backup warning. Eliza drops her basket and runs to her tree. Maize dumps the beetles and squishes them under his bare heel. He sends the jar flying into the woods and then takes off running toward the bulldozers.

Martin races after him. I'm thinking, they shouldn't be hearing this. Then I realize it's too late for that. There is no sheltering from it. We will not only hear it. We will see it and feel it. We sit down together, pulled into a family huddle. Eliza is shaking underneath her skin. Her lips are moving. One tear hangs trembling in the corner of each clenched eye. She squeezes them tighter.

Maize whispers, "Stop them." His voice cracks, like it's trying to break through the wall between frightened and angry, "Stop them, Dad."

I don't think Martin even hears him. He is staring. His skin is drained of blood. I don't know what to say. They are too young to be learning that their parents are not all-powerful beings who can protect them from everything. "We can't stop them." I say. "They own it, but we are going to buy our own farm. We're going to move to a new home and land, and I promise you, no one will ever bulldoze it." I don't know when, or where, or how. But I know we will do it.

"I don't want a new farm," Maize says. "I want this one."

Eliza and Martin sit mute, just holding on to each other.

We've been waiting for Bluebird Valley to dry after a perfect soaker. We go out to check it and find the field is flooded with water, three inches deep. It makes no sense. This valley is well drained, has never held water, and there is no reason for it to be flooded—it only rained half an inch, not a biblically proportioned deluge. We wade and muck our way across and find they have dug a trench from the swamp at the school site into the valley. They are pumping the swamp water into our fields.

"They don't have the right to dig through and dump water on land they don't even own," I say. "Don't they know the line between what they bought and the rest of the farm?"

"It's the school district; we can't say anything," Martin says.

We go out to harvest the first broccoli from the Swamp Field next to the school construction zone. As we pull over the hill, something doesn't look right. It should be green, but it is brown. As we get closer, we see the topsoil has been scraped into a pile that is speckled green and red with broccoli heads and cabbage leaves.

Cousin Rosemary and her sisters still own this land. We rent it.

The bulldozers don't have any right to come in here. Just a day ago I walked this field counting what was ready to harvest, then sold it over the phone to the food co-ops. Where yesterday I walked between rows of leafy mature plants, now are parallel lines of bulldozer tracks in exposed subsoil. The drought did not prepare me for anything like this. Life did not prepare me.

The kids climb to the top of the pile. I ask Martin what he is going to do. "Nothing," he says. "The City of Eagan can destroy us if we make trouble."

"Trouble! We're hardly the ones making trouble here."

"We're not opening that door. Do you have any idea how many code violations we have? They could put us out of business in no time."

"Open your eyes, Martin. They are putting us out of business."

We're heading back to the house to call the co-ops and cancel the order when we come upon a couple and two children strolling across the Plains of Abraham. The man is carrying two onions and a cucumber. The children are running around like puppies on a lawn, regardless of rows.

"Can I help you?" I say.

"We're just walking over to see the new school site. Our kids will go there." They sound proud. Like they made something happen besides a baby.

"This is private land, not a park. Where did you get the vegetables?"

"They were just lying on the ground over there."

"This is a vegetable farm. We don't operate a pick-your-own, so in the future you'll need to come to the roadside stand, but since they're already picked, it's five dollars."

"We didn't know. They were just lying there being wasted."

I look the length of the field and see a trail of broken plants. "Actually, make that twenty dollars for the vegetables and the plants your kids stepped on."

Almost every day we have a conversation like this. The people in the new houses adjoining the farm have no concept that anything is here. Land without buildings is perceived as free and open; vegetables growing in a field are being wasted. We come over a hill on a tractor, and there are children playing in the road sand. Not all of our field vehicles have good brakes. I don't know. Even if we could stop the development, would I want to keep farming here, the only farm surrounded by suburbia? It would be good for sales, but it is not a rural community, and our kids don't fit into the suburban culture.

I call the food co-ops and tell them, "I'm sorry, the broccoli and cabbage got bulldozed. We don't have any." The lump in my throat settles in like it's planning to stay for a long time. Instead of thinking about ways to get rid of it, I'm telling myself to get used to it.

The school development opens up access to the south half of the farm, owned by Ruth, the widowed second wife of the widower husband of deceased Aunt Margaret, who bought it from Uncle Bill and Aunt Ann with her husband Uncle Aubrey back in 1971. Whew, I can't keep the relationships straight. It doesn't matter anyway. It has been sold to developers. Before long, bulldozers are there too, ripping up the Plains of Abraham.

At least we still have Uncle Jim's half of the land.

There is no logic to taking land out of production to build soil when it is going to be bulldozed in a year or two. Plus, we don't have enough land now. Instead of planting legumes and Sudan grass for fertility, we side-dress with Suståne, dried and pelletized turkey compost in a bag. We are grateful to have it, it is the highest-quality organic fertilizer available, and Craig Holden makes it just down the road in Cannon Falls. Yet, it feels wrong to not be rotating in fertility crops. I understand the dilemma, but still, I feel like we are just taking from the land, not restoring it. And that feels worse than a sin. I tell myself, this soil doesn't matter anymore—soon it will be bulldozed. But then I feel like crying, and I don't believe my own advice. All soil matters. It's not a natural resource; it's a precious gift, and it's being squandered.

I'm lying on my back with eyes closed, feeling the soil, and asking where do we go from here, when Martin shows up and says quietly, "I spoke with Rosemary this morning."

It can mean only one thing: Jim's land—the last piece left—has been sold. I don't want to make him say it. I just ask, "When?"

Nomads

The developer, Ryan, sits in our kitchen with a map of the housing project that covers the entire table. He shows us where the roads will be and how the land will drain. The work will be done in three phases. The first year they will bulldoze and build the infrastructure on the back third, next to the school. Martin puts his finger on the map and mouths to me, "Fox's Grave." In phase two they will take Bluebird Valley, the Bee Field, Jim's, and the Clearing. The third year, Treasure Hill and Christina's, even the Ball Field and the Nest will sprout houses instead of crops. He agrees to let us use the fields until they are developed.

This means the developer is our landlord now. The rental agreement is long, but there are two crucial points. If the development process affects our crops in any way, they are not liable, and they retain the right to change their minds about what they bulldoze at any time without advance notice.

"There is no such thing as a new farm," Martin says. "All Minnesota farms are used. That's the dilemma."

I had never thought about it this way before; it is an entirely different perspective. I was focused on getting away from the bulldozers, on putting together a home and outbuildings, fields and greenhouses, creating a new family farm, and this time we will be the owners. "This is a little like buying a used car," Martin says. "We need to look for all the things the seller doesn't point out. But unlike a used car, we can't take it for a test drive. We have to know clearly what we want and need before buying."

He adds, "We need to look at how the water moves and how the neighbor's runoff comes on and affects it. It won't be looking to see if there has been erosion, but how badly. We have to look for old dumps—every farm had one. If we are lucky, it will just be a pile of broken glass bottles and tin cans. Usually it's near the rock pile, at the edge of the woods or the mouth of a gully. They can have old chemical containers that are empty now but weren't when they were discarded; there might be appliances or engines leaking fluids. In land ownership, it's not the person who polluted who bears responsibility and liability for cleanup, but the present property owner."

Martin's main criterion is a deep loam soil with high organic matter that is not highly erodible and hasn't been excessively abused. In particular, he is looking for Waukegan silt loam. We need diversity in topography: southern slopes for early, heat-loving crops like tomatoes, peppers, melons, and cucumbers; and northern slopes for the cool-weather crops, broccoli, lettuce, and kale. He talks about drainage, fields that don't sit wet, and hedgerows. I know he will see to our agricultural needs. I list a southern exposure for the house with a tree windbreak on the northwest side, a long driveway, an old lilac bush, and a bridal wreath. I'd like to have at least ten acres of woods, and I wish we could have a lake or a stream. We know we won't find everything. We prioritize.

We want to stay in Dakota County. It has some of the best soils in Minnesota, it is close to our markets, and, perhaps most important, Martin is fourth generation, Maize is fifth—our roots are here.

One of our marketing philosophies is a goal of fully meeting our buyers' needs from the start of the season until the end. To do this, we intentionally overproduce. If the weather is cool and crops ripen slowly, we still have enough. But this requires sufficient land. We both say, "one hundred acres." This will be enough room for cash crops, soil building, and biological diversity habitat. We're on the same goal now. We'll grow on rented land until we find the right piece to buy.

I know it won't be the same, and I don't have an image of the landscape or what it will feel like. I'm confused to find excitement mixed in with the loss. When I think about a new place that's really ours, not his relatives' and laden with family history, I can see a lot of personal growth in it, especially for Martin. The change will allow him to drop patterns long ingrained into his ancestral structure. Maybe there is no such thing as a new farm, but there is new opportunity.

I feel guilty about it though. Like my impatience to move on, to build our own farm and find the positive is a betrayal to land that I love, to nature, and to Martin and the children. And first we have to find it and keep our business going for years on rented land.

We're organic farmers. Where will we ever find enough land to rent that will qualify for certification—no prohibited substances for thirty-six months?

Just north of Rosemount, on gravel Dodd Road, Martin pulls into a driveway. The yard has been taken over by junk trees and burdock, but there are beautiful shade trees and a massive oak. It would clean up just fine. The classic lilac hedge runs along the road, and I can smell a bridal wreath blooming somewhere close. There is an old water-pump windmill with grapevines growing to the top. The barn looks like it held a lot of cows and hay in its day; the house was a real family home. There must be good soil around here with buildings like this. The farmhouse needs work, but I like the sagging porch. It looks like a comfortable lap. I can see us sitting there, all together, at the end of a long, hot day of harvest.

The pasture is dotted with mounds of beautiful black soil where pocket gophers have dug. I picture giant broccoli, creamy Peruvian Gold potatoes, fat leeks, and luscious sweet corn. Martin starts digging. Two and a half feet down it is still black, loose, well-aggregated loam. I know the color black absorbs all light, but this soil black must absorb and hold all nutrients. The organic matter must be 5 to 6 percent.

"This was Jack and Marie Daly's farm," Martin says. "We're related through our grandparents. It's Quam silt loam. The same soil as the Crown Jewel."

It feels like our new home, and this soil will grow anything. "Is it for sale?" I ask.

"It's slated for development in a few years," his voice wavers.

I see how hard he's working to hold back tears. "But we rented it," he says. I look at my blackened hands. It's not the same as owning, but it's a refuge and a start in the right direction.

Every week now Martin finds another field we can rent, land that will qualify for organic certification. Most of it is owned by people he has second- and third-generation relationships with, but some he finds in unanticipated places, like a stranger at a gas station or through word of mouth. He has secured five acres just up the road from Murphy, half an acre below at Louise's, a rich field from Louie Sachs. Much of it is slated for development, and it too will soon be gone.

People offer us larger pieces, but they don't qualify for organic certification; thirty-six months of no prohibited substances or practices is a long time. We have always been organic farmers, and we always will be. We consider growing less until we get onto our own land, but then we'd lose our place in the market, and how will we buy land if we drop income? By spring planting Martin has secured eighteen different properties, spread out, thirty miles apart. We call each field by the name of the owner we are renting from. It's a managerial nightmare, but it is just for a few years, and we can still use some fields at home until they are bulldozed.

It used to be the birds and sun that woke us in the morning; now it's the diesel engine roar of bulldozers starting. All day long it's a perpetual racket. Soil and rocks tumble against the blades. The incessant beep-beep-beep of backing is a relentless, battering invasion. They don't shut down for lunch, just switch drivers. When they finally stop, we are numb. I hear the crashing rumble all night.

I don't lie down in the fields anymore. It frightens me too much to feel the earth vibrate to the bulldozers instead of the life force. But it's the trees that most affect us, the shatter of trunks snapping, the crash of branches hitting the ground, the crushing whimper as bulldozers shove them into piles. Rosemary's daughter, Colleen, is running the roadside stand. Between customers she reads *The Giving Tree* to Maize. He's memorized every word and reads it to himself perched in the branches of the crab apple tree.

Eliza's daily outfit now is a frilly white communion dress from Grandma Corinne. The waist is soft layers of white netting. The skirt hem, sleeves, and neck are edged with lace. It doesn't matter what we are doing, she puts it on every morning. She never wears shoes unless we make her, and then it is only with resistance. Dirt on her feet, legs, or arms is not a problem. One drop of water or a speck of soil on the dress, she runs to the house and changes into her second favorite outfit, a maroon velvet gown with a lace collar from the 1940s. Before coming back out, she sprays liquid soap on the spot and soaks it in the washtub. It's not the dirt she objects to but the act of staining, of becoming soiled.

I wonder about the fact that it is a communion gown that she doesn't want to take off or spoil. She is the same age that Catholic children receive their First Holy Eucharist. Seven or eight—considered the age of reason. This is the land where she first received the holy sacrament of nature, where she connects with creation in the making. But instead of receiving her first spiritual union, she is being cut off from it, learning the sacred will not always be protected. What will happen when they bulldoze the Corn Fort? Or her Chicory. Will she still hear the world speak? Will the stars still listen?

We have a five-vehicle caravan lined up, ready to go when the crew shows up an hour before sunrise. Two box trucks shelved full of hundreds of flats of transplants and two thousand pounds of potato seed, a truck and trailer loaded with tractors and planters, a water truck with hoses and a pump to fill it from a pond, and the most important vehicle of all: the tool van. Now that we are nomadic farmers, instead of loading tools and spare parts for the job, we store them all in one vehicle—a traveling shed—and take it everywhere we work. One never knows what odd thing will be needed.

We're a regular farm parade, our lives and work on display. Kids stop and stare, wave at our procession. Adults beep their horns. People are always saying they saw us and want to hear where we were going.

"Portable farmers," I tell them. "You provide the field; we'll grow the crop."

This isn't so foreign to me. When I worked citrus as a migrant in Florida, we picked all over the state. The crew has the act down. We pull into Charlie's Pasture and everyone hops to opening chain binders and come-alongs, pulling strap-downs off the equipment, putting ramps in place, and unloading. Our quiet days of Martin making holes with a dibble and me hand planting seem so long ago.

It's a lot of work and energy to haul everything here; we make the most of it with two planting teams moving across the long field at the same time. Martin works ahead of us all, prepping land with a digger and drag. My sister-in-law is riding the one-row transplanter pulled by an International Super A. Every eighteen inches she slips four pumpkins seeds half an inch deep into the fold being carved by the trenching shoe. I'm with a four-person crew, planting broccoli on a two-row transplanter. The trenching shoe cuts a planting furrow that fills with water. We slip the root balls in and then slide our hand up the stem as the packing wheels close soil around the roots. There is a bodily felt tempo that keeps us on time, holds our plant spacing in a pattern. The turning of the wheel and the vibration of the engine provide the rhythm. The speed needs to be just right. Too fast and we can't keep up, too slow and there is an unnatural pause that throws off our spacing. Just right is a steady pace we can hold all day.

When the broccoli is finished, we switch to potatoes. I hop in the truck to haul the hundred-pound sacks of seed to the planter, but I can't find the G6666-4y yellow potatoes that we market as Peruvian Gold. Instead there are fifteen sacks labeled Yukon Gold. I'm thinking the vendor made a mistake until I open a bag. They look like cloned copies. It doesn't take long to figure out what happened.

Our number variety just got a trade name, Yukon Gold. It won't be long now before we lose our position as the only grower with them in Minnesota. We can't complain; we had a good four-year run with the Peruvian Golds. I look up and see Martin on the hill planting corn with an Allis WD45 and a 494 John Deere four-row line planter. The back of his shirt is full of air and billowing behind him. Our days of planting corn with a check wire are behind us also.

At lunch we lounge in the hedgerow with pasta salad and sourdough bread. After eating I lie flat on my back and soak in the bottomless sky. It is so quiet here. I can hear the voice of the wind again, and even better, the earth doesn't shake from bulldozers.

By sunset we are caked with mud, and every flat and potato sack has been emptied.

We are so tight with land; there is only one field open for lettuce. But big problem: it has a regular deer highway through the center of it—a main thoroughfare. Young lettuce to deer is like arugula to flea beetles or cantaloupe to bees. It has a powerful lure. They cannot stay away. We don't have the money to buy an electric fence, and I know of no other effective way to keep them out. Planting this field to lettuce is a generous act in favor of the deer.

We plant it anyway. We have the plants and a crew, the food co-ops are expecting the crop, and we have nowhere else to put it. If there was ever a time we needed the help of the nature spirits, it is now. I sit in the middle of the freshly planted lettuce. With eyes closed I visualize deer approaching and a sawhorse blocking the path where it enters the field. I imagine a sign hanging from the wooden frame depicting a full head of romaine with a do-not symbol crossed over it. Deer mass behind the sign. After a large group of them have congregated, I stand up and address them.

"Hi deer. I am here to propose collaboration as allies in this development challenge. Just like you, we are being squeezed out and losing habitat to bulldozers. If we work together, all our families will benefit. We need the money from this crop to buy land. You need food. If you eat this lettuce now—just planted—you won't get much, just a few small leaves. If you wait until we are finished harvesting, we will save it—and every other crop we grow—for you to eat."

I visualize the deer cutting a sharp right turn at the sawhorse and running along the edge of the field. I hear the mothers admonishing their young to stay out, to wait until they are invited to the feast. I see the lettuce, mature, and us cutting and packing gorgeous, crisp heads.

It works. The deer shift their trail to run around the edge of the field. I have never seen or heard of deer changing their route. Their highways and lanes are as old as their culture. Martin says, "I'll believe it when I see it." However, there is not a single footprint in the field. Where the path runs into my imaginary sawhorse, the deer veer right and then left to run alongside the south edge. At the end of the field they cut back up to their old trail.

The field produces: heavy, dark-green romaine—the nicest I've ever seen—bushy pillows of green leaf, red leaf, and butterhead. After weeks of harvest we are finished cutting, and there are giant heads, bolting to seed, still in the field. I picture again the sawhorse on the path, the deer congregating behind it, milling about. I reach over with my mind. The sign crumbles into vapor and exists no more. I say, "Come on in; the field is yours. Thanks for waiting. Good health and good luck to you and your children."

The next morning the field is full of hoof marks. There is not a single head left—not even a leaf. It has been eaten to the ground.

I'm scouting a broccoli field, counting cabbage loopers, when I smell the sharp acidity before I hear it or see it.

I look up and see a sixteen-row sprayer emerging from a cloud of mist, heading straight toward me. My head stops. Some kind of current runs through my veins. There is no thinking involved—just reaction, like a tiger protecting her young. With all this rented land, we now have fields next to conventional corn and soybean rotations.

We have thirty-foot buffer strips for protection from pesticide drift, but we don't live in an organic bubble. I sprint into the field, stand in the path of the tractor, and wave both arms wildly. He's coming so fast, and the wind is at his back; it looks like it's just going to push him right into me and our crop. Just when I'm thinking I better run, he stops. We stare at each other through the bug-splattered, dust-coated glass, until finally he crawls out of the cab.

"What do ya want?"

"Hi, can you tell me what you're spraying?" I have my notepad and pen in hand, ready to write it down. My intent is to sound pleasant, like a friendly neighbor, but it comes out more like a snarl.

"What's it to you, lady?"

"We're growing organic tomatoes in the adjoining field. I want you to know they can't be drifted on."

"I don't control the wind."

"That's true, but you could lower your boom height. You could stay back from the property line and pick a time to spray when the wind isn't out of the west."

"That's close to never. I gotta spray today. These weeds are getting away on me."

"It's illegal to drift." Minnesota has a strict liability legal standard for enforcement of cases involving pesticide drift: if drift occurs, the applicator is responsible, and no showing of negligence, carelessness, or intent is required to bring an enforcement action against the applicator.

"Oh ya. Well it's illegal to piss behind a bar."

"Tomatoes have no herbicide resistance. If you drift, they will be hurt. These are high-value specialty crops, and they're certified organic. If you drift, you will be liable for three years of loss. That would be a whole lot of money."

"You can't squeeze blood out of a turnip," he says.

"You own land, don't you? It's too windy to spray today."

"Who do you think you are? The tank's mixed, and I'm going to spray it."

He climbs back into the cab, puts the tractor into gear, and lets out the clutch. I walk backward to the property line holding a beady eye on his face. If I stand here, he surely won't spray to the edge. Maybe suburban residents are easier neighbors after all. I'd rather have people not recognize our existence than drift us with herbicides and pesticides.

He comes straight on, waving at me with his right hand to move, but I don't. I'm still too mad to feel anything but rage. It is like a flood of indignation that washes out any kind of fear. Just when I start thinking he's going to spray right to the end, he cuts to the left, missing the headland. I stay on the line. He keeps spraying, farther away each loop around. It's not until he pulls out of the field that I burst into tears.

We're not the only species that should have a right to a chemical-free environment, but we are the only species that has rights in a court of law. If we want to protect something in nature, we have to prove a loss to humans. What if nature had a right of its own? It should.

Some states do not consider pesticides strict liability. The injured party must show negligence on the applicator's part. Negligence means there is a standard that has been violated, such as spraying at the wrong time or not following the label. It helps if the grower is certified organic because they can show damage and loss whether or not the applicator was negligent.

Next time I come down I'll plant basil in our buffer strip. It can't tolerate any herbicide. If it is drifted, it will show. The task of purity falls to us. But we aren't the ones using the chemicals. Imagine if it was the other way around. It is illegal to damage another farmer's crops. What if the person using the chemicals had to have a buffer instead of the person claiming the right to be pesticide-free? Why does such a smart species spray its food with poison?

I think of what Anita and the suffragists faced. *The system works— why change it?* Works for whom?

As If It Never Existed

I accompany Eliza across the farm for a ballet class at Pine Wood Elementary. The brand-new school, built in the Swamp Field, has just opened its doors with community education classes.

One minute we are strolling a dusty field road between vibrant crops of kale and tomatoes. Birds are calling from the trees. Martin with Maize on his lap is cultivating corn with an IH Super C. We wave at the crew hoeing onions.

Then we are cutting through the bulldozer work area. There is no life here, just sand-gravel subsoil for a base, and beeping, rolling machines without a human face. It feels like a no-man's-land between disputed borders, a separation line between disparate worlds.

Next I'm opening the door of the school, and my shoes are squeaking on a shiny tile floor. It's so new there isn't even kids' art on the walls yet. I peek in a classroom and see desks in a row where there used to be vegetables. Instead of the sun, fluorescent lights shine from the ceiling. I have to check myself. I want to grab Eliza's hand, run out the door, through the transition zone, and back to green. It is so strange living and farming in this interface, but maybe it is better than neighbors who spray pesticides. I don't know, and it doesn't matter anyway—they are both reality right now.

I offered to take her on the tractor, but she declined. She is wearing a shimmery-blue dance leotard underneath a cotton sundress. Her ballet slippers are in a black bag slung over her shoulder. I am wearing work clothes. What I live in. There is a group of women in the hallway. I see them look at us, put their heads together, and whisper. The word "dirty" jumps out from all the rest and hangs—a black cloud between us.

"I know the way back from here," Eliza says. "You don't have to come for me. I'll walk over to the field."

I tell her, "It doesn't matter what anyone else says. They don't know you."

She glazes over. I think about the me who stood up to the sprayer, but that was a different threat. I was her age once, equally embarrassed by my mother's stained hands, and it wasn't so long ago that I faced my own shame of being a dirty farmer. She runs around the farm by herself all the time. She's old enough. She won't get lost or hurt. "All right, but stay far away from the bulldozers. Remember, they can't see you."

When I reach out to hug her, she pulls away and runs into the gym without looking back. I turn around, and my face flushes bright red when I see the trail of dirt clumps that mark my path. The women are staring. I still have to walk out—past them—alone.

Once I'm out of the door, I run all the way back to our side, hop onto an IH 140 tractor, and start cultivating cucumbers in Bluebird Valley. I'm finishing the first row when bulldozers roll out of the woods and start flattening trees on the edge of the field. Five minutes later the job foreman pulls up in his truck. He rolls down his window and waits for me to drive the tractor over. I feel the cool air flowing out from his air-conditioned cab as he shouts over the noise, "We are working in this field today."

"Here? Where the cucumbers are? We have the right to this land yet this year."

He repeats himself, carefully enunciating each word. "We are working here. Today."

The second time I get it: the rental agreement says they can change their plan. Anytime. "You'll have to wait while we pull the plants," I stutter.

He doesn't agree. He doesn't argue either. I tear off running for Martin and the crew. We dig each cucumber plant with a shovel and carefully place them into harvest boxes; they are just starting to vine. First yellow blossoms. The bulldozers are right next to us, pushing trees into one giant pile, topsoil in another. Clouds of insects fly out of the woods. Birds are right behind them, screeching as they go. Against the noise of the bulldozers the trees are screaming for help. It's not a crushing whimper now. It is a legless, angry plea. But I can't do anything for them. Their time is up. I am working bent over, eyes to the ground, when a vole bumps into my boot, straightens up, and runs off, away from the destruction. A family of rabbits race across the field. All along the edge of the woods are moving shapes, animals escaping.

It is a mass exodus—the animals, birds, and insects are fleeing; we are pulling the cucumbers. But the trees and bushes can't run, nor can the soil life. It just lies there, an innocent victim, and after all it's given us. I wonder what sound it's making. If I put my ear to the ground, I think I could hear it. The trees are sobbing now. Maybe I should stand in front of the bulldozers and stop them. But what good would it do? They'd shut down for a while, eventually I would get arrested, and they would go back to work.

I don't want to hear the soil. I don't want to listen to one more cry that I can't answer. I have to pick my battle. One I can win. Eliza arrives—completely out of breath—in the middle of this. She is still wearing her ballet shoes. The slippers, her legs, her dress, and her bag are coated with dust. I know why she didn't take them off. She wants to stay in her dance world—everything is clean and quiet and safe there. I shout, "Can you walk home and change into farm clothes?" I don't want her watching this. "We'll pick you up and take you along to Marlin's."

Once she gets to her Chicory and then over Treasure Hill, she'll still hear the bulldozers, but everything will look like it has her whole life. I watch her take off, then run to catch up. She shouldn't be alone right now, and she's far more important than saving these cucumbers. There has to be a way I can reach her and let her know the world is a good place, even when bad things happen. That's she's not alone, we are all in this together, and we'll get through it. When I reach her, I take her hand, and we run together all the way. I tell her we are going to move. It won't always be like this. Life is good. But she just looks at me. I know she doesn't believe any of it.

We replant at Marlin's. They'll be safe from bulldozers there. Eliza surprises me by throwing herself into the work with her old farm-kid gusto. I know the entire time we are planting that it won't work. It is too hot, and there is no water here. Cucumbers don't transplant well, and these are too large and already vining. We do it anyway. We have nothing to lose except time and labor, and it is worth a try. I am more than willing to be wrong.

The plants wilt in the heat. They don't revive. In three days they are dead. Eliza says she won't go to ballet anymore. I tell her in the future I'll shower and change my clothes. We'll drive on the road instead of walk. I'll even wash the car. She just says, "I'm not going."

Are we already vining? Is it too late to move us?

Hills are dirt blemishes to be moved—as they will. They are flattened, reshaped, and resized. Trees are flimsy sticks, pushed into piles to be burned or buried.

I look out and see loam soil. I see hedgerows of sumac, plum, and cherry. I see bluebirds flitting and mice eating weed seeds. I see spiders, ground beetles, beneficial fungi, and worms. I see places and relationships that are holy, that humans are not meant to enter or change.

The bulldozers don't seem to notice the homes of the other species that live here, or maybe they are of no consequence. The land is a blank canvas waiting to be painted with roads and houses. Shaping it into its new reality is just their job.

In the Clearing we circle tables around the hollow, all that is left of the original cabin. There is a seat for each aunt, Martin's siblings and cousins, our kids, and us. The woods are blooming with jack-in-the-pulpits and mayflowers. The grass is thick. We serve sweet corn frozen last summer and salad from the garden sprinkled with violets picked in the woods. Eliza walks around the table and hands each guest an arrowhead from Aunt Mary's collection—all of them found here on this land. Maize follows and plants a kernel of dried corn in each palm, seed that Martin saves each year, seed that was passed down from Uncle Bill.

This is a wake for the land. Everyone tells his or her memories. God is thanked. Irish ancestors are toasted. Hard work is romanticized. Aunt Betty is now the land's elder: "It just brought us all together, land and God's country. We saw nature in every form, whether it was in planting grain or cutting the wood. We had to depend on everything from our land and from God."

Martin's cousin Rosemary is Betty and Jim's eldest daughter. She has been responsible for managing the land that she and her sisters now own, and she is the only one of them still living here. The developers are at the table, sharing this food and hearing these memories. She introduces them and says, "I went into real estate because I knew that eventually we had to do something further with this land, rather than just let it be, because of the development of Eagan. It took some real searching to find developers who would do something with the property and preserve as much as possible our memories, the trees."

Her parents farmed, but she didn't. I realize her relationship is centered in the woods, not the fields. Some of the Oak Woods immediately behind her house will be preserved, which shelters her from the development. Her children are caught between the past and present, between the dream and reality. They grew up living on the land, but they never counted on it for food, shelter, heat, or livelihood.

Rosemary's daughters speak of growing up secure in a community of relatives, of having a special spot they called their own, of knowing their place in the world. Teresa works in economic development. Her spiritual relationship with the land is clear as she talks about what she carries with her. "That close witnessing of the life process, which is so embedded in me because of the wonderful opportunity I had to live in this place. The rootedness this land has given me absolutely cannot be taken away, no matter what happens to the land." Her voice slips. She wipes her eyes.

The dichotomy of emotion is too huge; she uses her talk to sort the confusion, the conflict between work, loss, and spiritual. "Change is not bad; what if the people never came from Ireland here? We never would have had this. We do move on. But I have a lot of sadness that it's going to change, that my land is going to grow houses instead of corn."

Martin hops in, "I'd like to make a toast to this land, the spring flowers, and the trees, our ancestors."

The challenge comes when the talk centers on opportunity. "It's so oddly American, the whole ownership of land," Teresa says. "It gave people an opportunity, and now it's liquidating it that gives the opportunity. And it does provide opportunity for all those hundred-some houses. That's an opportunity for all those people in their individual lives, to have something that they want."

I want to scream—stop trying so hard to make this OK. It's not, and it never will be. But I think she knows this. She is just trying to cope. Aunt Betty brings us back to the soil and the land's history of growing crops. "If anyone ever put their hands down in the dirt . . ."

But my mind gets stuck and stays there when Martin says, "I guess the question I've always had is, at what point does it stop?"

Maize's voice when the bulldozers first started still rings in my head, "Stop them. Stop them, Dad."

It doesn't take long with the big machines. The Clearing is erased. As if it never existed. Framed by the trees that formed the shelter, acres of mature oaks, trees that have been part of this ecosystem for hundreds of years, now scraped into a pile, burned, and buried. The land that grew them is shaped and smoothed according to lines drawn on a thin piece of paper.

It is a high, blue-sky summer day. Martin, Maize, and I are driving down to Charlie and Mary's to check on the crops. I still think of

Charlie as Mr. MoorMan. "The pigs will be happy to see me," Maize says. "Can I stay with Mary and the pigs while you're in the field?"

We pull into the driveway to the home and animal buildings. We're barely off the road, when Martin slams on the brakes. A massive bull is charging, head down, horns pointed directly at us. Charlie comes chasing up from the side yelling, "Block the driveway. Don't let him through." Mary is behind the bull, shouting and waving her arm.

Martin reacts by pounding the side of the truck door with his open palm. I copy him, slamming my fist on the passenger side. Maize holds down the truck horn. The bull freezes in motion, weight balanced on his right front leg, a thick, rooted oak log. His massive shoulders are pointed in line with the horns—at us. His eyes lift and lock onto Martin, who just keeps pounding but looks out the side window while he says to Maize, "Never, ever look a bull in the eye. If you do, he'll try to kill you."

Charlie is standing wide-legged, not giving an inch of ground, and yelling, "Get on, Brownie; get on." He moves closer, and his voice becomes sharper. The bull jumps up and turns in midair. He lands twisted, ass toward us. Mary sweeps her arm in the direction of the open pasture gate. The bull glares back at us. It was his avenue of escape, but now we're here, a barrier making a racket. He dashes into the fenced pasture. Mary runs over, slams the gate shut, and latches it. She and Charlie are laughing, as if chasing a mad bull around the yard is a jolly lark. "Hey, you guys came at just the right time."

We stay in the cab and listen to the story of how the bull got out. Maize sits silent, slouched between us, watching our faces. It's not until we've left them, checked the crops, and are back in the truck that he says, "Why are bulldozers called bulldozers? It's not like they're sleeping."

On the way home we stop to look at a farm for sale. It is immediate. I love it! The house has a sunny kitchen with wide cupboards surrounding a round oak table. The sink window views a yard of summer flowers and shade trees. The driveway is long. It is quiet and peaceful. I can see our family here and happy. Martin walks around the fields looking for areas of erosion and rocks. He digs through the topsoil to see how deep it is, takes a handful and squeezes it into a ribbon that runs out of his clenched fist, then rubs it between his thumb and forefinger and smells it. "This would be a tough piece for vegetables, poorly drained, tight and heavy clay. Compaction and disease would be constant challenges. It's badly eroded, and the soil is cold. We'd have late crops."

"This is like the thirtieth piece we've looked at," I complain.

"A beautiful house will not pay for land, but good land will pay for a house and everything else we need, a pack shed, irrigation, equipment."

"You are never going to be satisfied."

"It might take another thirty, but we'll find the right one."

We have this same argument every time. Maybe he's just making excuses because he doesn't want to move. I don't know, but I'm tired of it. I will do whatever it takes to get us out of Eagan and onto our own land.

On the way home we pass a billboard south of Rosemount that states the current lottery value. Maize says, "If I won, I would buy the farm and make them put everything back just the way it was—every hill, every tree, every field, every plant, even the weeds." I'm sitting here thinking, a five-year-old shouldn't have to think about saving the family farm—that should be our job, and one of us isn't trying. But Maize goes into detail: "The strawberries, the wild cherry trees, the blackberries, the artichokes, Eliza's Chicory, the hawthorns, the nettles, the Clearing, my mud puddle, all our forts, even the stones on the roads—just exactly like it was before the bulldozers."

His list of what has been lost amazes me. Maize is always taking things apart. Nothing is sacred. I go to wash my hands, and the handles of the water faucet are gone. I turn on the radio and find it is just a face; the insides have been removed. We get on a transplanter, and the wheels are missing. He wants to know how everything works. He takes it apart to see inside. Sometimes we find the faucet handles and the wheels and the radio parts put together in new creations. They don't work, but that's not the point—his inventions are about learning. He sees everything as raw material; nothing is junk to him, and if it isn't raw, he makes it raw.

But an organic farm is not a machine to be taken apart. Interactions between the components, the crops, animals, insects, soil, everything in the natural ecosystem, are as important as the individual species. When one thing is changed, it affects the entire structure. All the parts are necessary for the whole.

This is one of the zillion reasons I have to find him new land.

But what is a farm? Maize has identified some of the land-related components with his child's list. That's all gone now, but we're still farmers, and we still have a vegetable business. We're still a farm, right?

I don't talk to Martin all the way home. A bull is an active animal with a reputation for charging ahead, but Martin is frozen. When we pull into the yard, everything is noise. I can hear the bulldozers in the fields. Cars and trucks are racing past on Highway 3. Customers are jabbering about corn varieties. All I can think is, I will do whatever it takes to get us out of here. But then, when we are falling asleep, Martin says, "They bulldozed Fox's Grave today."

Instantly, I'm not mad anymore. I feel like a complete idiot. He's doing the best he can to find us the right land, and his loss is so huge. All I can do for him is try to hold him here on earth. And while I'm lying there, just squeezing as hard as I can, feeling his silent tears soaking into my arm, I realize Eliza's Chicory is next.

In the morning I look it up in the dictionary. Farm: A tract of land devoted to agricultural purposes.

No. The land is not the farm. That is so clear. How could a major dictionary have got it so wrong? The land was here long before the farm and long before the people or the business. The land is completely its own. The people and the business need the land. The land does not need either.

The farm is a synthesis of the land, the people, and the business.

A blending. A new entity with a personality—that is the farm. No two combinations are the same; each farm is unique, with its own character. The land contributes its climate, topography, soils, precipitation, biological diversity, and ecosystems. It is fixed in a location. Maize understands this with his child's list of what the bulldozers have destroyed. The people bring their passions, skills and labor, their relationships, creativity, and emotional patterns. The business brings its financial capacities, its reputation and earned goodwill, the culture and market it operates within. There is no one-size-fits-all. Each farm has to develop its own strength and place.

For now, the land part of our equation is temporary, rented around the county, but we still have the people and the business. We just need a permanent home. I look up the bull symbol in an astrology book: "Strengthening and a desire for solid ground, form, and structure. Preservation is important. The 'fixed' motivation is inspired to stabilize, to produce; feelings have very deep roots."

Martin is such a bull. I know what this feels like for me, but I'm triple fire, elderberries, and dandelions. I always come back in spring. It must be absolutely soul breaking for him to be a bull uprooted.

The bright spot in all this is a problem, but it makes us so happy, we don't even care. We go to dig Yukon Golds from the deep-black rented field at Daly's. The first time I saw this soil, I envisioned gorgeous potatoes, but the first forkful we turn up uncovers tubers as big as my foot. The second plant is the same. We cut them open, and they are good to the center, no hollow core. I bite out the heart, and it is crisp and moist and delicious, but we can't sell these to the food co-ops. I say, "No one will buy a potato this big."

"The Riverside Café will love them for hash browns," Martin says. I'm looking at the field and thinking it would take ten years for the Riv to cook this many spuds, when Martin says, "Imagine how this is going to look on paper!" We break out screaming with laughter. An entomologist from the University of Minnesota is doing research in this crop on a lady beetle that eats potato bug larvae. He'll be documenting this yield. We dig a few more plants, and we have a full bushel.

When we get back home, we go out to dig Jerusalem artichokes. On the south end of Treasure Hill the land slopes steeply for ten feet, then flattens out into a tiny field that lies nestled into the side of the hill. The hill shelters the field from the wind, and we call it the Nest. Martin planted Jerusalem artichokes here in 1973; he's been digging these tubers every fall since.

Jerusalem artichokes are native to North America, in the same genus as the garden sunflower. European settlers called the plant girasole, the Italian word for sunflower. They are also called sunchoke, sunroot, or earth apple. We dig the roots before freeze-up and eat them all winter. They are not for sale, just our personal use. In spring, fresh plants spring up from the roots that break off when we are digging. We weed them through the summer, and the next fall we come out and dig them again.

Martin, as the original planter, pushes the potato fork in with his heel and flips up a nest of fresh sunchokes. Maize, the last Diffley born on the land, picks up the first tuber and puts it in the basket.

I say, "This will be the last season we dig them."

"Artichokes are more persistent than a farmer," Martin says. "The only thing that lasts longer than a farmer and his life on the soil is the artichoke."

Next spring this field will be destroyed and he is still talking about persistence?

What to Hold On To

The last of the Diffley land will be bulldozed this season—right up to our one-acre property line. None of our crops will be on the home farm. We are true migrants now, but we do have one rented field that we can walk to. Louise's Field is a pasture that Martin's father sold in the 1950s, along with a house he built at the base of Devil's Hill.

Devil's Hill, the wildest spot on the farm, has a fierce energy that sets it apart from all other land formations in the area—a mingling of uncontainable passion and independence, as if it is self-made, a land formation with self-determination. The east face is a cascading series of slope and jump. Rocks squat firmly in scattered clusters, as if they rose up from the interior of the hill, too powerful to be contained by the thin skin of topsoil and grass. Halfway up begins an entanglement of sumac, hawthorn, and wild plum. Near the peak of the ruggedness, oak, birch, and poplar come in, and the slope gentles but continues climbing, until finally it eases into the asparagus and chive patch and then settles out flat as Christina's field.

Martin and I are at the foot of the hill in Louise's Field, checking the potatoes. "That's a magic hill," he says. "It's always been that way. I was captivated by it when I was a boy, and my father and his father before him. Now look at Maize and Eliza."

It's true. They are halfway up the slope, flung out on the ground with limbs wild. As we watch, they climb onto a rock, jump to the sky, soar for a second looking like they believe they can fly, then curl into a ball and roll bouncing down the hill until they smack into another boulder. They lie there laughing hysterically, then scramble up and take wing again.

Martin loved sledding on it as a boy, but his mother worried; someone always got hurt. Now I'm the mother. Today there is no snow to cushion a blow; the day's heat is blistering; the rocks shimmer as if they could scorch. How soon will it be before one of them gets hurt and comes down crying? I am afraid to allow it, but even more so, I am grateful for what the hill gives them.

I see Devil's Hill as invincible. When everything has been tamed and domesticated, when the bulldozing is complete, the houses built, and the lawns planted, this hill will still emit its fierce individuality. It will serve as a reminder of the time before the settlers, when the people living here had minimal impact on the landscape. It stands powerful, a barrier between the suburb and this fertile valley. We can visit, and we can play, but the hill makes the rules.

Louise's Field is small, little more than half an acre, but rich. It is easy to look at the soil and plants and see what the hill gives to this field. It is dry now, but the knee-high potato plants are in full bloom. We dig a few and find a heavy set of quarter-sized Yukon Golds. I pull my skirt into a basket and pick them up for dinner.

"Look at those clouds," I say. "If we have a good rain tonight, in two weeks we'll be harvesting."

"With this heat, ten days," Martin says.

Louise Mueller, the widowed owner, comes out to talk. This is a multigenerational relationship. Martin's father built and sold this house on land he inherited from his father; this field was once Diffley land. It's a funny concept, but if Louise's Field hadn't been sold, right now it would likely be under the weight of development. The developer owns Devil's Hill, but it is too steep for houses, so it too is safe.

In the 1950s, Louise and her husband, George, were horse breeders and traders; often there would be a dozen horses of different shapes, sizes, and breeds in this field, which was then a pasture. George bought them green broke, and Martin would help Bruce and Bobby, the Mueller kids, break them for pleasure riding and games. Louise was never

The Diffley homestead on the northeast corner of Diffley and Dodd Roads in Eagan, Minnesota, was settled in 1855 by Martin's great-grandparents from Ireland. Photograph circa early 1900s.

Uncle Bill, one of Martin's many "old-timer teachers," plows the home garden with a 1939 Farmall A.

In 1981, Eagan still had a rural community and Martin's roadside stand was called a "community market." Photograph by John Croft, Minneapolis Star Tribune *News Negative Collection, Minnesota Historical Society.*

Martin used this New Orleans French Market label from the 1930s for wholesale during the 1970s and 80s.

GARDENS OF EAGAN

Martin V. Diffley
4355 So. Robert
EAGAN, MINN.
55123

CERTIFIED ORGANIC
VEGETABLES

Eliza and me during our first spring farming. Photograph copyright 1985 Liz Welch.

With one-week-old Maize in the Woods Field planted to onions, June 1986.

For more than three decades this sign pulled in customers, and Martin and I used "Turn here" as an opening line for conversations about changing how our food is grown. Photograph copyright 1989 Helen De Michiel, from her video essay Turn Here Sweet Corn.

Martin checks parts availability and price, while listening to the history of a tractor he considers purchasing. Photograph copyright 1991 Nick Lethert.

In 1990, the Gardens of Eagan roadside stand was a lean-to roof attached to the family barbershop and an adjacent walk-in cooler.

The corn sales table and blackboard were the social and business center of the roadside stand. Photograph copyright 1995 by Dennis Nolan;

The Diffley family land in 1987, taken from the Plains of Abraham overlooking Cottonwood Valley, Bluebird Valley, and the Bee Field; the Big Oak Woods are in the background.

Martin and I watch developers' bulldozers and encroaching suburbia alongside sweet corn growing on the Plains of Abraham. Photograph copyright 1990 T. L. Gettings for Rodale Institute.

Checking Yukon Gold potatoes for maturity and signs of pests or disease two weeks before harvest will begin. Photograph copyright 1990 T. L. Gettings for Rodale Institute.

A few days later, the developers' bulldozers stripped the adjoining hill of plant cover. That evening a heavy rain eroded the hill into the potato field and destroyed the crop.

The Diffley land, after the development and school were built. The farm relocated, but the Gardens of Eagan stand continued on Highway 3. Imagery by Pictometry International Corporation.

We knew the soil was fertile when we saw this 300-year-old bur oak on our new land in 1991.

Maize and Martin introduce Maison Diffley in 1993—our one dollar, moveable, brick home.

In 2005, the 43 small fields on our new farm produced approximately 2,895,738 food servings. A year later they faced the threat of eminent domain for a crude oil pipeline. Our land is the center one-third of this image. Photograph USDA National Agriculture Imagery Program.

Martin on a point of purchase sign used in the food co-ops from 1994 through 2007. Photograph copyright Nick Lethert.

Tomato plants greet the dawn from the shelter of the greenhouse, spring 1995. Photograph copyright Dennis Nolan; all rights reserved.

I deliver fresh sweet corn to Linden Hills Co-op in 1991—a "direct-market" relationship.

Martin purchased five Farmall tractors on a lucky auction day in 1999.

Martin in a field of hairy vetch, a main component of our renewable fertility system that feeds the soil microbial life and captures atmospheric nitrogen and the energy of the sun.

On a Super M, Martin chops sorghum-sudangrass, adding organic matter to the soil.

In 2007 we had 200,000 cabbage and broccoli bare-root transplants in outdoor nursery seedbeds.

Transplants ready for planting thirty-five days after seeding.

Noah Engel and Laura Frerichs transplant cauliflower.

Sorting clean Heart of Gold squash is the last quality check before it leaves the farm. Photograph copyright 1995 by Dennis Nolan; all rights reserved.

Winter squash, solar-cured in the greenhouse, stored for delivery through December.

Yellow strips of canola, rye, and vetch provide habitat for beneficial insects that help control pests in this kale field. Photograph copyright 1995 Dennis Nolan; all rights reserved.

Martin and Laura Frerichs harvest cold-hardy broccoli during an early November storm in 2003.

Attorney Paula Maccabee represented Gardens of Eagan when Koch Industries threatened eminent domain for a crude oil pipeline. Photograph copyright 2006 Leora Maccabee.

At our harvest party and public hearing energizer, Martin's band, the Pheromones, play "Tequila" while the crowd performs the Corn Dance. Photograph copyright 2006 Camille Maize Diffley.

Martin and me in the kale field: the kale was our ally and expert witness during the MinnCan crude oil pipeline lawsuit dubbed "Kale Versus Koch, Soil Versus Oil." Photograph copyright 2006 Greg Thompson.

big, but now she's tiny. When we are working in her field, she often invites Maize and Eliza in, turns on cartoons, and gives them cookies and milk. She sits and laughs with them. It is cool in there. The kids don't get any of this at home, the cookies, milk, and cartoon treatment or the sitting in soft chairs in a cool house. They consider her a loving grandmother. Sometimes when we are ready to leave, they stay behind; it is an adventure for them to be there alone and to walk back, just the two of them. It touches Martin's heart to see them coming home, hand in hand, on the old horse path through the valley of his childhood.

Louise tells us the city will be running the sewer and water lines across her property to serve the development. Although she doesn't plan to tap into them, because she can't afford the additional hookup fee, she has been charged an assessment. A lien has been placed against her house and property. She lives alone and gets by on Social Security. "Will I lose my home?" She asks, "What can I do?"

All day we hear bulldozers working north of our house. In the evening, after they shut down, Martin and I walk back to check out what they did. We cut across the ripped-up Ball Field and through what was Christina's. The bulldozers are parked on top of the chives. It takes us a while to see what is right in front of us. We only sense that the light is wrong. It is too bright.

The trees on Devil's Hill are gone. We stand in the pungent scent of crushed chives looking down the now-open slope. In the short span of a summer day, the east face of Devil's Hill has been completely stripped. The trees and brush have been shoved into a pile. The rugged slope has been scoured into a slide of rock, silt, and sand; plant life is nonexistent. It looks like an oozing wound hanging above Louise's Field and the valley below.

In the darkest part of the night, the heat and humidity clash into a midsummer storm. Rain pounds the thin shell of our sleeping cabin. The kids press against the screens. A crack of thunder shakes the walls. "That's really close. It sounds like it struck Devil's Hill," Martin says.

The lightning lashes are white hieroglyphics written against the black. The brilliant flashes race the sky palette from crown to floor, no boundary between horizon and universe. It burns on for what seems like hours. The rain is a fluctuating torrent. It alternates between hard and soft but mostly stays in the rhythm of loud. Eventually the kids lose their excitement and fall back asleep. Martin lies down, but I know he's still awake. For him, the louder and rougher the storm, the more he worries about hail. I know the crops are fine. I am happy that the kids love a good storm instead of fearing it. Martin is right—ten days until harvest. I fall to sleep dreaming of the potatoes in Louise's Field below, reaching out with thirst and drinking, the tubers swelling.

When the kids and I wake, Martin is already up and out. We find him with his head under the hood of the Ford F150 pickup. He closes it but doesn't say anything more than, "Hop in."

Where yesterday a lush crop of potatoes grew in Louise's fertile valley-loam is now a soggy mess of subsoil and gravel. Green leaves poke through the surface. It is easy to see what happened. The heavy rain washed down the exposed slide the bulldozers made of Devil's Hill. There is a deep gully where the heart of the hill slid into here, the valley field below. Last night the hill looked like scraped skin oozing. Now it is gutted and bled out, its arteries removed.

This was an act of complete arrogance; humans should not be trusted with such powerful machines. How could anyone have missed how sacred this spot was? Some places are simply not meant for humans to change. And if Devil's Hill can't resist them, can't command their respect, what can? There must be something I can pin trust onto that will hold it secure until we get on the other side of this.

I start digging in the wet mess. I'm thinking we'll still be able to harvest and just market them as small, new potatoes; at least we'll have something. But it is not possible to determine where a plant was, much less a row. The fork cuts through twisted and broken plants, eighteen inches of silt and sand. Eventually I excavate what I am sure is the stump of a potato, but when I dig it out, it leads to no tubers. It is a dead end. There will be no harvest here.

I have never seen Martin like this. He doesn't eat and he doesn't talk. It's not the loss of the crop. This was the pasture, valley, hill, and neighbor he grew up with, one of his favorite places in the world. It was the first area he played as a kid, a valley full of giant cottonwoods fed by three ravines. There was a spring full of salamanders and frogs. The horses came right up to the fence line, not far from his bedroom window. Their whinny was often his morning wake-up. In the winter he would sled down and ride a horse back.

Devil's Hill is gone. Her spirit has departed. Once she was a pinnacle of wild vigor and the centrifugal force of the farm; now they have carved her down and shaped her remains into the gentle roll of a soil wave. It is not even the taming of a wild animal. She and her influence are only a reminiscence. What took an eon of time and mighty glaciers to create has been altered beyond recognition in a few short days. I watch Martin with Maize and see him trying to pass on what is left of the Diffley history, but when I ask him to talk about his feelings, he says, "We always knew it was coming. Every year was one more gift to cherish."

I know this is just a defense. I say, "It will always be with you, it's what you are made of, and you will pass it to your children." But they are just words. I don't even know if they are true. With the land gone, and now Devil's Hill, I don't know what is left. And I don't know who Martin will be.

Ryan, the developer, calls at the house with hat in hand. He apologizes for the devastation to our potato crop but says, "That is all part of development and is covered under the rental contract. I can't be held responsible for it." We go to look at the field. He says, "I see leaves, but where are the potatoes?"

An Irish last name and he doesn't know that potatoes grow underground? No wonder he has the ability to scrape this land bare. Martin says, "They are under a foot and a half of compacted sand and silt sediment. The crop is a complete loss. This field is not part of our contract. It belongs to Louise. You have to pay for this lost crop and the damage to her field."

"Who's Louise?"

"The most dangerous woman in the township—a horse trader.

I've seen her dish out lashings and whippings; her sons received the strap same as the horse. Consequently, her son was just paroled for such a heinous crime to another human that I can't bring myself to describe it, and he's now living at home. You'll be dealing with Louise and her son on this matter."

I can't believe he said that. And why? Louise is a sweetheart. Maïze and Eliza love her. There is no way she ever whipped her sons. They do have motorcycles, drink, and get a little rowdy, but I've never heard of any heinous crimes.

"My God," Ryan says. "What am I going to do?"

"You're going to go down there and offer to buy this field from her that you've destroyed with your development and your callous attitude. It's not just our crop that is lost. Your silt and sand have covered well over a foot deep her rich valley. This field is ruined."

Ryan is watching Martin's face. "She is the witch of the neighborhood," Martin says. "Her other son is a tough-ass biker. If I were you, I'd make it right with her damn quick."

The developer's insurance company makes a settlement offer for the potatoes based on conventional wholesale price.

We reply with invoices documenting our organic price as six times higher than conventional, along with our organic certification and a written description of our potato-growing practices.

They offer to pay twice the conventional wholesale price but at half the yield. They seem to believe that organic growing systems are not as productive.

Martin calls the entomologist who did the lady beetle research in the foot-sized Yukon Gold potatoes grown in Daly's field. He mails us yield documentation on University of Minnesota stationery. We send a copy of the letter with our calculations: our organic wholesale potato price times the university-documented Gardens of Eagan potato yield. A satisfactory settlement follows.

■ ■ ■ ■

Maize is riding his bicycle in circles around a display of pumpkins. He is a golden blaze. His hair is corn silk flowing behind, his body a collection of innocent energy and concentration as his sinewy legs pump the pedals and he leans into the corner. If I squint my eyes, I can't tell where the bicycle ends and the boy begins, a bicycle body with a boy's head, shoulders, and arms. Women come in with pre-school children to pick out a pumpkin and take pictures in front of cornstalks. They stop and watch this centaur racing in a circle. When he finally parks the bike against the corncrib, he is radiant. "I won the race," he says. "I won the golden pumpkin."

Louise walks into the yard. Maize skips over and hugs her. When they get up to me, I see that her body is shaking. She holds out an envelope. "He just came up to the door and held this out to me," she says.

"Who?"

"The developer. Said he'd like me to sign it."

I open the envelope and find a purchase agreement for the field at a fair price, plus payment of the sewer and water assessment and of the fee to connect her up to city sewer and water. "It's like *The Giving Tree*," Maize says, "only it's 'The Giving Hill.'" He hugs Louise again and then runs into the pine trees behind the house, where his last fort remains. I'm surprised he understands so well.

After this, Martin is a little more present. Knowing Louise is OK somehow helps with what he can't do for the land. I wonder though, will he always carry the loss like a failure of duty?

Subsoil Is the Mineral Base

There is a pair of robins I have been watching. The tree that held their nest was flattened. They moved to a new branch and started over. A few days later they were treeless and nestless again. Three times now—they just build anew and lay another batch of eggs. They make it look so easy.

Just wake up each morning and sing the same song. The bulldozers have ripped the development right up to the edge of our one acre—a green refuge pushed tight against the border of destruction. The robins have made it to the cottonwood on our side. I feel superstitious when I say, "They should be safe now."

An acre has never felt so small. There's the family house Martin's father built, our greenhouses, toolsheds, and roadside stand. The farm equipment, chased off of Machinery Hill, is crowded next to the summer kitchen. My herb garden is undisturbed inside a white picket fence. Purple spike flowers of anise hyssop poke between the boards. The Dolgo crab apple is right there full of birds. Our sleeping cabin under the cottonwood is resting in thick grass. The clotheslines stand firm beside the spruce trees that Martin's parents planted in 1941.

But I don't recognize anything when I look out at the open expanse of gravelly subsoil beyond our acre. Where are the wild plums that marked the edge of the field, the artichokes and blackberries? I can't even work out where big landmarks, like Treasure Hill, used to be. It's all just a big, dirty, bare space. There is nowhere for a bird to perch and nothing for one to eat. A sparrow would have to pack a lunch box to land there. The developers must have stood on the Plains of Abraham and looked down into Bluebird Valley with the woods behind in fall glory. They have named their housing project Autumn Ridge. Then they flattened the ridge, and the valley, and most of the trees. The only thing left of what was here is in the name. The other half is called Hawthorn Woods, but there are no hawthorns left.

The cottonwood is right next to the line—roots now disturbed—and its permanence feels threatened. The only thing that feels invincible between our house and the naked dirt are the clotheslines. The new lots have covenants on them that regulate the color the houses can be painted and what trees can be planted. Outdoor clotheslines are forbidden. This restriction completely violates my perspective of justice and reality. Hanging clothes should be a human right—it is an act of environmental responsibility. I am stunned to realize there are people so disconnected from nature that they accept this constraint.

We are next to these covenants, but they have no authority on our acre. My protest to these bulldozers ripping up our fields and our lives is to hang angry red union suits and old diapers. These people can't even have clotheslines—ours will be a symbol of resistance. I see the clotheslines as a fortification between our home and the destruction, the first line of sanity between us and the suburban sprawl creeping ever closer, like a moving wall.

Maize hides behind the sweet corn table. When a customer comes up, he jumps out and holds an ear of corn against his shoulder like a gun, making repeater rifle shooting sounds. He twists and leaps around, as if avoiding being hit himself. Where did he learn about guns? We don't have a television, he's never been to the movies, no one in our family hunts, and he doesn't go to school yet. Enough, I swoosh him off to play somewhere else.

One of our regulars, a bricklayer with arms like rocks, is picking out an onion when he jerks and blurts a startled, "Ooh." There is a small potato lying on the ground behind him. I hear Maize giggling and see him tucked up in the crab apple tree. I haul him down with a stern voice and send him into the house for a time-out. For Maize, not being allowed outside is the worst consequence imaginable. The man laughs and says, "Why punish him? Boys will be boys."

When I have a break between customers, I go in to talk with him, and he promises, "I won't do it again. Please can I come outside?"

Less then twenty minutes later I am talking cabbage with a frail old lady when she startles slightly and her eyes grow big. She calmly selects a new potato from the display in front of her, whirls around, and whips it at Maize perched in the crab apple. He screams, jumps out of the tree, and runs into the house sobbing. She winks at me and says, "You looked like you could use a little help." Who knew angels had such good aim?

After that there is no more trouble with Maize play-shooting or throwing things at customers, but he sneaks around the stand taking bites out of peppers and putting them back in the display—bite side down. He pokes holes in watermelons, squishes tomatoes, and then stacks fresh ones on top. Maize and Eliza used to spend their days running around the farm, house to field, to fort, to woods. Now they must choose in the morning where their day will be spent: stranded on our one-acre island, or at a faraway field, with no permanence, and no relationship. They are cut off from farming and the farm as a way of life—as home, playground, church, and school. Farming is now just their parents' job, and fields are just a place where vegetables are grown. They want to be part of the farm, but they don't want to go to work with us. I set up "day care" with neighbors. Maize stops acting out at the stand. We are still a farm family. But we are no longer a family farming.

Maize is standing in the tall grass on the edge of our acre, right up on the line between brown and green, between theirs and ours, between death and life. I marvel at his boldness, facing down the open expanse of empty, flattened dirt that has smothered out what he once knew. He doesn't cross the line the bulldozers have drawn in sharp contrast, as if touching the stripped earth will violate his spirit.

His body is quiet. Only his eyes move as he watches the bulldozers

drive back and forth, pushing soil from one place to another, digging
deeper here, smoothing there. The work appears mindless. I know
they have a plan, but I can't see it. Maize looks so peaceful. He blends
into the backdrop of the barren landscape; the dirt, marked with a
maze of crisscrossing bulldozer tracks, is the same color as his skin.

Suddenly, he explodes upward with the seething ferocity of a
confined typhoon, "Damn-shit-ass-monkeybutts-badbadbad-ugly-
gotohell-buttholes-biguglyassholes-dumbdumbdummys-Ihateyou-
hateyou-hateyou."

Strong language is not his only tool to curse them. With arms
and fists he pummels the air in repetitive screams of rage. His face
pulses red. His feet pound a rhythm of fury as his legs seethe with a
tumult of wrath. His back is a rigid line of resistance, muscles tense
with proven strength. I don't know if he thinks he is powerful and
will change what is happening, or if he is expressing his loss. Maybe
it is both. I touch his back and say, "I'm right here—backing you,
whatever you need—go for it."

He stoops down, reaches across the line, picks up clumps of dirt,
and throws them in the direction of the bulldozers. They leave his
hand with anger but crumble upon hitting the ground—mere dust
against the scale of the void. He keeps shouting big, ugly words, loud
and angry, coarse and base. The words hold the expression of his
blazing loss and allow him to lay it on the ground of his heartbreak.
He is hitting and kicking the air against the vacant hole. He is a burning squall, a foaming tempest, a howling fever. His emotion is a wild,
consuming force, leading him, somehow intact, through the fire.

His voice grows hoarse, his kicking lower. He keeps shouting and
hitting but weaker and smaller. I pick him up. Tears swell under his
eyes, and he huddles against my chest. There is no way to return to
before—before no longer is. I lay my palm across his forehead and
say, "Go ahead, let it go. I'll hold on to you."

It comes up and out then, with the force of a charging bull, from
where I do not know. Sobs deeper and bigger than could possibly
be inside him. Every cell in his little body is quivering. There is

no stopping it now, only riding it through as a coursing wave. The scream is no longer denial and anger. It is the deepest vestige of grief. But the anguish is immense, as if a loss for the entire world. A passing that can't be returned—only expressed and accepted. It feels like we are straddling a line between life and death. There has to be a way to cross it, to grieve the end, and love again.

His sobbing and shaking are coming from some place of spirit that I have never before seen in a human. It is so much bigger than him, but the absolute truth of him, and completely from within him. I turn my back to the sterile emptiness. His sobs eventually subside. He is not awake, but he's not asleep. I don't know where he is. I watch a dung beetle pulling a twig. An ant climbs a blade of grass. I don't hear the bulldozers, though when I check they are as loud as ever. He's going to be resting a long time. I carry him up to the roadside stand, wrap him tight in a cotton blanket, lay him in the hammock, and go back to packing produce.

When he wakes, he is serene. He wants to know when we will go again to look at land for sale. He asks what kind of tree I love the most. He tells me, "I love plum and cherry, oak, sumac and hawthorn."

When he says, "I love," the tears well in my own eyes. Thank God he is loving again. Thank God he left hate behind. Oh thank God he is going to come through.

I wish I could mourn and move on like him. I feel frozen at the center. Like I have to hold everything together for everyone and keep moving us forward. I am afraid if I grieve like Maize, we'll never be put back together in one place again. But I don't know what to say when he asks about looking at land. I don't believe anymore that we will move or that we will someday be a family farming again. I can't see beyond this acre, beyond this property line, beyond this life as a migrant farmer.

Eliza's reaction is the opposite of Maize's. When she walks out of the house, she turns her back to the bulldozers and the raped landscape a hundred feet from our front door. She does not play in the yard, just stays in the house or helps at the stand. And she cleans. She keeps everything tidy, vacuums and washes floors, takes responsibility for the family laundry, always using spot remover on our work clothes. She stares off in the distance and hums when I encourage her to talk about the bulldozers.

I have been worrying about what will happen when they take the Chicory, but she stopped visiting her holy spot long before the bulldozers reached it.

I find Peaches, the cat, on the side of the road—dead—hit by a car.

He never went on the road. It is a busy state highway. He knew better. This was not a pampered house feline. He lived here for thirteen years and hunted the entire farm. He knew every detail of the landscape, the dangers, the food and water sources, and he never, ever crossed the road. As the bulldozers got closer, he reduced his range. We never saw him on land after it was stripped. I guess it just got too close for him. He was used to 120 acres. One was just too small. I don't want to tell the kids or Martin. Peaches was a homeless alley kitten, scrounging for fish scraps behind Cafe Kardamena when Martin coaxed him into his delivery truck in 1978.

I bury him behind the kitchen herb garden, safe from the bulldozers, and mark the grave with a flat rock. When Martin and the kids notice he's missing, I'll show them the spot. They don't need to see one more thing of beauty destroyed.

After the kids are asleep for the night, I go down to the property line. The grass is still matted where Maize stood and kicked. I place my bare feet in his prints, hoping I'll feel it if I stand in the same spot. I squat down to his height and get his little kid view—but I'm an adult. I am bigger and older. I'm supposed to be stronger. I cross the line and walk out onto the bare land.

It's a strange kind of dark. The moon is full, but the clouds are dense. The light filters as if through a sieve and falls in tiny, separate particles like a fine mist. There is only the hard subsoil for it to land on, and there it runs off, like rain on concrete, wasted. There is really nothing here that I can see. I know there are houses built now on the west side by the new school, and oaks still left along the road. But here there is not a tree, not a plant, not a blade of grass. Not even an insect or a bird. It is completely devoid of life. The contrast between now and the past is so much more than just brown versus green. It is the complete absence of any ecological system at all. I try to imagine it coming together again, after the homes are built, the sod is laid, and the landscapers have planted, but it feels like a child's toy village. I can set in key elements represented by model block figures, but the invisible species and complex relationships, those I can't imagine returning, and they aren't in the kit.

When the farm was whole, I never once thought about where the nucleus might be. Now I am compelled to lie in the center, as if that is where the understanding is. I walk due west. It feels surreal to move in a straight line, to not have my path affected by a hill or a tree, by a field or a crop. When I find it, it's a magnet. There is no doubt I'm there.

I remember a night like tonight during our first year farming together. The kind of warm that is so close to perfect it is not even part of the sensory. Martin and I lay side by side in a field of leeks, basking under the rays of a full moon, our backs against the topsoil of Bluebird Valley. Everything was so alive. The soil had the scent of fresh rain and grass and happiness. The tree leaves were whispering. In the Big Oak Woods the great horned owl was giving an evening dissertation on the day's events, mostly about who did what, and we could hear the fox kits that used to den on Treasure Hill making strange, but cute, whistle-like purring sounds. We lay without touching or talking, just soaking in the light, moon-tanning. "It is possible to experience the divine wherever you are," Martin said. "Anywhere the moon can come—there it is."

I must be close to there now. I take off my clothes and lie on my back, face to the sky. If I'm going to move through this—cross the line from death to life and come back to love—there can be nothing between me and it. My back feels as if it's touching earth that has been peeled of its skin and drained of its blood. The smell is sour and stale; without the living topsoil the odor is of death. I lie motionless, trying to feel the anguish I watched Maize express. Why could he do it and I can't?

I just want to mourn and move on. I'm afraid of what I'll become if I don't, if I stay in this place of grief. I fix my eyes on the clouds, calling the moon to break through. But there is no response, just a truck jake-braking down the Diffley Road hill. We never heard road noise back here; the animals and the plants were the sounds of the land. Their absence now is louder than their presence was.

I can't. I can't see any life, and I can't see any way forward, only this destruction and death. Maybe there is no way. Maybe I just need to stop caring. Maybe the best thing to do is put the kids in the car and drive away. Then, when I know my heart will be a rock forever, when I'm on the edge of falling into a hole that has no bottom and no exit, when it's the only thing left that will get me through the rest of the night, then, the moon pries open the clouds and comes streaming down, searching until it finds me, the only life present for the divine to enter, and, finally, my tears gush, though there is nothing here for them to water.

By late afternoon on Halloween, there is half a foot of heavy, wet snow on the ground, and it doesn't look like it will let up anytime soon. Just a few hours to go and we'll be closed for the season.

Maize and Eliza trudge off, dressed in snowsuits to "trick or treat." They won't be going to a zillion houses like the future kids of this land will after the new community is built. They will visit just the Wachters and Louise, neighbors who have known them most of their lives. It won't just be a minute at the door with a piece of candy dropped into a sack. They'll be invited in and will sit together at the kitchen table visiting, with cocoa and something special to eat.

The snow has created a monochrome winter world. It feels as if we are in a sepia photograph with color highlights on key items in the picture. The vibrating orange of the pumpkins, the red crab apples dangling, the glowing Christmas lights on the stand roof pulsing throbs of pigment against the bland background. Cars pull into the stand. Doors open. Men and boys jump out. This is not the typical afternoon crowd of suburban mothers with their young kids. The Twins just won the 1991 World Series, and these men want to celebrate and bond with their sons. They aren't wearing coats or hats, boots or gloves. They lift their feet through the heavy snow and call over, "Do you have any pumpkins?"

I do believe we have the only pumpkins left in the county. I point at the dwindling circle of frozen and misshapen jacks. They are the most disgusting pumpkins we have ever sold. But there is nothing else. "These are the last of them," I say. "They are frozen and have rotten spots. Keep them outside until you are ready to carve. Don't let them thaw out." I believe in truth in marketing.

The typical pumpkin-buying scene with boys this age is the parents say, "Pick any one you want." The boys wander around until a warty or misshapen jack screams their name. The parents grimace and say, "Oh, you don't want that one," then point to a completely uniform, round pumpkin. "Here, how about this one? It's perfect." After that it can go two ways, depending on the family. Either the boys or the parents accept, or there is a power struggle.

Today's scene is not typical. It's me, roundly bundled in snowsuit and Sorel boots, scarf, hat and mittens, broom in hand, sweeping snow off of the frozen jacks. Visibility is about four feet. The snow around the pumpkins is trampled by shivering pairs of anxious fathers and disappointed sons, circling the ever-dwindling pile, looking for the best one or, I should say, the least rotten one. The father says, "How about this one?"

The son says, "That's really ugly, Dad."

"It's the best one, and everyone else is out."

While they are discussing, the pair before them grabs it out from under their feet. They then grab the next least ugly one from under the discussion of the next father-son pair.

I say, "Don't let it thaw; keep it outside." And so it goes, until every single hideous, frozen pumpkin is sold.

Another season—finished. I turn off the stand lights and put up the closed sign. Martin is in the kitchen with the kids ready to serve hot squash soup and bread. The windows are opaque-wet from the steam. We light the pumpkin candle. The grinning face links ours in a circle of orange flickering light. We can hear the cars and see the headlights rolling across the wall as they continue to pull in and out for hours.

In the morning we go out to shovel. Our traditional routine on November 1 is to take down the display tables and signs and clean up all supplies. We line up the last squash, potatoes, and onions in bushel baskets. Regulars come in for last-chance purchases. It's a holiday of sorts, an end-of-the season celebration.

But this year the display tables are frozen into the ground, and it's still snowing.

Corn shocks lean buried against the crab apple tree; broken tassels poke out of the drift. Dried flowers under the stand roof swing in the sharp breeze. Blue jays cut off abruptly from their fall diet of weed seeds and berries have eaten the Indian corn. It hangs stark— lifeless bare cobs. By the time the storm blows out, we have twenty-eight inches of heavy, wet snow. All winter long the stand sits frozen in place, a white winter ghost of summer past.

It feels wrong. As if there are still tomatoes and watermelon sitting on the tables, rigid under the snow. As if a human story was buried under an avalanche of time. There is no sense of completion. The season sits frozen, like our lives, waiting to move on. How long can we keep doing this? Living on a carved-down acre of land, migrant farming all over the county, every day looking out at what once was and now is lost. A farm family but not a family farming. When will I breath deep again? Or is the question, will I ever?

Eureka

Chris, the Viking-looking drummer from Martin's high school rock-and-roll band, is pounding the drum solo to "Wipe Out" on our front door.

I've told Martin I don't want him around the kids. He always was trouble, but I've heard he's now peddling stolen goods and hanging out with the local drug dealers. Plus he owes Martin $1,500 for a van. He was going to pay within a month, but it's been over a year. It's just after Christmas, and I'm sure he's not here to make good on his debt.

Martin goes out to talk with him on the front steps. Chris starts in with his usual prattle. "Hey Smarty Marty, I've come by to make things right with you. I've found Jesus, man. I'm taking care of my old debts and bad deals."

"You got my money?" Martin asks.

"I've got something you want more than money," Chris says.

"A guitar? A Fender Broadcaster?"

"I've been circling a piece of land for a couple of years. I was hoping to buy it for myself, but my city wife won't go for the long driveway. You've always been good to me. I decided to do right by you and the missus. If this works out, I'll trade you the lead for the money I owe you."

I confess—my irritation that Chris is at our door subsides when I hear "long driveway." But paying for a tip on property?

"You're sounding as desperate as I feel," Martin says.

"This is like being able to buy Willie Nelson's 'Crazy' song for fifteen hundred bucks, a barn burner of a deal."

"My wife already knows I'm crazy for having extended you credit."

"The place is a winner, a diamond in the rough. I know you and your bride can turn it into a little love nest."

"How long has it been on the market?"

"Two years, all the neighbors know about it."

"Why hasn't it sold?"

"It did. Guy held it up for a year with a purchase agreement contingent on selling his own place. Now it's back on the market. The owners are eager to sell. Deal?"

"Yeah, deal. If it works out."

Martin comes back in with a real estate flyer in hand: *Fixer-upper home on 31 acres with beautiful bur oak in front yard.* There is a picture of an abandoned farmhouse. Fixer-upper is a stretch. It looks more like endless work and a financial sinkhole, a knocker-downer. The oak, however, they've understated that. It is so beyond beautiful. It is ancient.

But we can't live in a tree. "It's in the area that has been identified as a potential site for the new airport," I say. "We might fix it up and then go through development all over again."

"It doesn't hurt to look."

"You're not really willing to pay that loser for a lead on property?"

"It won't be paying him, just forgiving a debt I'm not likely to collect anyway, and only if we buy it. We'll just check it out. I have a really good feeling on this one."

We study soil maps in the *Soil Survey of Dakota County, Minnesota.* There is Martin's sought-after deep and fertile Waukegan loam, along with a warmer, southern-sloping Cylinder loam, and cool, black Merton silt loam. He's grinning, "This is soil of the Giants."

There is even a mixed woodlot. But I wonder, is there such a thing as too fertile? And it's not enough land; only about sixteen acres are tillable. Martin calls anyway. The realtor is not interested in meeting us; she is from Hawaii and is busy getting ready to fly home in the morning. She says, "I'll show it to you when I come back in three weeks. There's no hurry. It's been on and off the market now for two years."

"We are very serious buyers," Martin says. "If it is the right property, we will make an offer tonight with money down."

He heads down to meet her. I pick up the kids at school and drive over with them. It is hard to determine where the driveway is. I find what I think might be the mailbox, but there are no numbers on it. I get out to look and find recent tire tracks entering what seems like a field. Ten feet in they disappear, filled by a ground blizzard whipping loose snow. I can see a cluster of trees and buildings about half a mile into the middle of the section. I pull in and start driving toward them, but it's so bumpy, it feels like I am moving crosswise through a moldboard-plowed field. Maize has his seat belt off and is hanging over the front seat, "Is that it? Up there? Those trees?" Eliza is hunched over a book, pretending disinterest.

It's impossible to tell if I'm on the driveway, and it's not worth getting stuck or breaking an axle. I tell the kids we are going to walk. I tighten their hoods down over their foreheads, wrap scarves around their necks and mouths, and tuck their mittens secure into their jacket sleeves. Our tire tracks are already filling in with snow. I should just pull out right now and take the kids home, but I need to see it. Martin already wants to buy it. We sink halfway to our knees, and snow falls in our boots. The wind is sharp. Maize runs ahead, and Eliza lags behind. I feel as if I'm pulling her through the snow on a sled of words.

"It's too deep," she whines.

"Walk right behind me. Step in my boot prints."

But it's not the snow that's too deep for her. It's this place we're stuck in, and she can't step into my prints. She's a kid and she's not me. It feels like the longest walk of my life. It's not the weather—farming has taught me to ignore physical discomfort—it's the searching, the responsibilities of mothering, the feeling of landlessness and being spread too thin, not wanting to hope and then be disappointed. And this is a little too crazy. Who buys land on a day like today?

I've lost sight of our goal. I'm just putting one foot in front of the other. Right now these feet are following Maize and dragging Eliza toward a cluster of trees that Martin believes might be our future. Up until now, no land has been good enough for him. It's impossible to imagine he's going to go for this piece, especially when he can't even see or touch the soil frozen under snow.

The wind drops, and I look up. We've made it to a stand of straggly lilacs and locust trees. I follow Maize's tracks around the windbreak, and I am stopped by the majesty of the grandfather bur oak—broad, dark branches spread wide in every direction. It must be centuries old. Talk about permanence! Prairie fires, windstorms, lightning—and it's still here. Even with the three of us holding hands we can't circle it. Maize is laughing, "It's bigger than any of the trees they bulldozed."

Beyond the oak are outbuildings—a granary, corncrib, pump house, chicken shed, even an outhouse. Some of the roofs are collapsed. Walls are leaning. A mature tree stands proudly in the middle of the corncrib. Between the buildings, rusty implements, tires, and tools show through the snow. Box elder trees are growing everywhere like weeds. Behind the barn a paintless tractor has a sapling growing through the steering wheel. The tires are hanging off the rims in rotten strips, and the rear fender is slapping against the seat. This looks like someone's lost dream. How could it ever restore ours?

Martin and the realtor come up from the barn. She isn't dressed for the weather, doesn't even have a hat on, and no boots, just thin dress shoes. "You don't want to see inside the house," she says.

"Can we go home now? I'm freezing," Eliza says.

"Yes, we do want to see it," I say. "Come on, Eliza; it will be out of the wind."

The front porch roof is caved in, but the main body of the farmhouse looks intact. We go in through the enclosed back entryway. The door into the kitchen is hanging half-open. There are glass shards on the linoleum floor from a broken window. Loose floor tiles slide as we walk across the room. Maize starts to kick them around, and I tell him to stop. There is mouse shit all over the floor. I don't want him to kick up the dust. Martin says, "That's too big to be mouse shit—more apt to be rats."

The root cellar is dug beneath the kitchen, served by a handmade wooden ladder. We crouch around the trapdoor, peering with a flashlight; water on the floor is three or four feet deep. The fieldstone walls, held together with cracking mortar, are covered with rough-cut wooden shelves. Old, aqua-blue Ball Mason canning jars, filled with pickles and tomatoes, still rest on them. Martin says, "There is probably a crock of sauerkraut under the water. The floor is surely dirt."

Off the kitchen is the living room. Large areas of wallpaper have peeled off, revealing a hand-plastered wall. Wood lath shows through in spots. The picture window frames the oak tree. "It must have been a beautiful room," Martin says. "Imagine a family here."

I test each step going to the second floor before I let the kids up. They creak but hold firm. At the top we find a short hallway and three bedrooms. The floors are fir. The ceilings are slanted with the pitch of the roof. I look out the window of the largest bedroom—there's the oak again. I'm already thinking of it as the Oak. I imagine fields of vegetables behind it. The view would be fantastic. I fall in love for a short second with the idea of fresh wallpaper and a big brass bed. It's not logical. It would be too much work to fix up, but it has such a cozy feel. It's a real farmhouse. The fields are right there next to it. Maize picks a long, narrow room with a window that also frames the Oak and says, "Here's my room."

Eliza and I look through the door to the last bedroom, and a long shape darts into the closet. I close the door but not quickly enough. She says, "I will never, ever live here."

Outside again we walk around the house looking at the foundation and roofline. The top trim of a window frame has fallen off. On the now exposed siding is carved *EUREKA—Ole Olsen—1880.* "That has got to be from the lumber yard," Martin says. "The wood was ordered to build this house, and the pile of lumber was marked for delivery. They used the marked piece of wood there, under the window trim."

I know it would take a huge amount of work and money to fix it up, but I do think it is beautiful. For a second short moment I feel like I am in love. I remind myself never to trust infatuation, which is all this is. I am so tired of Eagan I'd go for anything right now. We need to be careful. Whatever we buy we'll have to live with for a very long time.

The realtor waits in her AMC Eagle wagon while we look at the outbuildings. They are packed full of junk, but I can't tell what most of it is, as everything is coated with the thickest, grimiest layer of dirt. The barn foundation is made of giant boulders. The main body is home-sawed lumber, added on to a much older log structure. We go in, but it's hard to see. The filthy windows don't let much light in. A rat darts under a tire. This is a good infatuation check. Martin says, "We'll take them all down and start over."

We follow him out to the field behind the barn, where he scrapes away the snow with an old board, then thaws the ground with a flame torch until he can pry a chunk of soil free. I know he's not going to buy land when he can't see the fields. He's just window-shopping. But he stands up, hands me the torch, and says, "We can't wait till spring. Between this sample and the soil map we can get an idea of what's here."

After that we all squeeze into the realtor's car to ride out. I ask her how long it has been since anyone used the buildings. She tells us the house has only been empty for two years; Mrs. Hammer was living here alone, without running water, when she died in 1989. The equipment and outbuildings, she doesn't know for sure, but she thinks it's been decades.

At home we pore over everything the realtor has given us. Martin says, "It has the long driveway, fertile soil, gentle southern slope, and a woodlot."

"It's not enough land," I say.

"We can rent or buy other land in the area. The important thing is a solid base."

"The house is a wreck. There is junk everywhere. All the out-buildings are trash." I can't believe he is interested. Is it just a matter of timing and he wasn't ready before?

"Are we going to buy the Oak? Are we?" Maize jumps up and down. Eliza shouts from the bathtub, "I'm not going to live with rats."

I don't know why, but I am fighting the very thing I want the most. I am in love with it. I know it is our new home, yet I argue with Martin about every aspect of it.

"We can clean the place up," he says, "but even if we spent the rest of our lives at it, we couldn't grow an oak like that. And that oak tree is a clear indicator of the soil's fertility and value. Weak soil does not grow mammoth oaks. I want to make an offer tonight. I feel more kin to the land than any we've looked at. Chris is right; it's a diamond in the rough. We can bring it around with sweat equity."

I lie in bed all night but don't sleep. It is perfect. It is horrid. What if they accept our offer? What if they don't? How will we ever clean up such a mess? How soon can we move? The rats! I don't understand this confusion. This might be it—the family farm for future generations. But what if we're wrong?

We go to the library to look at old plat maps. I'm flipping through the *Atlas of Dakota County, Minnesota*, compiled in 1964, when I find an article about rats, right there in the center of the plat book.

> One pair of rats can breed five times—produce over fifty young per year. How can a farmer estimate the number of rats on a farm? Dr. Harold Gunderson of Iowa State College has suggested a method. "If you see no rats, but see occasional evidence, the population is one to one hundred. If you see an occasional rat at night, but never during the day, one hundred to five hundred. If you see them during the day, and a few at night, five hundred to one thousand. And if you see numerous ones during the day and night, one thousand to five thousand."

"Martin! Look at this! According to this article, the property has somewhere between five hundred and five thousand rats!"

Oops, everyone in the library is staring at me. Martin looks at the book for a second and whispers, "Hmm, that's interesting, how they put the information in the middle of a plat book. Most farmers kept one in their homes back then." Then he points at a map in the current plat book. "An Adelman owns these two adjoining parcels. I know the Adelmans from Eagan. Our families go back a century."

He shows me that there is an adjoining twenty-nine-acre parcel of farmland and another of thirty-seven, both owned by a Mr. Nick Adelman. They look perfect on the soil survey, more Waukegan loam and four other types, all rich, deep prairie soils. When Martin calls, Mr. Adelman recognizes the name Diffley. They have never met, but they know each other's relatives.

Nick tells Martin how his family came from Germany, settled in Richfield, grew potatoes and onions, and sold them at the Minneapolis Farmers Market. They were developed out of Richfield after the Second World War and have since moved twice. "It was hard work to farm and raise a family, but we were truly farmers," he says. "We knew we had to go to another piece of land, and it was for the good; our new land was richer soil, and our yields increased. You are making the right choice to come to Eureka. It's a good community. There are not many rocks, and it's productive. It is still zoned for agriculture, and there are many fourth- and fifth-generation farms."

Martin says, "If you are interested in selling the two parcels, we are interested in buying."

"It's possible," Nick says. "I'll talk it over with my sister."

The granite boulders that make up the barn foundation are troubling Martin. There are so many, and they are so huge. All he can think is the land has to be full of rocks. Octer, a lifelong neighbor of the property, tells him, "You have rich soil there. It always gave good crops. The boulders came from the next farm south." Octer's eyesight is poor, but he can still see the land. "Now that oak tree is quite an attraction to play under with the kids and the family, but if a storm comes, get out from under. It's been hit by lightning seven times."

Octer introduces Martin to the neighbors, Lyle and Henry. He says, "This here fellow wants to hear what you know about growing vegetables on the old Hammer place."

"Do you have a German wife who likes to farm?" Lyle asks. "That is what that place will take. It needs to be cleaned up and put to order."

Henry says, "It is productive soil and hasn't been abused. It will make it through a drought, and it will dry out enough in wet weather to get in."

Martin is convinced. It's the right piece. There are two sisters and a brother who have to agree on the offer. The brother doesn't have a phone in his home and can only be reached on Sundays at a particular bar in Wisconsin when the Packers are playing on TV. He holds the phone and asks his barstool buddies for advice. His distinguished council advises him, "Hold out for more. You only sell it once."

They counter. Martin reminds them that there are easement issues, the abstract is not current, the driveway needs to be completely rebuilt, and the buildings and all the junk need to be cleaned up. After weeks of waiting for the brother to be reached in the bar, we settle on a price.

But I've worked the numbers inside out, upside down, forwards, backwards, and sideways: we do not have the down payment, and we can't afford the monthly payments on a mortgage with what we are now making. We receive good prices and have a reliable market partner in the food co-ops, but driving to fields all over the county is inefficient, and we're not making any money, just surviving. Land prices are going up, and we've been looking for years. If we don't buy it, we'll either quit farming and get jobs, or be tenant farming all over Dakota County for the rest of our lives.

Martin just says, "Don't worry about it." A few days later he lays a stack of cash on the kitchen table, "I sold my 1950s Blackguard Telecaster."

"But that was your favorite guitar."

"I can always buy another Tele, but we can't always buy land. How many years have we looked? I'll tell you though, what was almost a deal breaker was he wanted the guitar strap I made in the '60s, of flowered upholstery material. It was like he wanted that as much as the guitar. The strap was the vintage patina. But I couldn't let go of it. There was too much of myself in it."

He sells a tractor for the rest of the down. He's not concerned about the fact that it isn't enough land or that we can't afford the payments. I am lying awake worrying when suddenly it hits me. I don't know why I never realized this before. Grandma knew she was dying years before she told us. Instead of coming back, she spent her last years earning and saving so she could help my parents realize their dream of buying land. If she was here, she would tell me: go for it; don't worry about the money. You'll work hard, and you have a committed partner.

Anita would remind me: self-determination. It's better to fail than never try.

We have purchased our land in Eureka Township. Maize has his Oak. For me, the long driveway and quiet. Rich Waukegan loam is Martin's dream. Eliza feels better now that she knows we won't live in the house, nor with rats. Mr. Adelman is willing to lease to us, with an option to purchase, the adjoining parcels. That makes a total of ninety-seven acres. We will continue migrant farming on our eighteen-field rented circuit until the new land is ready to certify organic in thirty-six months.

But thirty-six months is a long time. We now have the added work and expense of cleaning up the house site and transitioning the fields to organic, plus paying a mortgage on land that brings in no income. And I have no idea when we will be able to live there. We can't afford to build, and until we do, we will still be a farm family, not a family farming.

If Soil Is Virgin

Coming down the driveway is like going through a gateway to paradise. It's hard to believe it's the same place. The snow and cold are gone now. The soil in the neighbors' fields is so black, the gopher mounds look like giant chocolate drops. I feel like I am hopping from mound to mound, being led in to a new life. We come up to our property line, and the land lies before us, like a book open on display waiting to be read. The soil is glistening, wet still from the snowmelt. Dave Frattalone's voice is in my mind: "You need some soil as black as your Mamaluke's hair."

Eureka! We've found it. We stand just looking, like we are perusing the rest of our lives in the lay of the land. This soil is ancient. The mineral parent rock once sat naked. Time and water, sun and cold broke the rock into stones, the stones into dust. For a very long time the earth sat aging, then the life process started, and living soil was created. Thousands of years of plants have left their condensed energy and captured time stored in the organic matter. Farming it in present time is a relationship with the past.

Imagine the soil has a heart and we're walking all over it and talking about it. Martin points at a small field next to the woods, so deep and so black, and says, "Imagine kale there!" We come to an eroded clay knoll, "We have to get this covered as soon as it dries out. It can be our machinery hill." On a south-facing slope it's, "We need strips of grass here to prevent erosion."

What is this like for the soil? It doesn't get a say. People walk on it, talking, making human plans, like it is ours to open up and do as we want. Think how long this has been going on here. Since they broke the prairie off of this land, one hundred forty years of doing this to soil.

What was it like for Ole Olsen the first time to pick up handfuls of virgin prairie loam? What did it smell like? What happiness did he feel? Imagine if today there was an entire continent of land that wasn't heavily inhabited by a chemical-based society. If we knew what we know now, what would we do different?

If soil was virgin, what is farming? Do we choose a love affair, or is it a coarse taking? It's clear what needs to happen here. Its base potential is strong, but its metabolism is sluggish. It's just waiting for another chance to be alive.

Most of the tillable land is one big, bare field worked the length of the three parcels. The same tenant rented them all, and he has been farming end to end, through the waterways and up and down the slopes regardless of the topography. An intermittent stream runs through the center. Hundreds of upstream acres drain through it, and it too is bare. It is rushing now with soil-filled spring runoff. We walk the entire property, marking the water drainage with stakes based on signs of erosion. As soon as it dries, we will seed all the waterways to a permanent mix. We'll sleep a lot better once it is established with secure roots and we know that the water and soil are protected.

We check for compaction with a homemade soil penetrometer, a length of rebar with a handle made from a piece of scrap wood. In most areas it goes in less than six inches and then hits hardpan. We expected this; compaction is a common problem on land that has had years of mono-cropping, anhydrous ammonia, and salt fertilizers. Thirty-six months suddenly seems short.

It's simple to understand what compaction means to a plant if you visualize single particles of clay, smaller than the thickness of fine hair. It is bacteria and fungus living in the soil that hold these particles together into loose aggregates. Without this microbial life the soil is hard, compacted, and lacking in air. Roots have a difficult time penetrating. Rain cannot enter, and it runs off wasted, leaving soil droughty in its wake. We have serious work to do here. We need to bring microbial life back to this soil, and to do that, we must provide food, air, water, and a hospitable environment.

Transitioning land out of herbicide addiction starts with breaking the soil out of chemical dependency. Before we can begin soil-building therapy, this land needs to go through detox. Martin works the field with a digger and drag to stir up weeds and create a moist seedbed. Shortly after, it germinates thick with weeds that have been lying dormant, suppressed by herbicides for years—pigweed, giant ragweed, lamb's-quarters, sedge, and foxtail. These weeds are not our enemy but our allies, nature's system to protect, repair, and purify the soil. They are an important first step in breaking down the chemical residues that may be here.

The weeds also serve as indicator species, providing clues about fertility, soil conditions, and temperatures. The foxtail, a grass, is the thickest we've ever seen. Foxtail is nature's tool to remedy compaction, and it is commonly seen when land is taken out of herbicide use. It will dig deep channels with its roots, fiberize the soil particles, bust through the hardpan, and create paths for water drainage, working it into looseness better than deep tillage can.

Pigweed indicates high fertility, and the fields are thick with it. Its extensive roots develop quickly, laterally and deep, breaking apart compacted soil, taking up loose nutrients and storing them secure in its leaves and stems. Reaching down into the subsoil, the roots bring up minerals. When the pigweed dies, it becomes long-lasting humus, and the nutrients stored in its tissues become available for the next plants.

But it's the purslane that I am the most delighted to see. It needs warm ground to germinate. The first place it comes up will be the earliest spot for heat-loving watermelons and tomatoes.

The crucial trick to managing annual weeds is never letting them go to seed. We dig them in before they flower, the digger brings more seeds to the surface, they germinate, and the process begins again. Doing this repeatedly reduces the weed seed bank. This is one of numerous strategies that organic farmers refer to as "weeding the soil, not the crop." As the soil becomes biologically alive and remineralized, the weed pressure will diminish. We don't need to eradicate them, just manage them.

Perennial weeds, however, require a completely different strategy than annuals. These we do want to eradicate. The back nine-acre field is solid quack grass, one of the most tenacious perennial weeds in this bioregion and an indicator of hardpan. Quack grass roots can drill a hole through a potato or a carrot, and it's very hard to kill. If a tiller or digger cuts the rhizome, which is an underground stem, new roots shoot out from the nodes, and each piece produces a new plant, multiplying the problem rather than diminishing it. It's going to take serious attention to get rid of it. We can't do everything at once, and right now it is too wet to kill the quack. It will have to wait for dry weather.

After we've worked with the weeds for a few months, we'll spread composted turkey manure. It's an effective way to reestablish healthy microbial life and will also suppress plant disease. Then we'll plant canola. It will further loosen up the hardpan and compaction with deep taproots that can go forty inches down. We'll incorporate it into the top few inches and follow it with a fall planting of rye and sweet clover to overwinter. We will continue this process of feeding and building the soil until the thirty-six-month transition to organic is finished. And then our migrant farming days will end!

Eight inches of rain, too much and too fast. Once it starts, I can't go back to sleep. I'm confident that the fields are OK—the weed cover will protect them from erosion—but the waterway seeding just germinated, and it has no roots yet, nothing to hold it in place. In the morning we ride the thirty minutes to Eureka in silence. I have never seen Martin look this sick.

It's as bad as I feared. The intermittent stream is running huge and dark, full of soil and plant residue. The old streambed has filled with silt, and the rushing water has carved out a new route, taking soil with it. I still can't believe the former tenant was plowing through it.

Where the stream leaves our land, it passes through three culverts beneath the downstream neighbor's driveway—John. Except the ripping current has torn the culverts and his driveway out, and the stream is flowing through his greenhouses. He is on a B Farmall with a front blade, driving through floodwater a foot deep, pushing gravel and silt into a dike.

This is not a great way to meet our new neighbor. Before we even have a chance to introduce ourselves, he says, "Every time it rains, the water comes rushing off that land, full of cornstalks and soil, and plugs my culverts."

Martin explains, "We seeded the waterway to a permanent cover, but it hadn't much for roots yet."

"Well that's great," John says, "but not good enough. When it rains, your soil is so tight the water can't soak in. All it can do is run off or sit in a puddle until it evaporates."

We tell him. We are working on the compaction. Martin talks about organic matter, how it supports microbial life, which will increase the aggregation of the soil particles, improve the soil structure and thus the hydrology.

I say, "The organic matter will act as a sponge, taking in moisture when it rains and releasing it when it is dry."

Martin says, "The roots will go down into the subsoil, break up the plow pan, loosen the compaction, and allow rain to soak in deep."

"In two or three years, this land won't puddle or run off anymore," I add.

"As soon as it's dry enough, I'll be reseeding the waterway," Martin says.

"Great," John sneers, "as long as I don't lose my driveway again."

Now in Eagan, instead of bulldozers, we listen to air hammers, generators, and electric saws as the construction workers frame up the new homes.

Today I learn the buildable lots don't come with topsoil. When the land was bulldozed, the soil was scraped into piles and sold. The new homeowners have to buy topsoil and haul it in before they can plant their yards. This seems even stranger to me than a home with a covenant against clotheslines. I can't comprehend topsoil and sub-soil being treated as separate salable components. They just belong together. They came from the same parent rock. Think of the millennia they have spent touching and interacting.

It's strange to think of all the soil we cared for spread around the county. I guess it's a migrant now, like us, except it will never come back together in one place again, and we will.

This is the coldest, wettest spring ever. The fields are rarely dry enough to plant, and when they are, we have to do it on eighteen rented properties, plus rebuild the new land. Field conditions are so miserable, it is actually ridiculous. We do whatever it takes to get the crop in, which often means slopping plants in by hand in soil that is so completely saturated we don't even have to dig a hole. We just push the roots down into the muck. June and July are just as wet. It's rare to have a day that is dry enough to cultivate, and when there is, we spend it in a mad rush, using every second of light, each crew member on a different tractor, on a different property, cultivating as fast as they can, without hands-on training, and Martin, racing from field to field with the truck and trailer hauling equipment to keep everyone going.

When it's too wet to do anything else, we work on cleaning up the house site. We pull junk out of the sheds and separate it: rotten wood goes in a fire, paper and metal are recycled, plastic we haul to the landfill. Trailer loads of rusty implements are sold as scrap. Empty Old Crow Whiskey bottles are stuffed under all the buildings; we fill fifty-five-gallon barrels for recycling. The only thing we find worth keeping is a crystal-glass cake plate beneath the granary.

I'm working behind the barn, pulling scrap metal out of the old pasture, when I come upon a pile of coyote feces. I have never seen anything like it before, a heap reaching to my knees—a coyote toilet. I've always thought of them on the move, leaving bits of hair-filled scat to mark their trail. This must be a coyote base camp. Maybe they are eating the rats.

Martin calls the fire department and offers the rotten buildings for a practice burn. They aren't interested. He gets an estimate to have everything knocked down and hauled to the landfill, $35,000. We consider a burning permit, but they'd have to be pushed away from the woods, and we don't want nails in the fields. He says, "The fine for burning without a permit is $300."

We start with a crowbar, pulling rotten boards and hosting bonfires, but it's too slow. Soon we grow bolder and torch whole buildings, small ones like the outhouse and the collapsed corncrib. The fires are easy to control. Everything is damp. Martin lights the chicken coop, then the granary, finally the barn, which is so wet it smolders for four days. The embers reflect on the silo, and the orange glow is visible for miles. Neighbors stop in, and we ask them if they mind us burning. They all say the same thing, as if they discussed it at the local coffee shop, "We're glad someone's finally cleaning the place up."

I think about the role fire plays in replenishing prairies, and I realize it's the best way to cleanse this land for a fresh start. By midsummer we are down to the house and the concrete-stave silo. I try to talk Martin into saving the silo. "We could have a multifloor apartment for the crew. It would be the summer of their lives, to live in a silo on an organic farm."

"It's completely rotten," he says. He drills holes around the base and explodes it with dynamite. Neighbors Henry and Octer come racing up the driveway minutes after the blast.

Henry says, "Every time you take down a building over here, I get another flush of rats. I should be charging you my poison bill."

"I was here helping when they built that silo," Octer says. "Sure is good to see you breathing new life into this place. I hate to see a good farm run down."

All that's left now is the house, but it's too close to the Oak to take a chance with fire. We'll have to knock it down. I'm driving to Eureka with the kids and lunch for the crew. Miles away we spot a pillar of smoke. I don't know what could be burning. We're halfway down the driveway before I realize. Damn it anyways. Why did I think he was listening to me?

Orange-yellow flames are shooting thirty to forty feet out of the house roof. We round the last corner and see that the Oak's branches are being licked by the blaze. Martin is on the M-loader tractor, and his partner in crime, Scott, is on the ground directing him. I can't believe what I'm seeing. They have chains wrapped around the flaming-to-the-sky house and are pulling it away from the Oak.

Maize is bouncing all over the backseat. I can hardly pull out now and pretend he doesn't know what his father—his very own personal role model—is doing. The crew comes over to the car. "One match," Ann says. "I was standing next to him, and he just tossed a match—one little match—at the back porch."

"We had just finished pulling the windows out," Kari says.

"I was over in the woods pulling scrap metal and heard a gigantic whoosh explosion," Lynne says. "It's hardly been on fire for fifteen minutes."

"He's pretty worried about what you're going to say," says Ann.

They are smeared with ash, dirt, and sweat. I don't want to know what they were doing before I pulled in. If the Oak dies, I don't think I'll ever be able to forgive him, and what if the tractor blows up? He's driving through coals and flames, pushing the burning house with the front-end loader, and the kids are here watching. I lay out a picnic of pasta salad and chips and guacamole because there's really nothing to do now—except gawk. When he finally gets off the tractor, he is a bizarre mix of defiant, shy, exhilarated, relieved, and scared. He says, "It wasn't as wet as the other buildings." Then he sits down and proceeds to eat everything he can find.

I'm sitting there about to blast him when I realize the clothesline poles are still standing less than ten feet from where the house is now a glowing pile of coals. They are the last structure left standing at our new homesite. This is a very good omen.

It's not until every dish is empty and he's lying on his back with eyes closed that he says, "Dumbest thing I ever did."

Maison Diffley

Ryan, the developer, stops by the roadside stand. I wonder what he wants. We haven't seen him since the debacle of Devil's Hill and Louise's Field. "How's your land search going?" he asks.

"We bought land in Eureka Township," Martin says.

"Congratulations. When will you move?"

"We put all our money into the land," I say. "There's an old house. Well, there was an old house. We'll live here until someday when we have the money to build."

Ryan's eyes circle the yard, dart at our clothesline, and move over the equipment. "I suppose you'll be moving your tractors and tools down there?"

Martin says, "No, it's more secure here. We'll haul it when we need it."

Ryan stares at the roadside stand. I turn around and look at what he is ogling. I see beautiful organic produce. I look at his face. Perhaps it looks a little different to him. "Would you like a brick rambler, for one dollar, to be moved?" he asks. A house, a mile away, on other land he's developing. If we don't want it, they will landfill it. "It doesn't fit into the character of the new development."

A dollar and a notarized agreement about our one acre and roadside stand: "to move, organize or generally clean up all spare parts, inoperable equipment and other possessions, . . . make every reasonable effort to make the appearance of the property more compatible with the new single family neighborhood, . . . install a six-foot-high, solid wood barrier fence, along the entire west property line, . . . and, first right of refusal, if we should sell our Eagan home."

There is no mention of the clothesline. As soon as he's gone, Martin says, "I earned my first paycheck in that house. The owner was an auctioneer. When he saw what a serious worker I was, he started taking me to auctions as a ring boy. I'd hold up items and watch for bidders. I learned a lot about auctions and people. Every week, he'd go to his rolltop desk, pull out the biggest ledger book I ever saw, and write me a check for twelve bucks."

To Martin, the fact that he received his first paycheck in the house means without a doubt that we'll experience financial success in it. "It was built on top of a kame hill by a French family named Chapeau," he says. "My parents called it Maison de Chapeau, the Hat House. It really was like a hat on top of a hill."

It's a beautiful house, built to last, brick. I find it hard to believe they were going to landfill it. So it doesn't fit in with the new development—neither do we. Martin and I decide to walk the farm-suburb. Perhaps it's knowing we will be moving sometime soon, but up until now I didn't think we'd ever walk on the land after there were houses on it. I'm not sure, is it still land? By definition, yes—it is land. For me—no.

As long as we can see our home, we have a sense of where we are. We walk along and say, "This is the Ball Field." "Here is where the blackberries grew." "The goldfinch nest was there in the hawthorn." We turn a corner, and I become completely confused.

My eyes see suburban homes, streets, and sidewalks. They tell me that I am in the middle of a housing development. But my body insists I am standing on Treasure Hill. I feel the cool breeze at the end of a long, glorious day, coming up from the valley, blowing dust against my sturdy legs. My feet know the old path; I have urges to turn in the middle of lawns. Double images overlap. The past is superimposed over the present. Hills rise through homes and yards. Trees stretch their limbs through walls. Leafy fields of kale grow in garages.

I can't tell if I'm walking a ghost farm or a suburban street. I see a row of artichokes growing at an angle from an unfinished house. The rest of the lot is weedy subsoil. "Look, we are in the Nest," Martin points. "Wow! The artichokes and the weed seeds are the only thing that survived the bulldozers—besides us."

Hearing him say "besides us" makes us laugh—hard. We not only survived; we will thrive.

Martin comes home from an auction with two old school buses. When we are finished with each tool for the season, we pack it into a bus. When it's time to move, it will be a simple turn of the key and a thirty-minute drive. Everything will already be loaded.

The house is moved in the middle of a starless night. Strung with bright visibility bulbs, it is a rectangle of light rolling slowly through the deepest black. By sunrise it is resting behind the Oak and overlooking the new fields. Putting it together is old-home week for Martin; his community comes down to help with the Maison Diffley. The Weierke brothers install the septic system. Their families go back three generations, and they did a lot of excavation for Martin's father. Marv Schwanz works on the old windmill well and brings it around. They have been family neighbors since the 1880s, and even lived on the original Diffley homestead. Dave Tousignant does the basement cement work. "Do you know the story about your father and the bread box?" Martin asks Dave, as he sets up to pour the basement. "He was born premature, and those old houses were cold. My Aunt Mary told your great-grandmother to keep him in the bread warmer of the woodstove and feed him with an eyedropper." That baby, who survived with Aunt Mary's advice, grew up to be the Rosemount chief of police and saved Martin's life in turn during his wild teenage years.

Even though the land is gone and we're moving, the relationships will last. By the time we're having our winter meeting with Dan and Barb, the produce buyers at Mississippi Market Co-op, the house is ready to move into. We sit on upside-down five-gallon tahini buckets squeezed into the corner of the produce back room. The cooler compressor kicks on and off behind us. We have to shout to be heard above the noise. "The land is ready to be certified," Martin says. "We'll be farming and living there next season."

Barb and Dan are beaming as they say, "That's fantastic." I realize how much this means to them too. The food co-ops have stood behind us all the way. We're in this together. I pass out spreadsheets showing their annual purchases for the past ten years. These numbers reflect so much more than just the sales between one farm and one store; they illustrate a history of the organic movement, weather, seed availability, development pressure, customer awareness, and food co-op growth. Barb says, "Amazing how well the watermelons did considering the wet weather."

"That was Martin's foresight," I say.

Saying it out loud, I am struck by just how much insight he has. This spring he insisted on planting the melons on a gravel hill with beach sand for topsoil. He said that with the wet weather, the only chance they'd have was well-drained soil. Then all fall, while we were harvesting melons by the truckload, our watermelon-growing neighbor came round scratching his head, wondering how we pulled off the crop in the cold and wet without using fungicides. His were planted in a low, airless, wet spot, and he'd sprayed three times a week to prevent fungal disease, but lost his crop anyway.

It's not only planting melons on the right ground. We wouldn't be sitting here, ready to move to our own farm, without the prescience and courage he's used since the beginning, starting as an organic farmer when the rest of agriculture was racing in the opposite direction.

"What can we expect next year?" Barb asks.

Martin says, "Same crops. We want to settle in a year before we make any changes. What growth should we plan for you?"

"Ten percent," Barb says. At the same time Dan says, "Fifteen." They order the same way.

Barb says, "Our board is exploring the idea of a new store."

"That will be wonderful for everyone." I'm thinking, we're like kids, growing up together. Are we teenagers now or young adults? I write 20 percent on my notes, better safe than sorry, and we'll actually have enough land. I pull out our grower-store agreement; it lists the certified-organic crops that we agree to plant, produce, and deliver for their retail store. They agree that we are their main supplier during our season of availability, and they do not hold us to performance in the case of an Act of God.

While we are passing it around and signing on our knees, Dan asks, "What are you most looking forward to?"

"Rich soil," Martin says.

"Quiet," I say.

"Watermelons," Barb says.

"Can I come down and drive the Super M?" Dan asks.

Right now, there is no place I'd rather be than sitting on a plastic bucket in the crowded produce back room of a food co-op.

I'm cleaning out office files and packing them to move. When in doubt, throw it out, is the mantra I'm using. I come upon a receipt from Lengsfeld's Organic Farm. August 16, 1990, four bushels of green beans for the roadside stand. It is signed with the big first printing of a child's—Maize. I burst into tears. The day those beans came was the first time I ever left Maize to run the stand "alone." It was late afternoon, and I had dashed out to the Ball Field to pick two sacks of sweet corn. Martin was twelve feet away packing peppers. When I came back, Maize was beaming. He'd had two customers and one delivery, and he'd handled them "all himself."

It's not only the memory of Maize at the stand making me cry. He received the beans from someone he's known his entire life. Evelyn was working here when he was born, and she called Martin "Uncle Happy." She met third-generation Inver Grove farmer Duane Lengsfeld at our fall harvest party. They transitioned his farm to organic, and now we are buying their green beans. It's never going to be like this again. So what if endings come with new beginnings.

I take everything I'd thrown in the trash and put it into the packing box. The invoice I put into my dresser drawer with my most valuable possessions.

The optimistic, forward-moving part of me is screaming with excitement. We are taking down the Eagan clotheslines poles to move to our new home. My oppositional defiant side feels we are admitting defeat, taking down the symbol of our resistance.

We take turns swinging a pickax. It doesn't take long to work the poles free with a base of mud clinging frozen to the bottom. They seem eager to get out of here and move to their new home, though they want to bring a bit of the "old sod" along with them.

"My dad put these in the summer of 1941," Martin says. "I'm not sure why, but we always painted them green."

"Green's a good color."

Maize runs circles around us with the line. "Good omen," Martin says. "You and me tied together by a clothesline as we are moving to our own land."

February 24, 1994, is moving day. The first thing I do is put a whole turkey and cut-up butternut squash in the oven, our last meal to be cooked in the Eagan kitchen.

We have plenty of help, and before long everything is loaded and we're on the road. By early afternoon the trucks are empty, the furniture is in place, and we're seated in our new kitchen ready to eat. The food feels like an inoculant. Cooked in Eagan, transported to Eureka, this feast with family and friends—only the first of many festive meals we will share in our new home on our own land. After we all have our plates filled and are settled into the laughter and joy of the meal, I say, "Time for a speech. Look who's here."

I pull out Oz, push the on button, and set him in the middle of the table: "Mostly clear, with a high near eighteen. Southeast wind around five miles per hour."

"Clear from here," Martin says, as we click water glasses.

"That's a warm breeze," I say.

The meal is loud and boisterous. We have cause for celebration.
Only Martin's sister Teresa is quiet. Afterward she goes out to the
Oak and stands with her back against it. I watch her from the window and realize that her familial attachment to the Diffley land is
being transferred to here. Even though she won't ever live here or
work directly to make here happen, it gives her a place to attach her
emotional investment—a piece of earth that carries a bit of home.

By evening even the clothes and kids' toys are put away. It's just
Martin, the kids, and me relaxing in the living room. A full moon rises
up so heavy it is dripping light. A line of deer bound leaping out of
the woods, then brake to cautious tiptoeing, their hooves nervously
crunching the brittle snow. They sense something is different. Humans
are here. The fawns and yearlings feel the change in the mature does
and pull in closer. The herd cuts across the yard, all eyes on the house
until they are past and into the front field, where they drop their necks
and eat yellow clover still green beneath the snow. The alpha female
stands guard. Martin whispers, his voice deep, "Look, toward the
woods, the biggest buck I've ever seen."

He is on the edge of the woodlot, half in, half out, framed between
two trees. His heavy rack spread wide mimics the massive Oak. He
turns his head, checking all directions with nose up in the air, and then
saunters boldly into the yard, proud, proclaiming his authority as he
parades past the house. He takes a position separate from the herd but
watching over. His ears twitch slightly at the sound of fast-hitting feet,
but he doesn't send a warning.

Coyotes come streaking across the fields, as if we are a magnet
drawing them to center. They merge beneath the Oak and continue
on together, chasing each other around our house. The Oak stands
watching, silent witness and wise sage, recorder of history. The graz-
ing deer don't even glance up. The coyotes are not their threat.

"Prairie wolves," Martin whispers, as they sprint past in a loop,
their sharp, erect ears pointing straight up and open, their bushy tails
bouncing behind in attack position. Their mangy fur looks mean and
piss-yellow in the open moonlight, but their long limbs are youthful

elastic strengthened with steel, forelegs meeting hind, as they bound in midair, lean creatures of the earth pulling toward the sky. The only sound is the coyotes' paws treading the snow. It's not a thud but a delicate contact; the firm push-off is louder than the landing.

Each coyote, as it passes us at the window, swivels its head and glares into our eyes—their round pupils shine greenish-gold, scorching fire. Then it is gone, and another flows into its place, challenging our presence with a defiant stare. I can't count them; I don't know where the line ends and where it begins. Around and around, until they melt into one blurred chain of pointy heads, fur bodies, bouncing tails, and glaring accusations, burning a demand louder than words.

Just when we've gotten to the point where we're holding hands in a half moon and asking each other how long they'll continue circling, Eliza is crying and saying, "forever," Maize is still trying to count them, and Martin and I are pretending this is everyday normal, then, they slow their sprint and gather into a ragged group in front of us.

The largest throws its pointed, narrow muzzle to the sky and opens with a tenor scream that cuts through the firmest denial. The group joins, yowling harsh with crackling voices—a torrent of falsetto stabs that pulsates through our bodies and sends cold spasms down our backbones. An urgent, discordant staccato, no Western theory of musical scale applies to their composition. Then, for extended lingering seconds, they merge into a unified chorus, intoning together with sharp, snapping rhythm.

If the race was the opening ceremony, this is the public address. I feel pushed back against a wall, facing the ultimate judgment. I know the truth of what they are saying, and it's not convenient.

The leader springs high into the air, twisting and snapping, and the others join, all the while primordial voices chanting. We are on the second floor, and they fly up even with the window, snarling with sharp canine teeth exposed. The moon casts their leaping shadows against the house, imprinting their message in brick and mortar. They settle finally onto their haunches and continue to glare, all eyes on us. Their mantra becomes a yammering, swelling low, then growing into a bawl. They morph into bullet form and take off again, a smoking ring, whizzing around the house. We are caged, prisoners of their burning spiral, wordless and listening. Their message is irrefutable.

This was their wild place. They are furious at our invasion. Circling the enemy is an intimidation tactic. I lose track of how many times they loop and keen, their long-drawn wail climbing as it changes from anger to pulsating grief. I stand helpless between their anguish and this new reality. This is a human habitation now. No longer wild enough for a coyote base camp. We have been pushed out of Eagan by the bulldozers, and in chain reaction we are now encroaching upon the coyotes' territory. We are the intruders.

Then, as if on a signal, they disperse. Melt into the night. Vanish. It is dead silent. All of nature is standing unified, backing the message. The quiet is the loudest voice I've ever heard. The spokesperson coyotes have spoken on behalf of all: *Remember always.* The most important law of nature is that we live in relationships. All of life is connected. We must be conscious of how our decisions affect all forms of life.

Spring Covenant, 1994

Should we call it the Gardens of Waukegan, or maybe the Gardens of Eureka? It would be confusing for our customers if we changed our name, but this land has a completely different personality.

In Eagan, the shelter of the landscape felt like our own private kingdom and ecosystem. Here it's like we are standing on the Eastern Edge of the Great Plains. The view is open. There is wind and prairie exposure. We see storms coming long before they arrive.

The ground is still frozen, and we need to get the greenhouses up. We buy time by starting the first seeds in Lengsfeld's Organic greenhouse. Martin burns charcoal where the pipes need to be pounded. We build the frame in one long day and install the plastic skin in a blustery wind early the next morning, making for a loose fit, but we just aren't willing to wait. The furnace man is still working on the hookup when I move in the seedlings from Lengsfeld's and start transplanting. "You really will have the heat working tonight, right?" I say.

This is not our normal cautious behavior. I'm noticing how change pulls us out of our patterns, and while I don't care for some of the decisions we have to make, I like having our routine busted up. I'm thriving on the jolt.

We've already established the waterways; now we need to lay out fields and harvest lanes. Ideally we would have done this last summer, and they would be ready, waiting for us. But nothing about this process has been ideal. I'm just happy we made it here. There is still so much we don't know yet about this land. It didn't come with the manual of passed-down family folklore that the Eagan land had. We study the soil map, paying particular attention to that which can't easily be seen—the subsoil. Clay versus gravel makes a big difference in drainage and soil warmth, and the map guides our decisions, but it will take years and numerous crops and weather patterns before we develop a deeper understanding of the land's variability. It's little things, yet they have a huge impact on yield and efficiency. Like knowing where the clay will ball if worked too wet, which are the first areas to ripen, which are droughty.

We start with the obvious. In front of the house is a gentle southern slope. The solar exposure and angled topography will make this an early, warm field, but we need to prevent erosion. Martin discs the standing clover for an eighty-foot-wide terrace, then leaves a strip of cover to serve as beneficial insect habitat, to slow water drainage, and to access the vegetables. Working his way down the hill, he creates five terraced plots. He moves around the farm this way, watching for erodibility and listening to his previous experience, his intuition, his relatives, and the old-timers who taught him.

I am pleased when I see the soil opened up. It is loose and friable, easy to rake my fingers through—a huge difference in only thirty-six months. I knew we could wake it up, but I didn't know we could do so much, so quickly. Seeing the change, I understand in a new and deeper way that for now, this soil is in our care. Without our human disruption it would care for itself. It would grow through a succession of plants based on nutrient needs.

First, the mighty soil builders, with long taproots digging deep and bringing minerals up from the subsoil, the annual weeds with their short and simple life cycles busting the clods and plow pan. Then the perennial grasses, the soil coverers, the verdant guardians and protectors. The soil would grow a complex system of multiple species. There would be no straight rows or naked soil. But we humans interrupt this natural process—we want to control what is grown here. We name the crop. Choose the cultivar. Add the fertility.

Farm soil is a wild animal held in captivity. Living in the soil are more undomesticated species than can be found aboveground on the entire planet. This soil life has simple needs: food, air, water, and shelter. Just like every other species. Prevented from caring for itself, it lies at our mercy, dependent on our long-term vision and integrity. Its future capacity is determined by our judgment. Anytime we open up the land—when we remove its protective cover of grass and forb, brush and tree, when we lay the soil bare, exposed to the elements— we embezzle its ability to command its own wellness.

Opening land is a covenant.

I think of Anita and her value of self-governance. The soil species can't vote. If we control what grows on it, then we also have the responsibility to meet its needs and preserve its future.

We need a field plan for the season, what crops and soil building, where and when. This too should be done at least one season ahead, but we haven't been able to plan in advance for the past six years. Soon that will change. This fall, when we have a more intimate understanding, we will be able to write a multiple-year plan. But right now, we don't know these fields yet, and it will soon be time to plant. We make a plan on paper, but I know us. I know what is going to happen. We will get the equipment, the crew, and the transplants out to the field. The first row will be staked. The planter will be pulled in, watered up, and ready to go. One of us will say, "This just doesn't feel right." We'll stop, reevaluate, and move to a different spot. The crew will think we are nuts. Flexibility and intuition will be crucial skills this first season. It will be a lot easier next time around.

The fields need names. But names are based on association, a link to a memory, a person, attribute, or activity, and right now, we have no history with this land. I realize someone must have had intimacy here before us, but they have left no markers, or if they did, perhaps we cleared them out unknowingly in our haste to make this our own. We still see and think of the land as we bought it—the number of acres in each parcel. We use names like the Back 29 or the West 37. It meets our needs for now, but it doesn't carry any emotion or connection. It's just a field, and nothing has happened to us there yet. It feels clumsy. Like we are stumbling around, trying to find our place, or like we are visitors, guests at our own farm.

I thought it would be instant joy. That just getting out of Eagan and away from the bulldozers would make my world bloom and turn us back into a family farming. But nothing feels like it used to. Martin says, "Give it time. It takes years to build a relationship—just like soil. There is a lot more to ownership than buying."

Bringing beehives in helps. A field name carries over to the new farm. We have a Bee Field again, and next to the now-gone barn is the Pasture Field. Maize is busy exploring, running around the fields and woods, getting to know every tree, rock, and magic spot. I don't know how he gets up there, but somehow he can climb the Oak. It's twelve feet to the first branch, where he has padded a nest for himself with a tiger-print blanket. His tree companions are squirrels and birds. Eliza—she is still keeping the house clean and shows no interest in the farm or the land.

I realize I'm expecting our lives to be what they were before the bulldozers. But we are on different land in a different community. The kids are older. I don't know what any of this is going to look like. Martin comes up from the Front 31, where he was prepping a field for lettuce planting. I'm surprised to see he is caked with mud halfway up his legs. It's not that wet out. "I found a seep," he says, amazingly cheerful for a man who must have just sunk a tractor. "Come and pull me out."

It's a mess. He points ten feet from the stuck tractor and says, "I should have guessed. Look at the sedge grass thriving there. It likes moist soil. The water is trapped in a clay path underground. That's where it drains out."

I've got my hand on the throttle, gradually increasing the gas to ease Martin out of the wet spot. I want to rip it open—full throttle—all of it, the settling in, finding our way, the kids making connection with the land and the crops. But I realize, just like this tractor, we have to pull out slowly or we'll just get stuck worse.

Maize decides that for one day he will only eat things that he harvests himself from somewhere on the farm. I suggest waiting—in a week or two there will be more options—but he is already set on it. He drills a hole in a box elder tree and places a kettle under it to collect sap. The edge of the woods is thick with burdock roots; he digs and steams them with ramps that he finds deeper in the shade of the woodlot. The nettles are still short, but they are up. I show him how to grab them firm on the stem to avoid being stung. I say, "Be sure to rinse them well before cooking, or they will be gritty."

He spots a bird's nest. "Is it OK if I eat the eggs? I could make nettle omelets."

"What do you think?" I ask. "What kind of bird is it?"

He hadn't thought about the egg's future as a bird, or what kind. He stops for a second, thinking with his head cocked, "I don't want to eat the singing ones."

"All birds sing," I say. "I think for the same reason people do. They can't help it. It is joy that is in them and has to come out."

That's the end of the egg idea, and he's hungry. In front of the house are pots of perennial herbs we've moved from Eagan. He nibbles chive tips, then spits out his mouthful and turns to the peppermint to clear his palate. It is just up and very strong. He finds a spike of lovage emerging, but it is the same, seasoning—not a meal. In the woods a few rose hips are still hanging. He sucks on the dried fruit while he searches the fields for lamb's-quarters and purslane, but it is still too early. There is a good inch of box elder sap collected in the kettle; he drinks it fresh and then puts the kettle back under the tree. He comes to the yard and picks plantain and dandelion leaves, which he steams.

"If I am going to live off the land, I have to catch some meat." Setting a snare is a first for him. The "rabbit" hole he picks is a gopher tunnel, but he isn't interested in my opinion on this. Not much later, he takes it down because "I don't want to kill a bunny."

He studies a survival manual and asks me if I know where there are cattail plants. I say, "Along the boardwalk on Chub Lake."

He says, "I'm too hungry to go that far." Next time I see him he is racing past on his bicycle and eating a peanut butter sandwich. A white egret follows right behind.

We've been so busy setting up the farm we haven't had a chance to put up the clotheslines, and we haven't done laundry since we moved. Washing isn't the hard part. It's putting up the poles. The equipment is still parked everywhere around the house, and no matter where we put them, I know they'll be in the way and have to be moved later as we build our sheds. But even bigger—and I don't know why—I have been afraid to stake the claim. Afraid to make the commitment that planting clotheslines poles on the land will be.

Martin says, "Go up to the rock pile with the wheelbarrow and bring back thirty stones the size of big potatoes." While I am gone, he digs holes. I hold the poles upright while he packs stones around the base then tamps in soil with an old two-by-four. "This will work for now. When we know their permanent place, we'll put them in with concrete. Little by little. It'll come together."

Now at the end of my first really dirty day here, I am sitting in the bathtub noticing the water feels different. It's softer, smooth. It hits me, it's the difference between sand and prairie loam. In Eagan the coarse, multisided sandy soil quickly settled to the bottom of the tub. Sand particles are larger and heavier than clay. It felt like we were sitting on grit. Here, the higher clay content of the loam soil stays suspended longer, making the water satiny. Somehow the tactile sensation of the soft clay illustrates for me that clay particles are flat, like a fish scale. They pack on top of each other, making for a tighter, less airy soil than sand. In Eagan, the sandy soil dried quickly. We could work it within a day of a soaking rain. Here, with the higher clay content, it takes three to four days of sun and wind before the soil is dry.

I knew this, but feeling the change in the water, I have a deeper comprehension of what it means to us as farmers. The change in soil is going to affect the decisions we make, how we manage our soils, and what we grow. I start to laugh. Our lives are completely dependent on soil. Here I am, lying exhausted in a hot bath, at the end of a long and muddy day, and studying the dirty water. Lots of things are going to be different here.

Sometimes it feels like the wind comes all the way from the Dakotas.

We are trying to transplant lettuce, but dirt is blasting our eyes and skin, and hair is blowing in our faces. It is the first week for our new crew, and I am trying to bolster them. It won't always be like this. But then I realize that I don't have a clue what it will be like. We asked the neighbors about the soil, but we never talked about spring wind.

This is far from ideal conditions for tender, young transplants to experience their first day in the field. Under a different forecast we'd wait for it to pass, but Oz is calling for a week of rain. Lettuce leaves are thin and tear easily; to an untrained eye, they look like they are dying, but their roots are young, strong, and healthy. This wet week will be ideal for root establishment. Once that happens, fresh leaf growth will be rapid. If we wait to plant, they will become root-bound, their potential stunted. I feel an affinity with this lettuce. I hope the bulldozers were merely the winds of life. Our leaves are a bit tattered, but once our roots are in, we too will flourish. I just hope we didn't wait too long. That we aren't root-bound transplants struggling to settle in.

In the evening I go out to check the lettuce, and the field is full of deer. They run when they sense me, but I know they'll be back. I sit in the center and visualize a sawhorse and a do-not-eat sign. I offer deals. We are allies. I invite them—just as I did in Eagan—to come eat when we are finished with harvest. When I get back to the house, the sun is low and the way the Oak's shadow is spread out, deep and wide on the lawn, it's as if I'm seeing the roots of the tree with their powerful grip on this land. Now there's an omen I can hold on to. The deer, however, just keep coming and eating.

Like they don't understand a single word I said. It is a different family. Maybe they speak a different language, or maybe we don't need the crop as badly as we did before. I don't know. We buy an electric fence.

Reducing the weed seed bank while the land was in transition to organic was a first step in weed management. Before planting the crop we do a fine-tuning.

Most weeds germinate from the top half inch of soil. If we kill them with very shallow cultivation when they are young, and avoid bringing deeper weed seeds up to the surface, we can create a relatively weed-free field before planting. But it was impossible to do last fall while we were farming on eighteen properties, and now the onions are a weedy mess. Martin reminds me, "We are in transition. Everything will get easier with time."

I train the crew to hoe down double rows for fifty feet and then turn around and work back up the next. It's just a psychological trick, but it helps. As soon as two or three short rows are hoed, there is a satisfying block. I say, "Never look at the unfinished area until more than half the field is done."

The weeds are in white thread stage, barely visible aboveground. This is the best time to hoe them; the thin roots will dry out quickly and die. I show the crew how to stay shallow so they don't bring up fresh seed. A smattering of white weed roots surrounds the onions spikes. I think it's beautiful. "But they look so benign. Why do we have to do all this hoeing?" David, an intern from Germany, is staring at the unhoed part that I just told them not to look at.

"In August, that benign weed will be as tall as you. One pigweed can have five hundred thousand seeds. Do next year's crew a favor, kill every weed."

He doesn't look impressed. Experience is the greatest teacher; his thinking will be different in just a few weeks. I start in on cultivating leeks. Here, too, we stay as shallow as possible. Digging deep not only brings up more weed seeds, but it is detrimental to soil

microbial life and ground-nesting pollinators, and increases the potential for erosion.

It's mesmerizing to stare at the plants moving evenly between
the tines. Before long I am glazed over with culti-vision. Suddenly, I
slam on the brake. Before the tractor is stopped, I realize that it is not
a naked human body lying in front of me but farm art.

Tony is an artist learning to be a software writer temporarily em-
ployed on this organic farm. His art shows up wherever he works.
Here it's a human figure made of soil, a woman lying on her back,
staring straight up at the sky. A line of leek plants grows down the
center of her body, marking it as two halves.

I get off the tractor and lie in the aisle next to her, copying her
form. Most of my time I spend looking at the ground. Now I'm staring straight up at the sky. I imagine myself marked in half and think
about the complications of personality—all the ways I am a contrast
in myself. But this soil woman is blended. Her two halves are clear,
and the leek roots join them. The roots bring all aspects of her up,
from this delicate work of art into the plant, which is nature's gift of
wholeness. The pungent medicine of the leek is a metaphor for life
itself. My roots will bring up everything I need, and I too can be as
strong as a leek. I lift the cultivator shoes and pass over undisturbed;
she fits right between the tires. Maize's footprints are here too.

A week ago, Maize and I made an insect trap out of a quart-sized
yogurt container. The majority of insects are beneficial, and we wanted
to see what is here. We dug a hole at the edge of a field, in the halfway
zone where the open soil meets the road grass, slipped the container
in level with the soil surface, then added rubbing alcohol so the insects wouldn't eat each other. With a piece of wire and a plastic bag, we
made a roof to keep the rain out. Now we are back with a magnifying
glass. There are springtails, assassin bugs, millipedes, spiders, and dung
beetles. Those are the ones I can name. But there are all these other
cool creatures, various species in larval stage, caterpillars and beetles,
and most exciting of all—because we've never seen one or imagined

its existence—some kind of worm that must live deep underground. It's as long as my foot, as thin as a thread, and brilliant white. How could something that white come out of such black soil?

We have a general rule: never kill an insect if you don't know what it is. These species provide many ecosystem services that benefit humans and the environment, including, but not limited to, pollination of crops and wild plants, recycling of nutrients, regulation of plant and animal populations, food for other animals, and our favorite— predation of pest species. Biological diversity is crucial to life.

The importance of diversity applies to seed as well. Martin is out in the West 37, planting the first Indian corn on the new farm. The seed was given to him when he was ten by Uncle Bill, a decorative corn with a diverse genetic lineage coming from Mandan Bride, developed by the Mandan Indians of Minnesota and North Dakota. Martin first grew it in 1959 and sold it in his Uncle Aubrey's grocery store. He has grown it out and selected seed from it almost every year since. Planting it here brings a small part of his heritage and the Mandan culture onto this land—old seed on a new farm.

It's the middle of the afternoon when the light starts to fade, like twilight. Martin thinks something is wrong with his eyes, but he wants to get the corn in, so he just keeps going. All of a sudden it is dark like right after sunset. He stops and turns the tractor off, thinking, did I lose track of the time? He glances up and sees the sun looking like a new moon. He realizes then, it is an annular solar eclipse.

This is a right omen—like the new moon—a new chance on a new farm. The moon is covering the sun, from which all light comes. Without light, what would be life? Martin is planting corn on land he cared for with plants and the renewable energy of the sun, the only source of fertility that is capable of eternal regeneration. For one long moment the sun is a shining ring around the moon. The unbroken circle is an age-old symbol of eternity. As the moon slides over, the crescent reappears; the sun is reborn, a new life, and a promise of perpetuity.

The past is behind him but going on in the seed. He thinks about the Indian corn—multiple generations of growing for him and for the people who lived here before. How long has corn existed as a food source, the husk for bedding, the silk for soup and medicine? Corn is entirely of seed; to eat corn is to eat the miracle of life. The plant will go on evolving genetically. Will he go on as the person he was, here on this new land? He sits on his tractor, aware of the entire universe from this little piece of the earth.

Maize shows up on his bike and climbs up. They start planting with the lights on. It's difficult to see the marking groove, but they keep going, putting the corn in for its start, together, here at the new farm while the sun is in this rare state.

Afterward Martin is inspired. He comes home with a chicory plant, but when he shows it to Eliza, she looks at him like it's dumb. She doesn't even want anyone to know her middle name. He tries to build excitement by taking her out and planting it together. She goes along but without enthusiasm. The plant doesn't take. Chicory thrives on poor soil.

Fertile Ground

It's hard to believe it's only mid-June; the crops are so much larger than normal. Even the weeds seem to be growing twice as fast.

It's just before sunrise. Martin has a light clipped to the rear fender of the Farmall Super C and is lying on his back changing the oil. I line up the cultivator shoes and tighten them, then check the tire pressure. By the time the tractor is set, the sky is light enough to see the weather.

Right now the way the clouds are roiling, it looks like just about anything could happen. Sometimes that's the way my life feels too. I mean that in a good way. I dreamed about farming, but I never knew it would be this satisfying, that I would be able to lean into it and find myself through the work. I feel a debt of gratitude, and getting up early to cultivate feels like a gift for the most part.

Day of the Weeds. What happens today will make or break weed control for the year. We won't stop until we've cleaned up every field or until we get rained out, whichever comes first. The soil is loose, not too wet and not too dry. I'm able to roll a gentle hill, burying the small weeds in the space between the plants. It feels so great to have all our crops in one place, like I'm a mother bird, sitting on eggs in a nest, each of the fields a different chick about to be hatched. I can see Martin from wherever I am. He's moving from cornfield to cornfield, hopping from tractor to tractor—rotary hoe, flame weeder, four-row rear-mount cultivator—cleaning up sweet corn in every stage of growth, from just emerging to last cultivation. We could never have done all this in one day on eighteen properties, hauling equipment and people to each field.

I move into the peppers, where the crew already hoed between the plants: now I'll clean up the aisles. In the first row the weeds are sliced off instead of dug out. Sometimes it is hard for people to believe they will grow back from the roots. I bring the crew out and show them the fresh leaves rising from the cut stumps. I demonstrate how to dig a little deeper, flick the weed—roots and all—smooth the soil. We start hoeing, and right away I can see that one person is still just slicing them off, not pulling out the roots. She's smiling, big, like she's real happy to see all these weeds alive.

Isn't she tired of hoeing yet? I explain again why the roots need to come out. I show once more how to dig a little deeper, flick the weed, and smooth the soil. She says, "I got it." But she keeps just cutting. I ask her if there is a reason she's not getting the roots. She flips to sobbing. I had no idea. "All we do is kill things," she says. "I thought organic farming would be about life. I feel like the hand of death."

"They're just weeds," I say. "Killing weeds is part of farming."

"They are living organisms. They deserve a place on the planet."

"Yeah, they're our allies, and our job is not to annihilate them—don't worry we can't—but we still have to manage them."

"You expect us to come out here and kill all day, every day. I won't do it."

What can I say? Life isn't possible without death, no matter what we eat. That's one of the great things about farming, daily lessons on the laws of nature: balance and relationship. "Every species eats, and every species is eaten." I wonder how she'll feel when it's time to cut off the broccoli heads.

We still have to deal with the quack grass in the Back 29; we can't use the field at all. Neighbor Henry is visiting. We take him out and ask his advice. Everyone else has said, "Spray Roundup." But Henry farmed half his life without herbicides. He must know some trick. He says, "I have never seen quack this thick. It's going to take some real wallop. Try atrazine; that'll knock her down. There's no way you're going to get clear of it without herbicide."

"No way?"

"Well, we used to field-dig it and dry out the roots; that worked, but atrazine is a whole lot easier and quicker."

Where do I even start with atrazine? Aquatic habitat and drinking water contamination, endocrine disruptor, neural damage. It is associated with birth defects at concentrations below government standards. He shakes his head when we tell him we are determined to do it without herbicides. "Your fields are going to be all weeds, no crop." I can see him making a little check next to weeds in his mental black book against organic farmers.

And it's not just about human health. There doesn't seem to be any value placed on wildlife unless it somehow serves humans. Atrazine chemically castrates and feminizes wildlife; it reduces immune function, induces breast and prostate cancer, retards mammary development, and causes abortion. This land is their home. It's not legal to walk into a human's house and spray atrazine, but we should use it in the field because it's the easiest and quickest solution? Where is the long-term perspective? Are humans the only species on the planet worth considering? If we claim to be the smartest species, why aren't we thinking?

Martin tries field-digging the quack. The dense mat of rhizomes and roots is so thick and so tight that the digger barely cuts through to scuff the soil. "It's a start," he says. Three days later the field is solid green, like it hasn't even been touched. He field-digs again, "Maybe it'll dry up now." The grass bounces right back. We can't use the field at all, nine acres, completely out of production. But it's too cool and wet to kill it. We'll just have to wait for a hot, dry year.

"They'll deliver it early in the morning," Martin says. "Let's figure out where to put it."

It's a four-room Cape Cod. Martin's expertise is putting together this farm in a fiscally frugal manner, and he's accomplished it again by

finding worker housing to move here. We walk around the yard trying to agree on a location. Our strength of diverse perspectives is also
our Achilles' heel. I point out a spot. He says that's where the pack
shed will go. I say that's too close to the house. He's just pretending
this is a mutual decision.

He's already set on a place: where the clotheslines are. "They
haven't even had a chance to settle in yet and you want to pull them
out?"

"There are lots of places to put clotheslines, and they are easy to
move."

Down come the poles. They won't have a permanent home until
this farm is fully put together, and it will take years to do that. The
next building we need is a pack shed. There is no point in growing the
highest-quality vegetables possible if we don't remove the field heat
quickly. Cooling produce is crucial to shelf life and quality. Harvest
will start soon, and if we don't have the pack shed set up, ready with
cooling tanks and a walk-in cooler, it won't be easy and it won't be
good. We placed an order for a pole building months ago, but every
time we call they say, "Next week. Don't worry; they go up fast."

But the crops come in before it does. We harvest at first light, before the day's heat, and set up in the shade of the largest trees to wash
and pack. Every few hours we have to move the scale, the washtub,
all the supplies, and the vegetables out of the sun. Once the produce
is packed, we cart it over to a refrigerated truck box, our temporary
cold storage until the pack shed is built.

Then the broccoli starts, and it's one more heat-sensitive crop to
handle in a clumsy, inefficient system. Martin says, "At least we have
trees and the refrigerated truck box. Imagine if we didn't."

Sometimes in life there is a fine line between challenging and in-
sane. I decide it is best to just function with blinders on. We are deep
in August harvest by the time they start building. It goes fast, just like
they said it would. The roof is on, and they are installing the metal
siding, but at least it's shade that won't move. I set up inside the shed
and start packing muskmelons. This is just the first load. Martin and

the crew are out in the field picking the rest. After a few minutes I can't stand the hammering and put in earplugs.

It is just me, a truck of melons, boxes, and a scale in an otherwise empty, half-built shed in the middle of construction. Somehow I find this to be hysterically funny. It will never, ever look this clean and bare again. Tony pulls up with another truckload. "Martin says to tell you there are this many again in the field."

They won't all fit into the truck cooler, and we don't have water cooling set up. I need to move them and fast. Who but Eddie at the Wedge Co-op would pop for this many? I've got his number on speed dial. "We've got the sweetest Saticoy muskmelons of the season—melt in the mouth, juice tender. If you buy fifty cartons and run a member special, I'll drop the price."

"Far out, how soon can you have them here?"

"A few minutes to load and thirty-seven minutes to drive—if I hit all the lights."

"I'll open up the front end, and we'll slip them right in."

"They are dead-on ripe, and I don't have a way to cool them yet. You'll want them out the door in forty-eight hours."

"No problem, they'll blow out of here."

"Great. It'll be a thank-you special to everyone for supporting us. Let me know if you lose any, and I'll make it right with you."

I hang up feeling like there's nothing we couldn't do—we are so completely supported. If I had only known where I'd end up when I was so unhappy locked into a marriage that wasn't working. It must be some kind of lesson on trust. I'm out here on the farm, doing exactly what I need to be doing. Eddie's there in the city, passionately promoting organic food, exactly who he is. And we're both serving the same mission.

The next day our new wet-brush pack line is delivered from Pennsylvania, where a Mennonite family makes them. The carpenters are still putting up the walls, but I'm not waiting another day to install this vegetable-washing tool. Maize pedals past while I'm in the middle of cursing a chain that isn't jumping into place like I told it to. He hops in helping. Actually he takes over. I'm assisting him. This is where he shines. He has an innate ability to understand mechanical functions. Though he helps with planting, harvest, and packing, and with a good attitude, it doesn't seem to be his passion. But when something needs to be fixed, built, or problem-solved, he's quick and right there, just seems to glance at it and have a solution.

He still lives to be outside. When he's not helping on the farm, he's inventing things, building forts in the woods, or flying his bike over dirt jumps. His highest need right now is to be airborne, and the closest he comes is on a bicycle. The first crop we run through the new washer is a truckload of Dark Red Norland potatoes. We finish in thirty-five minutes. It would have taken half a day by hand. We should have bought this tool years ago.

The crew brings in a truck loaded with cucumbers. I check our records and see we are harvesting almost double of last year. It's back to the phone. All the food co-ops jump at the chance to put them on special.

Eliza helps by feeding the cucumbers into the wash end of the pack line. I keep thinking if she is included in the work, she will re-root. We pay the kids for their farm labor, but when it's an option, she'll always choose unpaid housework over earning money with the crops or at the stand, and she has no interest in the land as a spiritual connection. Would this have happened anyway as she became a teenager? I just want her to accept her new home and settle in. Sometimes I feel like an unsuccessful hostess. I'm trying so hard to make her feel welcome and comfortable here, but she is determined to stay left out.

When the cucumbers are packed, I switch to tomato sorting. We could have the pickers field-pack them, which is industry standard, but they are highly perishable, and I prefer to personally pack every box right before shipping. Our name is on it, and quality is crucial, but it's not just that. We enter people's lives in the most sacred way possible. Our hands touch every vegetable that leaves this land. The food enters the eaters' lives through their mouths and nourishes their bodies. I need to be certain that every piece of food that leaves here is good.

The builders are gone for the day, and it's finally quiet. Eliza is in the house reading. Maize is who knows where, doing who knows what. Everyone else is out in the field. I'm appreciating the time alone, when old-timer neighbor Charlie saunters into the pack shed. "Pretty fancy building you got here. You two move fast." He picks up a tomato. "Sure is pretty."

He wants to trade: out-of-date Hostess Twinkies and Ho Hos for organic tomatoes. I have zero interest, but a little produce is nothing to give for a good relationship. His pickup is a jumbled heap of doughnut boxes. He tells me he fills it for five dollars and feeds them to his llamas. "I just dump them in the pen—box, plastic, and all. They eat the whole thing up and just love them."

He's stacking cartons on the tailgate when the crew comes in from the field with the last load of tomatoes. They see the colorful boxes, and their eyes light up, "We are so sick of tomatoes."

"Take some more," Charlie says.

Henry walks in holding out an ice-cream bucket half full of water and swimming with sunfish. "I brought these over for you and Martin."

Octer is right behind him with a tractor part. Is this the local old-timers convention? "Marty said he needed a magneto for his Farmall Super A. I had this one lying around doing nothing for nobody." He lays it on a piece of clean cardboard. "What's that growing in your front field? None of us have seen it before."

"Hairy vetch. It's a legume capable of 'fixing' up to 160 pounds of nitrogen per acre. Usually we incorporate it earlier, but we let it flower for the beneficial insects."

Charlie hops in, "We thought organic was going to be all weeds, but your fields are cleaner than ours ever were."

I don't have all these relationships and identities worked out yet. I see Henry as the conservative, respected leader in the community,

Charlie as the wild maverick, and Octer as the local repair genius. Suddenly I get it. If Octer is here bearing gifts of tractor parts, Charlie is trading week-old Hostess doughnuts, and Henry is offering a bucket of fresh-caught sunnies, then we just made it. We are being welcomed into the community as respected and valued neighbors.

I pack them each a bag of tomatoes, cucumbers, and potatoes and place a Saticoy gently on top. "If this isn't the best melon of your life, let me know," I say.

When I show Martin the fish, the Twinkies, and the magneto, he says, "It's hard to stick out in a small community like this. Remember, there is a lot more in common than different between a conventional farmer and an organic one. We all need the same tools to change a tire. We all deal with the same weather and the same weeds. They see that we are hard workers, and that is what they respect."

By fall we are deep in harvest of the most glorious winter squash. The set is so heavy that the fruit are lying on top of each other, every one big and thick and sweet. We weren't expecting this yield, and we aren't equipped or staffed to handle it.

We work sunup to sundown for weeks, cutting, hauling, and stacking it into the greenhouses three feet deep, layering vented tubes through the center of the piles. There we cure it for storage by closing the doors and allowing the sun to heat it, while blowing warm, dry air into the center of the piles through the tubes. Each week we put one variety on special. I change the size of the shipping box and pack the squash at sixty pounds per carton instead of the industry standard, a lightweight thirty-five pounds. My theory is the produce workers won't want to haul the heavy box twice, so they'll stock it all out, making a giant display. It works. I get buff, and sales triple. The Wedge Co-op makes a giant heap right at the front entrance. The staff walks around singing, "Oh to live on squash mountain. Where the Buttercups and Sweet Dumplings grow."

But despite the strong sales, it is the crop that just won't quit. It is January before it's sold out, and I'm finally in the office putting together the season's spreadsheets. It's not until I compare with past records that I realize just how productive our first year here was.

Squash sales jumped from 27,540 pounds to 93,960 pounds! We planted the same acreage. Kale nearly doubled. Cucumbers tripled. Sweet corn went from 123 sacks to 821.

Part of it must be the inefficiency we dealt with while farming eighteen spread-out fields. But the yields per plant from Eagan, when we were still an intact farm, weren't any higher. When I compare this season's numbers with the "Approximate Average Yields in the United States" as listed in the *Knott's Handbook for Vegetable Growers,* we are above average on many of our crops. When I show Martin, he just says, "Damn, we bought good soil."

"Just better soil? Our gross income almost doubled."

"They don't call it rich soil for nothing. Plus, we did three years of soil building."

I knew soil type and health make a big difference, but I've never experienced such dramatic results before. This raises all sorts of questions for me. The Eagan land was sandy, fragile soil. It would never have stood up to large-scale agriculture and continual mono-cropping of corn and soybeans, but 140 years of diverse agriculture existed there in conjunction with livestock, dairy, and vegetable crops. The richness and the soil's future were preserved by returning organic matter and by protecting the land from erosion. Now, moving to this different soil has increased our productivity and profitability. And beyond the yield increase, I can see many positives.

Together we're creating this farm; it's not just me coming to his family's land. We're a team on mutual ground. Our new home is private and quiet. We have plenty of fertile land, and we are in a township that supports agriculture through zoning and right-to-farm ordinances. We will be able to grow here and build an infrastructure that we couldn't have in Eagan.

But who is to say which is better, that one has more value than the other. It doesn't mean that development is OK. High yields are not the only criteria. There are so many ways the Eagan land contributed to wellness, so many reasons it should have been valued and preserved. The land had many characteristics that were positive. Sandy, well-drained soil reduces fungal disease and heats up earlier, extending the season. A farm producing food in the midst of the community is valuable not only from a food security perspective, but also its example is an educational resource. It was biologically diverse, providing crucial ecosystem services to the community. Much of the land was in grass, native herbaceous plants, mixed hardwood trees and brush, and berries and fruit. It was ideal habitat for native pollinators, beneficial insects, and wildlife; pests and crop disease were largely managed by the diversity of the ecosystem and our cultural practices.

The definition of *ecosystem services* is simple: the benefits people obtain from natural ecosystems. But the services themselves are complex and crucial to the future of life on the planet. They include provisioning services such as food and fresh water and genetic diversity; regulating services such as climate, flood, and disease control; cultural services such as spiritual, recreational, and cultural benefits; and supporting services that maintain the conditions for life on Earth, such as nutrient cycling, production of atmospheric oxygen, and soil formation. How does one put a dollar value on this?

Habitat loss through farming and development is the leading cause of both species extinctions and ecosystem service decline. Managing the land with organic farming preserved its ecosystem while also contributing food. Our customers and the broader community have experienced a loss that cannot be restored, nor can it be compensated. But most important to me, chicory thrived there.

So did Eliza. How would Eliza's and Maize's lives be different if we were still living and working on an intact, fifth-generation family farm? What was lost that can never be returned? I wouldn't take back moving here, and I would never have chosen to leave or bulldoze the land in Eagan.

There is no way to resolve all that.

The Difference

It is scorching hot. Martin is lying in a Mayan string hammock with feet up, drinking iced tea and eating cookies—so not Martin. Nothing is planted. The fields are tall with weeds gone to seed. I keep saying, "Come on, we need to plant."

"Mañana. Today is too hot," he says.

I scream at him, "It is August, and we are so far behind, not even the onions are in." Then I wake up—drenched with sweat and trembling.

I have this same nightmare every winter. If I think about everything it takes to pull off a successful season, it seems impossible. I just want to quit. I'm not even willing to start. If instead we have a plan in place and I stay in the present, then the work is manageable. It's the same psychology as hoeing a big field: little by little. At the end of a week I am amazed by how much we have done. I just have to remember not to look too far ahead.

Now with one growing season behind us, we have a better understanding of what crops thrive here. This soil is deeply fertile and moist. It is ideal for shallow-rooted, high-nutrient, and water-demanding crops. All of the brassicas—kale, broccoli, cauliflower, and cabbage—are well suited. Sweet corn has always been a keystone crop for us, and this soil produces huge ears, filled to the tip, glossy and juicy.

We can't start or stop the rain, but by increasing the organic matter, we can increase the soil's ability to absorb, hold, and regulate moisture. For every 1 percent of organic matter, the soil can hold as crisp, I suspect it may be flaccid. Lettuce needs to tolerate heat; if slow bolting isn't mentioned, I ask. Even when we have a trustworthy variety, we give others a trial; we need to be prepared in the event that a crucial cultivar is lost.

Our greatest fear as farmers isn't the violence of storms or the vagaries of markets. It's access to reliable seed. A handful of multinational, for-profit corporations now own the majority of vegetable varieties, and often cultivars that we have grown dependent on are discontinued, no longer available for farmers to plant. Without the seed we have nothing. This challenge is increased for organic farmers by the reality that the majority of seed is treated with chemical fungicides before sale. The selection of untreated cultivars is limited. Very few plant varieties have been developed in low-input organic systems, and many regionally developed varieties have been lost. Every time a cultivar disappears, it is a loss to genetic diversity and food security. We often have no option but to rely on seed that has been bred to perform well under high-input chemical systems.

Organic systems have different needs than chemical farming systems. For example, the size of a carrot's green tops may not seem important to a customer who doesn't eat them, or to a farmer who uses herbicides to control weeds. To the organic farmer, a fast-growing bushy top means the plant's canopy will shade the soil, protecting it from the sun and preventing weeds from germinating.

The market adds its influence to the decision of what to grow. When new crops emerge, one of the questions we answer is whether it will be a trend or a fad. If it is a novelty but doesn't provide better flavor, tenderness, nutrition, or convenience, it may sell well for a short time, but then either drop out of the market or settle into specialty status.

We don't always follow the trends either. Educating customers is part of our task. For example, seedless watermelon has become status quo, but it doesn't have good disease resistance, and it is highly susceptible to *Fusarium* wilt, one of the most threatening of watermelon diseases. The spores can remain viable in the soil for years and

16,500 gallons of plant-available water per acre. When it comes to a crop's need for water, timing is everything, and each crop is different. With broccoli, for example, we rarely irrigate when the plants are young in the development stage. We want the roots to grow deep in search of water. Once the plants have fifteen leaves, we watch them daily; when the leaves begin to cup inward, it is a sign that the plant is switching to head development. From then on until harvest, we make sure to keep the soil wet. We switch from focusing on root growth to producing large, sweet heads.

This soil is not perfect for everything. It holds too much moisture to meet the needs of deep-rooted, water-sensitive cantaloupe, which thrived in the dryer sands of Eagan. Here they are a complete gamble. Watermelons and tomatoes are deep-rooted also but not as sensitive. We'll grow them on the southern, well-drained slopes and prevent disease by laying rows with the prevailing wind for airflow and quick drying of foliage. Tomatoes are sweetest when grown on dry soil, which this is not, but if there is a large fluctuation in moisture, the fruit can crack. If watermelons receive too much water in the last two weeks before maturity, they can turn mushy.

Learning what crops will thrive here is an important step in adapting to this change in our farm synthesis of land, people, and business. And then there is the question of cultivars.

I am a child again when I hold a single seed in the palm of my hand. Not only is it miraculous that the characteristics of an entire plant are contained and held dormant in a package so tiny, but the genetic difference between two cultivars of the same species is staggering.

Having varieties that are well adapted to our local bioregion, with strong disease resistance, is a key factor to our success. We keep records of every cultivar we grow, with details on disease resistance, shape, size, flavor, quality, and consistency. Winter is the time to peruse seed catalogs and analyze cultivar trials. What a description doesn't say can be more important than what it does. I read between the lines. If a watermelon cultivar report doesn't describe the flesh can be transmitted on seed or through human touch. Many seedless watermelon growers have complicated fungicide treatment plans. Instead of struggling to grow the inherently susceptible-to-disease seedless watermelons in an organic system, we have explained to the co-op produce buyers why it is not a good choice environmentally. They have in turn educated their customers and have stood firmly behind marketing our organic seeded melons.

This relationship with the market goes two ways. Every winter we meet with our core committed buyers, the food co-ops, to plan and commit for the coming season.

We don't just tell them what we grow. We ask them what they want and need. When the crops come in, we take their order and pick to fill it. Our philosophy is, "Fully satisfy core customers. Quality, volume, and service as early, late, and consistently as possible."

To do this, we plant a little extra. When it is cold and maturation is slowed, we usually still have enough. When we have surplus, we offer it on special—a thank-you treat to pass on to their customers—but only to our contracted stores. We don't want to undercut another local farmer. There are many ways to work successfully with the market. What is crucial is a plan in place before planting.

One farmer I spoke with told me he is short on land and needs to sell every single thing he grows. He intentionally plants less than his market demand so that he can always sell it. When he doesn't have enough, he raises the price to drop the demand.

Every farm needs to develop its own personality based on its unique syntheses of land, people, and business. Our tagline is "Taste the Diffley Difference, Eat Local-Organic." We have found our strength is to be service oriented with highest-quality, popular crops and an added distinctive attribute. For example, our watermelon plan includes a family-size watermelon, the crisp, red-fleshed, open-pollinated Crimson Sweet, combined with specialty, icebox-size yellow and orange varieties.

Cabbage has long been a steady workhorse for us. Fresh harvest starts in early July and continues until late October, when the walk-in cooler is filled six feet deep with storage varieties. All the way through winter we are able to supply our accounts with organic, local cabbage, providing us with a reliable cash flow for nine months of the year. Our goal is a dense three- to five-pound head. But this year, with all the rain, the fertile soil, and being behind the entire season, the cabbage "got away on us." The entire crop grew to fifteen-pound heads too big to fit into a cabbage box. We pack them three each in net onion sacks. No store wants a cabbage so big, but as luck would have it, this year there is a national shortage. The food co-ops are so happy to have organic cabbage; they cut them in eighths and wrap them.

For the first time ever, we make it through the winter without off-farm jobs. This is graduation for us. We don't go to the bank until we borrow spring start-up money. The only long-term debt we are willing to carry is for land. Spring start-up is paid back in full when the fall crop comes in.

Martin supplements our income with buying and selling farm equipment. His philosophy is "Everything has a buyer." When I complain that he has sold my favorite tractor, he says, "There's always another sunrise," or "Nothing happens until somebody sells something." Just home from an auction, high from the excitement of the bidding and the deals, his adage is "You make your money on the buy. Don't worry about the sale."

His perspective is that Gardens of Eagan is borrowing the equipment inventory while it is on the Martin Motor Equipment Lot, and at favorable terms. If I object to what he buys, he says, "Can't sell from empty shelves," and "You'll love driving this one until I sell it." And if I get on his nerves about the yard looking like a junkyard, he holds up two fingers in a peace sign, "Grease for peace."

"Peace and grease in the same sentence?" I wince.

"You don't complain when a field is being cultivated instead of hoed by hand."

True, and I have to admit that Martin's strategy of a designated tractor for each task means we don't lose crucial time switching implements, and multiple jobs can be done simultaneously instead of waiting

for a tractor to be freed up. This can make the difference between getting the job done or not when rain is frequent. But his infatuation with
motorized equipment is beyond my understanding. He believes that
there is a strong link between humans and machines, and he truly loves
going to auctions to rescue abandoned tools and equipment. He tells
the crew, "Be sensitive to equipment; have a relationship with it."

To me, he says, "Everything you need to know about a person
shows up in their machines. If they are angry, it is in the throttle—
sticky and sputtery—uneven fuel delivery. If they are indecisive, the
steering is sloppy. Lazy shows up in battery problems. Rebellion
sounds out in the exhaust system."

When he approaches a tractor, his eyes are busy looking for leaks,
paying particular attention to the underbelly for drips and to the
ground for dark spots. He studies the fluid and reports how long it
has been leaking and the composition of the liquid. The attachments
are inspected for looseness and proper placement, tires for pressure
and wear. With the engine running, he feels the vibration, listening
for any misses, squeals, or thumps. He hears a sound in the front,
says, "Sympathetic vibration," then walks to the rear with a stetho-
scope to pinpoint the problem.

The normal smells of a machine are not a stink to him. It is when
something is wrong that the tractor's odor turns from healthy sweat
to sickly stench. A smell like acid? It is oxygen and hydrogen gas vent-
ing from an overcharged and potentially explosive battery. Check the
charging system—with caution. Smells like sulfur? It's the 90-weight
rear-end gear lube, leaking through the PTO seal. Oily burnt toast?
Someone has been riding either the brakes or the clutch.

His engines communicate with him in numerous ways, including
the clock. When he wakes up at the same time that is the number
of a machine he owns—say 5:04, like his Farmall 504 Hi-Crop—he
knows it is a communication, a call for attention. The oil or antifreeze
needs to be checked, a nut tightened, or a tire filled. Usually by lunch,
but always by dinner, he has a story about the engine that woke him
with its plea for help. Once he woke at 6:56 with a stomachache, and

sure enough, someone had operated the Hydro 656 with the choke half on and fouled the spark plugs; they needed to be cleaned and re-gapped. Another time he woke up at 7:06 with a pain in his lower back. Turned out his International 706 was low on hydraulic fluid. When he wakes at 1:40—his specialty cultivator tractor—he knows he will find and buy one within a week. But the best time to wake up is 5:55. Triple Nickels. He knows he will buy or sell something that day. There must be a word for this sixth sense he has. I know the definition: a subconscious awareness in relationship to a machine based on sensory input. Maize has it too.

My sixth sense is strongest in the greenhouse, and here Dave Frattalone's message is clear, "Water is holy and bless the plants." The work has an intimacy that is deeper than outside under the open sky—this close, quiet handling of the seed and young transplants. We are sheltered together, the plants and I, defying the bonds of winter, growing in warmth and light, getting an early start on growing.

It has been an incremental spring, appearing gradually, like a watercolor painter beginning with a blank white canvas, spreading tones of color, one scented layer at a time. Now pigment is returning to the cheeks of the world. The artist of spring started with the sky: singing winds pushed out the heavy clouds; brush strokes of blue appeared from behind the dense winter cover. Not deep summer blue, but soft pastel, the blue of change, of transformation, the blue of birth. Opening the sky releases the long arm of the sun, which draws open patches in the snow. This is a vulnerable time for soil. Often the surface is thawed, but a few inches down is frozen. Rain and snowmelt can't soak in, and if it is bare, there is nothing to hold it in place.

Last spring I felt like we had just been plopped down here to carve out a new way. We were always behind when the next task was upon us. Now, only twelve months later, we still have a lot to build and learn, but it's so much easier to see our future.

Martin and I go for a walk and stop at the corner of the driveway, where the neighbor's corn and soybean field has a drain tile flowing into our grass-covered waterway. We fill a glass canning jar with the spring runoff. The water is dark brown with eroded soil particles. Cornstalk residue floats to the surface. We walk to the other side of the farm and take a sample where the water leaves our land, after it has run through the now grass-covered intermittent stream. It is almost clear. I knew this, but I never saw it so visually before: ecosystem services, in only 1,300 feet of grass. After the water leaves us, it likely picks up soil again, but at least we are doing our part. Eventually protecting water quality will become the norm. Neighbor John walks over and looks at the collected water. "I've been watching how you take care of your soil. Would you be interested in renting my fields?"

Martin and I grin at each other. Extra land means more room for soil building, the highest-quality and least-expensive fertility we can buy, a profitable investment in the future. John's land is lighter than ours. It will give us soil diversity, but it will have to go through transition. "We wouldn't be able to harvest off it for thirty-six months, until it is certifiable for organic production," Martin says.

"You don't have to pay until you can use it," John says. "I thought your farm was just hard clay, the way the water ran off or sat in puddles. But now I rarely get heavy runoff from your land, only in spring melt like today, and when I do, it is almost clear, not full of crop residue and soil. You don't have standing puddles in the fields anymore either. You guys are smart. You keep your water."

Water is sacred. We don't want to waste it.

So is energy. It's early dawn, just before sunrise. I open the greenhouse vents and turn on the fans. It's 49 degrees outside. I learned this cultural system called "DIFF" in a workshop at the MOSES Organic Farming Conference. When the difference between daytime and night temperatures in a greenhouse is large, plants grow leggy and weak. By pulling in the cool, early morning air, we drop the greenhouse temperature below the nighttime temperature and the DIFF effect is counteracted. It doesn't take long, only an hour or so. The result is strong, stocky plants, and it saves the energy of maintaining high temperature in the cool night.

Plants have an internal clock. When they are transplanted, this reproduction clock is reset. This is reflected in a seed description's "days to maturity." The clock ticks off the days until blossom and subsequent maturity regardless of the plant's age at transplanting. This is where young plants excel. Their roots are still growing rapidly, and they take off quickly in the field. Older, larger plants often experience more transplant shock. The smaller, younger plants can pass them up. At the time that blossoms set, the plants that have the greatest root and plant mass will have the highest yield and quality.

Last year I experimented with three systems: transplants grown in 4-inch pots, fifty plants in an open flat, and plug trays, where each plant had a 1.25-inch square cell. The 4-inch pots, with the most room for roots, had the largest plants at transplanting. But it was the open flats that matured first and had the highest yields. Their roots were not root bound like the ones in the 4-inch pots and plug trays were, and they quickly established themselves after transplanting.

This is the first time we've ever had a pest infestation inside the greenhouse. The peppers are thick with aphids. My first thought when I see them is, did I use too much compost in the planting mix and attract the aphids with excess nitrogen? My second thought is, the lady beetles in the vetch field. How can I move them into the greenhouse?

Yesterday, Martin and I were checking the maturity of a field of soil-building vetch. We nibbled on the leaves to determine the carbon level of the plants, but it wasn't just work. We were floating on our backs like the vetch was a green pool. The plants were covered with lady beetles, and not just adults but larvae looking like miniature alligators and voraciously hungry. Now, just a day later, we need these predators. But we don't have to bring the beetles into the greenhouse to eat.

Meals on wheels—we can bring dinner to them. Eliza and I load the aphid-covered pepper plants onto hay wagons and park them in the middle of the vetch field. When I come back at the end of the day, it's hard to find an aphid, and the plants are loaded with lady beetles. That was so simple. This biological pest-control system cost the labor of loading two hundred flats of plants onto wagons, driving them back and forth to the vetch field, and then carrying them back into the greenhouse at the end of the day. We spent less money than if we had used a fossil fuel–based pesticide. At a glance it may appear that we spent more time, but we didn't.

We used present time and energy. The pesticide, using the stored time and concentrated energy in fossil fuel, is a very expensive net loss of time. Plus there is the long chain of damage to the ecosystem, which starts long before a sprayer hits a field, in the lives of the people and the environment that are part of the manufacturing and distribution of the chemical.

Too bad everything in life isn't so simple. Eliza helps. She works hard, carrying just as many flats as I do, but not with joy, only family duty. I'm starting to realize I need to change the question from how can I help her reconnect to the farm and nature to how do I accept she might not, and that's OK. I'm thinking about how she loves people and relationships when Martin comes into the greenhouse and says, "Cousin George wants to come back to Dakota County, buy property here, and set up a seasonal business. Do you have an idea of one he could start or one already existing for sale?"

George grew up just eleven miles south of our Eagan home. When he graduated from college, he traveled the world and taught agriculture in Nepal and Guatemala through the Peace Corps, then settled in Japan. Now he wants to return to his roots. "Let's sell him our acre in Eagan," I say. Martin looks shocked. "We don't live there anymore. We don't farm there. We don't need to own it just to sell there." After I say this, it hits me: part of Martin does still live and farm there.

"But my father built the house for my mother. I grew up there."
"So?"
"Everything important in my early life happened there."
"Martin, you're here now. We've always talked about developing a bedding plant business at the vegetable stand. We'll never get to

it, especially now that we live and farm thirty minutes away. He can do that. We can have a long-term lease of the stand for the vegetable season and keep selling there. We have everything we need here. We are in the green again."

This is a radical concept for Martin. I have just stomped all over the sacred cow. I don't know why I didn't see this sooner, but I'm realizing it now: he doesn't intend to ever let go of this last piece of Eagan. The thought has never even entered his head. But it's my turn to be surprised when he says in a contemplative tone, "He always did feel close to my home and family. But what about my mother?"

"George is a relative. Corinne will like that. We can sell it on a contract for deed, the payments can pass through to her, and she'll have a steady, reliable income to live on."

"What if he doesn't like the lease idea?" he asks.

"Then we don't sell," I say.

George jumps at the chance and names his bedding plant business Marvin's Gardens, which is his first name. Eliza helps with sales. She's a great resource for him; she's been working and living at the stand most of her life. It's good for her too. I watch her interacting with the customers and realize how much she has learned here, skills that will carry her far in life, communication, business, sales presentation, and confidence. She has always been about people. Since the bulldozers started rolling in Eagan, I've thought that she needs to somehow reconnect with nature to be whole. But it's not the only route. I can see a path for her through relationships with people. I just need to accept this and support it, stop trying to make her be like me. As long as I expect her to live by my parameters, I'm not respecting her.

Being tenants instead of property owners makes going there easier—one less obligation to the past. I drive up with the daily load of fresh produce, set displays, train the sales staff, and leave. I barely notice the houses pushed up around the stand. The farm is where I want to spend my time. It is good for Martin too. He's a little closer to being the "Uncle Happy" he was before the bulldozers. I wonder if this change will lift the oppressive feeling that still seems to be driving him, that he should be caring for land that no longer exists.

All spring was wet and cool, then in mid-July the weather flips to day after day of high blue skies and hot, drying sun—no rain in sight. Martin tells me, "Uncle Bill always said, 'The most accurate forecast is usually just more of the same.' This is our chance to go after the quack."

He trains the crew, David and Margie, on the digger. "You are raking the roots, not working the soil. Keep it shallow. Don't bury them. Expose them to the sun, and lay them out to dry."

They feel like real farmers, moving across the nine-acre field with a 930 Case and a Vibra Shank field digger. Every time they work it, the root mass is a tad bit smaller, the soil is a little closer to the surface, and the green comes back slower and thinner. I pick up a two-foot-long rhizome that is brown and shriveled. "Here's a goner." But when I scratch through the outer epidermis, it is white and succulent. I look for a root node and find a miniature shoot ready to push out. I pick up another rhizome, same thing. "Damn it anyway, we're not getting anywhere; these are still alive."

"Yes, we are. Look." Martin stirs through the thick mat of roots and rhizomes. "First step is separating it from the soil and starving the roots of water and nutrients. It's going to take time and dry, hot weather. If we keep flipping it in the sun, eventually it'll run out."

Six weeks later David comes in from digging. He climbs down from the tractor slow and deliberate, coated with dust. "I think we broke the quack's back," he says, so proud I think his throat will crack. "I didn't see a single root or blade of grass."

We go out and sweep the field in a line looking for living roots. "Here's one," Margie shouts. Then, "No, it's just a piece of dried weed stalk that blew in."

This is serious cause for celebration. Martin sends Margie and David back out with a grain drill full of rye and hairy vetch seed— our idea of a feast, a banquet for the field. We got rid of the quack, and we didn't use atrazine or Roundup. There was a cost though. The excessive tillage was detrimental to the microbial life and the soil structure. Now we have the task of regeneration before we will use this field for vegetables. It's part of the balance equation.

Organic farmers manage weeds and insects by understanding their life cycle and disrupting it; it's called "stress the pest." We do have bigger brains. We should be able to outsmart them.

For example, our first line of pest management for Colorado potato beetles is a trap crop. It is a trick of sorts. In spring we plant twenty leafy eggplants in the field that had potatoes the year before. When the adult beetles emerge from the windbreaks and wooded areas where they overwintered, they move straight to the eggplants, their food of choice. They are ravenous and must eat before they mate and lay eggs. Then it is a quick and simple task for us to brush them into a bucket.

One female can lay over five hundred eggs, and there are usually two generations per summer. Capturing the beetles and preventing reproduction makes a big difference. Some beetles make it past our eggplant trap and into the new field. There we have hay buffers, habitat for ground beetles, whose larvae feed on potato beetle larvae. We also have aerial support; I often see rose-breasted grosbeaks eating the potato beetle larvae. If they make it through that, we get out the flame weeder and roast them. The potato plants recover from the brief intense heat, but the beetles don't. This is also a great strategy for engaging Maize in the farm. Fire is exciting; add exploding beetles and you have a very interested nine-year-old.

Further on in the season, if the potato beetle population reaches a density of economic injury, we spray a naturally occurring bacterium called *Bacillus thuringiensis* (Bt). It doesn't affect any other species and breaks down quickly in the environment. The potato beetle larvae eat the bacteria, which then attack their gut cells; they stop feeding quickly and die within a few days.

We use a trap crop in winter squash too; only here we are trapping a disease microorganism instead of an insect. Aphids can be the carrier of zucchini mosaic, which causes stunted and deformed fruit with raised lumps and bitter flavor. Instead of trying to eradicate the aphids, we plant a strip of wheat around the perimeter of the squash field. When the insects enter, they chew on the wheat, cleaning their mouthparts of the pathogen. Aphid toothbrush. The aphids continue on into the winter squash and feed there, but their eating doesn't cause significant damage, as they are no longer vectoring the disease. We've had excellent results with this simple and nontoxic strategy, which we learned from Beth Kazmar of Tipi Produce.

As organic farmers, we recognize that when we allow some pest pressure, beneficial insects are encouraged to establish a foothold in the cropping system. The trick is to understand when the pest threshold is acceptable.

For example, research has shown that once broccoli plants have at least six leaves until just before creating a head, they can withstand up to 50 percent defoliation by pests without a decrease in yield. In fact, moderate defoliation of the plants—around 20 to 30 percent—actually increases yield. Defoliation causes certain plant substances to be emitted that beckon parasitic wasps and predatory insects to the plants. The parasitic wasps insert their eggs beneath the skin of cabbage worm larvae. When the eggs hatch, they feed on the worm.

It's not until the broccoli begins to head that we need to be particular about pest levels. If cabbage worms are present at heading, we spray microbial Bt. This will kill the worms but will not harm the beneficial insects or any other species.

An organic farm close to the University of Minnesota and the Department of Agriculture is valuable for entomologist researchers. They need fields that aren't sprayed with pesticides, and unmowed grass is crucial for beneficial insect nesting. Dr. David Andow is here studying *Trichogramma* wasps as biological control of corn borers on sweet corn, and Dr. Dharma Sreenivasam is researching the impact of a specific lady beetle on potato bug larvae.

Maize follows them in the field with a magnifying glass. He understands the simple elegance—every species is eaten by another, and every species eats. Today Dr. Andow shows him minute pirate bugs burrowed into corn silk. They're tiny, smaller than a flax seed. He tells Maize, "Know your friends. Minute pirate bugs are an important predator of corn earworm eggs and European corn borers."

This spring I gave Maize four seeds from the World Championship Pumpkin, the top prizewinner, which weighed in at over a thousand pounds. I don't need him to be a future farmer. It's this relationship with land and all the life on it, his experience growing up in a family business, his understanding of the seasons, of life and death—this is sculpting who he is as a person.

He took the task on with complete seriousness. Carefully he placed two seeds side by side in a greenhouse pot, growing tips down, a bit of soil between them; he measured the depth of cover with his pinkie, checking the moisture daily until they germinated. In the field, he fed the plants a blend of cow and turkey compost and watered the roots so gently. Frattalone must have been whispering in his ear. Every day he ministered small attentions—compost tea, hoeing, scouting for cucumber beetles. By the time the plants started to canopy, native squash bees had found them and were making nests at the base of each plant. European honeybees don't work in cold, wet weather. Squash bees do, and they live right where they will be needed; the males can actually spend the night inside the flowers. Maize spent hours watching them, until the pumpkins were fertilized and the fruit set. Then the spell was broken, and his bike and the woods became more interesting.

Now it's October, and two fairly large pumpkins surprise us, one weighing in at 125 pounds, the other at 142. We haul them up to the stand, and Maize prices them at $30 each. A few days later, the roadside stand clerk calls. He's apologetic. The price tag blew off. A construction worker driving an expensive pickup wanted them, so he charged $100 each. "Hope that's OK," he says.

I hand Maize two crisp new bills and ask him what he'd like to do with the money. I'm thinking he's going to say a new bike or Legos, or can I buy a PlayStation. But he says, "Put it toward the land. Next year I'll plant one hundred giant pumpkins, and we can pay it off really fast."

It's heartwarming, and I had no idea he thought about what it takes to buy land, but it would be wrong to let him think we can't take care of him. "We've got this one covered just fine, Maize. Nothing will happen to this land."

I'm so surprised that it brings me back to Eliza. I've let go of believing she has to reconnect with nature. But I realize that it would be wrong to assume that her strong connection with the land in Eagan isn't still part of her. Just because she's not showing an interest here doesn't mean it's not deep within. She is a beautiful, kind, loving teenager. She has a healing presence and loves to be with people. I wonder what she'll do with her life and how her childhood experiences will come through and guide her.

The Real World of Fresh Produce

Martin is in his typical rain-is-coming, corn-planting tizzy. I find it interesting that in some areas he is the complete Buddha of patience, and I have none, and on other details, we are the reverse. The first thing he said to me this morning was, "Uncle Jim called this 'the kind of weather where your best cow would kick you,' hot and muggy, dropping barometer, rain coming."

"This is the kind of weather where your best friend might kick you," I sassed back.

I still think God can be in the form of raindrops, and it is fascinating to me that I can pray for or curse the same drops. Right now we need rain, but first we want to get the planting done. The question of the day is not will it rain, but when, how much, and how hard.

Further complicating the corn-planting tension is the potential of cross-pollination with neighboring field corn. Pollen is light and is often carried considerable distances on the wind. Corn plants have separate male and female flowering parts; the tassel is the male, and the ear shoot is the female. Each ovule (potential kernel) produces its own strand of corn silk. The tassel anthers shed grains of pollen, which are caught by the fine, sticky hairs on the silk. A pollen tube then grows down the length of the silk until it reaches the ovule and fertilizes it, which then grows into an individual kernel. Pollen of a given plant rarely fertilizes the kernels of the same plant.

If our sweet corn is cross-pollinated by neighboring field corn, it is not sweet nor is it marketable. Martin manages this threat by recording the dates of all the developmental stages for our crop, as well as the neighbors' planting and pollen dates. He then adjusts his cultivars and planting sequence by what the neighbors plant and when. But cross-pollination is impossible to avoid completely. When there are field corn–pollinated kernels in our sweet corn, they are visible; they are larger, squarer, darker yellow kernels mixed in like polka dots among the small, tender sweet corn kernels. We can usually feel the bigger kernels through the husks, and we avoid picking and selling them. But now there is an even larger challenge and looming threat.

It is 1997, and our neighbors are experimenting with genetically modified field corn (GM). We don't want GM traits in our organic crops, and there is no controlling the pollen. We know from firsthand experience how readily cross-pollination occurs. We are concerned that eventually it will become impossible to find seed and food that isn't contaminated with GM traits. Fortunately for our customers and us, our neighbors are planting field corn. If it were GM sweet corn, we might not be able to see the different kernels.

Genetic modification is an experiment not of our choosing. But we all are participants. This is even more serious than pesticide drift. It's not if cross-pollination happens but when. There is no taking it back, and segregation in the field is not possible. It is a threat not just to our survival but also to the future of our genetic heritage and to nature itself. Right now it's field corn and soybeans. What species will be next?

Martin jokes, "Alfalfa."

"Nobody could be so foolish as to introduce genetically modified alfalfa," I say. "Bees and native pollinators carry alfalfa pollen for miles. Seed purity would likely be lost, even in wild alfalfa, which cross-pollinates with domesticated, and what about the 'hard seed'? It remains dormant in the ground and germinates years later."

He agrees it would be crazy, but asks, "How much precautionary principle are you seeing in practice?"

If an action or policy has a possible risk of causing harm to the public or to the environment, in the absence of scientific consensus that it is harmful, the burden of proof that it is *not* harmful should fall on those taking the action. In this case, the burden should fall upon the seed breeders and their companies to prove it is safe, and they haven't done that.

This has changed my message at the stand. Genetically modified foods are not labeled in stores. Now I tell customers that eating organic is the only way they can guarantee that the production of the food was without genetically modified organisms. Sometimes they ask, "How about all-natural meat? I can get that at my grocery store."

According to the USDA, "natural" means no artificial ingredient or color has been added and the product is only minimally processed. Minimally processed means the raw product has not been fundamentally altered. It may still contain antibiotics and growth hormones, and the animal has likely been fed GM feed.

It's not if, but when. Cross-contamination is as likely as the coming storm. The rain hits just as Martin finishes planting. A few days later we go out to check the corn. We dig through the damp soil and find the seed swollen and full, pregnant with moisture and new growth. A tiny nub of root protrudes, the first step in growing a roothold. We move down the row and uncover a few more. All are in the same state of moving from dormancy toward green, growing, and reproduction. Seed is sacred. We need to protect and preserve it.

I'm thinking about everything that goes into producing a corn crop while I'm listening to a produce buyer.

"I don't want local produce. It comes in warm and doesn't hold up," he says.

"You won't have that problem with us," I say.

"I'm not interested."

I have lived an unusually sheltered life as a fresh-market organic farmer. This is my first wholesale pitch to a non co-op. I'm thinking, welcome to the real world of produce, Atina. This is the reality most farmers deal with. This is my third sales pitch, and I've gotten nowhere. "Here's the deal," I say to the produce manager. "You're new in town, and you don't know us or our farm. It's only fair that we prove ourselves to you. We'll ship you five hundred dollars' worth of produce. If you're not satisfied, you can do whatever you want with it, and you don't have to pay for it. If you like it enough that you want to order more, send a check, and we can do business."

"Fair enough," he says.

"Here's our product list. We ship on Tuesdays, Thursdays, and Saturdays. I'll need your order by seven A.M., the day before."

"Most farmers want two to four days' lead time."

"We pick to order, cool, and ship within twenty-four hours. All we need is a one-day lead. We have a one hundred percent satisfaction-guaranteed policy. Just tell us if you have a problem."

He moves through his first order in three days and calls for more.

"Don't sell more than sixty sacks," Martin says. " We'll be lucky if we can get that out."

I make the phone rounds, writing each store's order on a chart, how many cases of each item, how many sacks of corn. I tell everyone, "Corn is tight. We'll do our best to fill your order, but we might have to short you a little. We should be strong with whatever you want by the next delivery."

Martin comes in over the walkie-talkie. "Got near one hundred sacks on the ground and maybe another fifty in the field yet. How many should we pick?"

"Jeez, Marty, how about a little warning. You've been telling me all week to stall them, and now you expect me to move a hundred and fifty sacks in two minutes?"

"It just got ripe—last night. It wasn't ready when I checked it before bed."

Am I really supposed to believe this? "I can't just sell that much without warming them up. It takes advance notice to clear out their back stock."

"Pick it or lose it. It just came in. With today's heat it will go over by tomorrow."

I can hear Julio in the background, "Marteen, Marteen—mucho maize y no gusanos."

Why, after all these years, do we still go through this almost every time we pick corn, like three times a week? I should do the field counts myself, or Julio should do them. He always knows what's in a field. If he is out there chanting "mucho maize," I know I need to sell. "Give me a few minutes anyway. Why don't you start loading what you have. Check back when you have it on the truck."

Where's the quickest place to move volume? I call Eddie at the Wedge Co-op. "Corn deal time, and not a worm in it."

"Fantastic! What have you got?"

"Sugar-enhanced, bicolor Temptation. As much as you could ever want—special it."

All the co-ops, except one, go for the deal; the order moves up to exactly 150. I'm about to walkie-talkie Martin and tell him to keep picking when the phone rings. It's Rick Christianson at Roots and Fruits, and he wants sixty sacks. "Yep, we got it, no problem. We'll drop it in the morning." Knowing Martin and his fear of overpromising, I might as well shoot for the max.

I walkie-talkie him, "Clear out the field—sold up to two hundred and ten."

"There's not that much out here, and if we clean it out, what will we sell on the next order?"

"Just pick it, Martin. What are you saving it for? You just told me it won't hold."

Only one store didn't jump at the corn special, but I figured they probably just "got long," need to "sell down," and will be ready on our next delivery.

After unloading their order, I cruise through the produce department to check how our vegetables are holding up in the store display. My gut flips when I see a huge pile of conventional corn on special— front and center—an overflowing, virtual mountain of dried-out, tough-looking cobs with a bright orange sign, *6 for a dollar.* I don't have to taste it to know it's dead. I look for our sweet corn and find it hidden in a corner at the back of the department marked up 150 percent from our wholesale price.

This co-op has been committed to organic and local for decades. This new guy needs an education—where is he from anyway? He didn't even use the same markup on the two. A higher margin on organic is not the normal food co-op modus operandi. I grab a random ear from both displays, breathe deeply three times, plaster a smile on my face, and head to the back room.

"I have something for you to taste," I say, and hand him the conventional cob.

He pulls back the husk and sinks his teeth into the big, tough, starchy kernels. He gags, spits the mouthful into the trash, and spurts, "That's complete shit; where's it from?" Then he whips the uneaten cob into the can.

"Your conventional sale," I say, smiling real friendly. "Try this one."

He peels back one side, takes a cautious bite of the tender kernels, then rips the husk off and eats the ear whistle-clean without stopping or talking. "Man, that's good. Where's it from? I gotta have another one."

"It's our organic corn. We have as much as you could ever want, and it's on special now." I think I've made my point. I don't want to grind it in; less is more in this situation.

But the next time he orders, it's a pathetic two sacks. When I deliver, the conventional pile is just as big and dried out. I taste it, and it's still inedible. "Why are you selling this crap? You know it doesn't 'eat.'" I have no smile left and no caution. "Where's your credibility? You're just going to burn your customers."

"All they care about is price," he says.

"That isn't true; your customers know quality, and they are committed to organic. They've been buying Gardens of Eagan sweet corn for decades. This store has never carried both organic and conventional."

"Then why is it selling five sacks to your one?"

What can I say to that? Because you're practically shoving it in their carts with your front-and-center display, because only the completely determined will even find the organic tucked in the back corner, because you're using different markups, gouging on ours far beyond what is acceptable.

For the next few orders I accept his piddly numbers and tell my-self, relax, you'll outlast him. I know this is true. He's not meeting the members' needs. But I'm thinking in terms of months. I'm surprised when two weeks later, there is a new buyer, who shrugs when I ask, "What happened to the other guy?" The conventional corn is gone. Ours is heaped in its place. The price is down where it should be, and the order is fifteen sacks.

After I finish delivering, I go into the store to buy breakfast. The general manager is at the register. "Your corn has been fantastic," she says with a big grin. "Thanks for all the years you've grown and de-livered it to us."

When I get back out to the loading dock, the Roots and Fruits driver is backing up. "Do you know what happened to the buyer?" I ask under my breath.

"The word in the warehouse is he got caught taking produce pay-ola from the conventional broker—color televisions and free seats to the Twins game."

I am thinking about these relationships we have with the food co-ops and the organic community they serve as I read the introduction to *Don Quixote*: "Literature's foremost appeal is to temporarily become another. To leave a typically embattled self for another closer to one's desires and aspirations. Experience and life's blows teach us our lim-its and erode the hope of living up to our dreams, but our hope never vanishes."

It isn't just produce our customers want and need. The opportu-nity to have a relationship with the farm has a value with a shelf life much longer than the fresh produce. We meet so many people who express their aspiration to farm. Our success serves their dreams by providing an example of agriculture not based on corporate com-modities and fossil fuel inputs. It supports hope and stimulates change by demonstrating the reality that organic farming works.

We've been living and growing on our new land in Eureka Town-ship for six years now, and we are thriving as a farm and business. We have a hard-working, committed crew, fertile soil, growing systems in place, and strong relationships. One of our greatest strengths is the support of the food co-op community. Their commitment to local organic food is bottom-up from the members; it is top-down from the general managers and storewide through all the departments. The food co-ops exist to serve the needs of their members. The success of their stores and that of the farms they support are interconnected.

For us, it means a solid wall that has backed us every step of the way. There are so many variables beyond a farmer's control. Having a secure and supportive market means we can take calculated risks. If we know what we need to produce and will reliably sell, we can make strategic business decisions and investments. We don't need to be pampered. We want feedback if there are quality issues, and we expect to be held to a high standard. We need to do our job of producing food, and we need to do it very well.

We've lost a few co-ops along the way. Powderhorn Co-op, the New Riverside Café, Whole Foods Co-op, and East Calhoun Co-op have closed their doors. But most of them are experiencing double-digit sales growth annually and are doing an excellent job of educating and satisfying customers. The Wedge, Lakewinds, Seward, and Linden Hills have all built gorgeous new stores, and Mississippi Market and Valley Natural Foods have ones under construction. The Wedge is starting a produce warehouse, Co-op Partners, which will buy from small, local organic farms as well as larger, name-brand organic labels.

It's exciting, and we have the production capacity to grow with them. Each year our yields and quality have steadily grown as our soil health continually improves. Martin once told me that 90 percent of success is being in the right place at the right time. "Good decisions and hard work are important, but opportunity is a key factor." In the 1970s and 1980s it seemed like the right time for organic food might never come, but it's here now, and we are ready for it. It is good to remember that when we bought this land, we didn't have sufficient income to make the mortgage payments, and Martin still worked off the farm. We are finally earning a good living.

With all this growth, sometimes it's hard to know if we've planted enough in spring. Both Martin and I have this challenge. We look at everything that is planted, and it doesn't look like much. Seed and labor are inexpensive compared to insufficient product. We would rather have surplus than fail to satisfy our customers. Each year I plant a little more than our plan—for good measure. I know he does this too, but neither of us admits it. Half the task of planting is prepping the field, setting up the equipment, crew, and plants. Once we're in place and rolling, it only takes an extra twenty minutes to put in another thousand transplants. The same with cultivating, what's a few extra rows? Harvest, however, is another matter altogether. Everything is picked and packed by hand. Then we're asking ourselves, "What kind of monster have we created?"

Somehow it all sells, and by the end of the season we're glad we planted it. When the next year comes, we need still more to meet the food co-ops' demands. Now we are starting to get tight on land again. I am interested when Martin comes home from an equipment auction at Bill Elstad's and tells me his land may come up for sale.

A Norwegian bachelor on his family's land, we've known him for years. When it was time to quit farming, he moved into a small cabin on his land and rented out the farmhouse to a couple, who run the crops and milk cows in the barn. The tenants are supposed to be buying the land, but not only are they not making the payments, they are borrowing from Bill. He is at a stage of his life where happiness matters more than money. He has become fond of the children and wants to see a family on the land. The tenants are in over their heads now. The bank is closing them out.

It's a raw day in late fall. The neighbors ask each other what the land is worth and discuss who will buy it. The kinder ones talk about how hard working the woman is, doing the milking morning and night and working off the farm during the day. After the auction is over, Martin finds Bill sitting alone at his kitchen table drinking black coffee, no heat on. The earflaps are turned down on his plaid wool cap. He's happy to see Martin but disheartened by the sale. "This isn't anything new," Bill says, "a family trying to farm and not able to make it. I've seen it a number of times where working hard doesn't pay the bills, doesn't satisfy the banknote. They earn more calluses than cash."

Bill's father was named Martin too, and he was blind. Bill was the eyes for his hands. He grew up here; his entire emotional life is tied to this piece of earth. "What's going to happen with the land now?" Bill asks. Questions like this aren't simple to answer.

Martin is at the Buckboard Café with Henry, Lyle, and Octer when they tell him the sad news that Bill's health is failing. They shake their heads and say, "He's been moved to the Odd Fellows Nursing Home. His sister and niece put the land up for sale, and it sold quickly, but shortly before closing they found out the buyer's bank would not cover the loan. It is back on the market now."

Once again, we are considering the purchase of land that is frozen and buried under snow. The soil is lighter, sandier; it would give us diversity and long-distance rotation. Over half of the seventy-eight acres is in hay and qualifies for organic certification. The rest we can clean up. We go down on New Year's Day and are welcomed by the perfect omen—a pair of robins singing in the open creek.

By late January we have closed on the property. We are rewriting our crop plan for 1999, moving the potatoes, melons, and early corn down to Bill's alfalfa ground and buying a second set of tillage equipment.

We slide out of bed and into our clothes. Minutes later we are rolling pallets of packed produce out of the cooler and lining them up on the loading dock. I love seeing the food all together in one place like this, ready to leave the farm and our care. So much has gone into getting it to this point. Soon it will be in the hands of the eaters.

It takes two trucks to get everything to town. Martin will drive one, and I the other. We hop right into the work, hand-stacking mixed loads in the order in which they will be delivered. Fortunately we have the routine down. At 3:00 A.M. we are too tired to think. I have the clipboard with each store's order and have to shout to be heard above the cooler compressor. Martin mishears me and loads a Sunburst melon instead of a Sugar Baby. I tell him it is the wrong box. He snaps back that he loaded what I said. I say he wasn't listening.

We have these foolish arguments every time we load trucks at three in the morning, which if we weren't such optimists we'd more accurately call the middle of the night. Neither of us will give in, so it continues until we are finished packing the truck. Sometimes I wonder if we have this clash just to build the energy to get the work done.

One truck is filled and insulated, and we start on the second. This is not what anyone would call "the life of Riley." My mother often told me not to take people seriously after nine at night. There should be some time off in the morning too, like anytime before sunrise on less than six hours of sleep doesn't count. And if two people, especially a married couple, get up and load trucks in the middle of the night, after picking all day under a broiling sun, and then wash and pack produce until after dark, they should just forgive everything each other says, no matter what time of day.

Somehow it works. It is rare to finish and find a leftover box. If we leave the farm by 5:00 A.M., we can avoid traffic jams and empty our trucks before the heat of the day. Someday in the future we'll have a refrigerated truck. We'll be able to load the night before. I think that "some day" better come this winter; we have reached a scale where this is no longer an option.

My first stop is Valley Natural Foods Co-op. It's too early for staff to be there, but I have the key to the store safety-pinned to the back of the seat cover. It is a huge trust. Every time I turn the lock, I am aware of the goodwill and relationship the key represents. It makes for a very quick and easy delivery. I back up, open the truck door, pull out the ramp, two-wheel the cold produce into the walk-in, set the tomatoes under the counter—careful to rotate the new ones to the bottom of the stack—put the invoice on top of the scale, weigh it down with the pen cup, lock the store door, close up the truck, and

I'm finished—less than five minutes. I think back to the days when Maize and Eliza were little and they took turns coming along on deliveries. They would have been in charge of the key and proud of it.

I park behind Linden Hills Co-op and finish unloading before the produce buyer comes out, signs the invoice, and waves good-bye. It's the same at every store. I stack the produce into their cooler, and the busy buyers sign without inspecting the boxes. They know we are reliable and pack quality.

The day is warming up. I want to get these vegetables into a cooler. I want to get out of town and back to the farm. And I want a refrigerated truck. I didn't care before. I thought it was beautiful getting up early when the world is fresh and quiet, but those days are over. I back up to the Wedge Co-op and drop the ramp through the doorway into the produce back room. The race is on, pushing a two-wheeler directly into the cooler, heaped with kale and cabbage, sixty-pound cartons of melons, and tippy sacks of corn. The produce buyer, Dean, sticks his head into the cooler and says, "All right! It's the speed queen!" I must look confused, because he adds, "You're the fastest Gardens of Eagan delivery person."

I just need to stop at the farmers market to pick up a few items, drive to the roadside stand in Eagan, unload, and whip through a display setup. Then I can get back to the farm. We buy additional produce for the roadside stand from local organic farms to provide one-stop shopping for our customers. When organic is not available, I buy local, display it separately, and label it in big, bold letters: *Local-NOT Organic*. Our sales staff is trained to inform all customers at the checkout if any of their selected produce is not organic.

At a stoplight, blocks from the market, a man stands with a cardboard sign cut from a produce carton. *Homeless. Please help. God Bless.* I hold four ears of corn out the window.

"Listen, lady, you don't understand. I really am homeless. I don't have anywhere to cook that."

"You don't have to cook it. It's delicious raw and good for you. I eat it in the field for breakfast every day."

He glares at me. I husk an ear and start to eat it. "Why don't you just try it?"

His look turns to skepticism. I glance down at the kale on the seat; that would really be a stretch. I hold the corn out again. The light changes. I let off the brake, and he takes it out of my hand.

I had hoped to be home before noon and take a nap, but it is after lunch when I roll exhausted out of the truck and am immediately greeted by the crew, ready to go out and transplant. This is the nineteenth sequential broccoli planting since late April, adding up to 125,000 plants and continuous harvest for five months. These August plantings are the most difficult. The spring thrill is long gone, and we're focused on harvest. It's a challenge to work up planting energy.

By late afternoon we're finished, and I'm in the pack shed sorting tomatoes. Brenda Langton from Cafe Brenda arrives with a film crew to interview Martin in the kale field for a cooking video. It is hot and it is humid. I don't want to do anything right now but lie in a cold bathtub and sleep.

"Oh, I love your outfit!" Brenda says as she hugs me and kisses my cheeks. "You look so good in that mauve silk shirt and your white cotton pants."

Kristina and Chris are behind her, tittering into their hands. My shirt is filthy with ground-in dirt, tomato juice, and green streaks of kale. Only two buttons are left. The rest is held shut with safety pins. I'll be lucky if the tear in the armpit makes it through the rest of today, and these pants cannot with any honesty be called white anymore. Chris swoons to Kristina, "I love your straw hat. It is so chic."

I glare at them. "Are you finished picking the peppers?"

"We just came in to change our outfits."

Brenda has no idea. She turns around and beams. "Oh you girls look so cute in your little shorts and T-shirts." She's so happy to be around fresh produce and farmers that we're all beautiful to her. Martin comes in, and they go off with the film crew. Kristina, Chris, and I lie on the pack shed floor laughing hysterically. I say, "We must have heat and exhaustion stroke." This sets us off even more.

Martin has a theory that since we start at three in the morning, by noon we have one day's work in. Then we have lunch and a short nap, and work again from one to nine in the evening—miraculously living two days in one. "But I didn't get a nap," I complain.

"We'll have twice as much life this way," he says.

"More like we have no life."

"I only get one morning a day. I like to make the most of it."

"You think loading a truck on four hours of sleep and arguing with your wife is making the most of your morning?"

"Always look at the positive," he says. "We don't have to drive to work. We just walk out our door."

It is worth a lot to me that I can roll out of bed, slide into my clothes, and be at work instantly. But I don't get it. Where is this life of Riley that people think we have? I am brushing my teeth when I remember—dang, I almost forgot my dad's birthday. I have to call him before it's too late. Somehow the conversation goes to women working. He says, "Women don't need to work outside the home; it's a lifestyle choice."

"Dad, some women have to work, and some women want to work. It's OK if women work."

"It's a choice. Women belong at home taking care of their children. All my daughters stay at home."

"Dad, I work." As if working so hard that there is nothing left of myself isn't enough, I have this familial message that women who work are neglecting their families.

"No, you work at home."

"I'm not exactly in the house baking cookies and ironing hankies."

"You work on the farm. That's at home. That's OK."

For a short second I have a really strong desire to get an off-farm job, any job, waitress, secretary, I'll even clean toilets. I look at my watch. There's mom's message again. Don't take it seriously. It is not about me.

Next week the homeless man is at the corner again. When I pull up to the stoplight, I ask him, "How were they? Did you eat them raw?"

"I cooked them," he says.

I'm ready this time, and he smiles when I hold a muskmelon out the window. I'm ripped through with the thrill I felt when I first started farming. It feels so great to feed people. Sometimes when I'm really tired, I say to Martin, "We could quit farming, you could have a full-time job, and I would be the best housewife in the world. Think of the fantastic meals that would be waiting for you when you got home."

He just says, "You would be so bored."

Living in the Relative Present

Dirt is just soil that's out of place. Soil has structure. Dirt does not.

I have been cleaning all week, as if dirt is the enemy, not a lost tribal member of our friend soil. Once our home is reclaimed from the summer's madness, the real fun begins. As part of our annual evaluation process, we formally quit farming for one week at the end of the season. Quitting is part of our commitment. When we farm again, it is a conscious choice. We quit to begin anew, to create larger lives. We intentionally lose the path in order to find our way. And today is quitting day.

I positively pop out of bed and jump into a bright orange and pink polka-dot silk dress—my special occasion outfit when I need something extra sassy and ultraclean. I shake Martin's hand, jumping up and down while I say, "Thank you for another glorious season. I, Atina Diffley, hereby solemnly do swear, as of this very moment, I quit farming. I will assess my goals and values, my assumptions and guiding philosophies. I will create a new commitment for my life and work."

Martin shakes back in ceremonial earnest. "I, Martin Diffley, quit farming. I will reevaluate my life's purpose and focus. I will not start farming again until I have made a fresh and deliberated commitment."

And that's it. We are free! For the next week we do not fix tractors, buy supplies, or read want ads. Talking farm, interviewing prospective employees, or doing fieldwork is prohibited. Even talking about the weather is an illicit act. We do scrub and manicure our hands and feet until there is not a speck of dirt or stain. Our clothes are spotless in the middle of the day. We spend hours cooking and listening to records, dancing in the kitchen, or we spend the day browsing secondhand shops. We stay up late reading and laughing in bed.

It doesn't really matter what we do, as long as it is fun, together, and doesn't involve farming. It is one thing to think we have a choice; we don't have to be farmers just because we own a farm. But it doesn't strike the heart of reality for us. Officially quitting, taking a holiday, and reevaluating create a depth of understanding and commitment that I can't match with imagination. Perhaps this is where the artist-gardener versus blood farmer distinction comes in. We have personalities separate from the work. Farming for us must be an evaluated decision and a unified commitment. If we get caught up in should, and must, and have to, then our passion and joy get lost in the slog of repetition and the stress of weather and management.

Instead of a duty to a lifetime obligation, we make a one-year pledge to give the farm our complete and best selves. We create a signed-in-ink, sealed-with-a-handshake, fifty-one-week commitment and plan. When we are too tired to take another step, we know it is not forever. There will be other time in our lives to develop different passions.

I don't remember anymore where the idea for this annual quitting and recommitting process came from; most likely it was a flash of inspiration that got us through a hot, humid day in August. I don't even know if I'd recommend it to others, because a long-term commitment is crucial to farming success. I just know that this exercise works for us.

It is the fifth day of our week off from farming. I'm cleaning up after a lovely dinner of borscht, bread, and organic chicken. With a fresh washcloth, I wipe the cutting board. It is a contrast of swirling grain. Touching the smoothness of the wood, I pause in movement; the beauty of nature's design and the pleasure of simple tools are experiences of connection. I forgot work could be so enjoyable, the contentment of a job well done, the satisfying sense of order and completion. You could knock me over with a feather is how I feel right now. Work and life are completely merged as one. I lose this in the heat of the harvest.

I immerse the soup bowls in hot water, and bits of moisture and soap foam on my forearm. I think of bedrock along streams where a pebble had spun for centuries in the tumbling water, carving small cups and bowls in the granite. The plates have an edge of green leaves; wiping them clean reveals the forest. I'm standing at a sink with my hands in dishwater. But I'm traveling through nature. Finally I understand the plaque on my mother's kitchen wall, "Thank God for dirty dishes."

Our quitting week is over. Now the most important task of the year comes: winter planning. We will evaluate the year's experiments, successes, and failures. We'll take a look at the reality of the farm and our lives, based on numbers and emotions, our backs and our spirits. Just making money isn't enough. We'll ask, what is working and what is not? What is joyful and what is drudgery? What can be changed to make it better?

Years ago we took a Holistic Management class taught by Audrey Arner and Richard Ness at the MOSES Organic Farming Conference. It made a big impression on us, and we incorporate many of the tools into our annual process. Our first step is writing "quality of life statements," an exercise I download from the Holistic Management website. The better we know where we want to go, the more likely we are to get there.

If we lived perfect lives in a perfect place, what would it look like? We close our eyes and imagine who would be there, what our surroundings would be, the colors and smells. I write a list of "I want" statements.

I want excellent physical, emotional, and relationship health. I want to eat healthy food. I want to spend the majority of my time outside. I want to be an organic farmer and feed a lot of people. I want to take excellent care of the land we own. I want to be self-employed.

Martin shares his list: I want to operate a successful and profitable organic farm. I want to spend more time with Maize and Eliza. I want to protect and cherish the environment and land. I want to be healthy. I want to live my passions.

Then we write personal essays answering the question, what do I really like about my life right now? This is a great reminder to notice all the good already present.

I am a creature of seasons. The structure of my life allows me to adapt and flow with the changes of nature. The results of my labor are visible and tactile. We have made our dreams real. We feed people and nourish health. I wake with the birds, ready to be part of the glory of life.

What would I change about my life if I could?

I would do a better job of staying in the present. I would be able to throw myself passionately into my work and ride the challenges and exhaustion without slipping into worry or stress. I would remember to take time to revitalize through nature.

Martin writes: I love that I'm doing what I've wanted to do since grade school. I live my life outside like I am at recess. I work with plants and soil, and I'm in nature. More than anything else I'm in a seasonal sensitivity. I rest up and enjoy a good night's sleep in the wintertime. My down blanket is like snow keeping me warm. I enjoy the sun returning, the spring energy, the first weeds germinating. I love the summer growing and jumping in the pond. I love the joy the food brings to the eaters, the return of cool nights, everything the seasons bring.

I would have more recess. I would take time to really enjoy the things that I like about being outside. I would lie down more often under blooming plums. I would stop and listen to the bees and look for jack-in-the-pulpits. I would take more time to inhale the dawn and feel the sun on my body. I would taste the sap in the trees.

This is a process. We give it an entire week. We update our Farm and Self-Inventory, a document we've created to better understand our resource base. It doesn't just identify our financial assets and liabilities. It includes everything that contributes to our ability to create the lives we want. It draws an image of the farm's personality separate from our own, the topography, climate, soil types, and signature crops. It includes lists of equipment, employees and market, and how much money we need to earn. We list very element that goes into the composite whole of this farm.

This all contributes to our Holistic Goal, which is a long-term, overall blueprint for what we want to create. It has three parts: quality of life, production, and resource base. What Audrey explained in the class is that our Holistic Goal should be 100 percent about what we want and 0 percent about how to get there. The best way to get what we want may change with time, and people argue far more over "how" to achieve goals than "what" those goals should be.

That fits Martin and me. Our goals are fundamentally the same, but our thinking processes are so different. Once we have the Holistic Goal firmly in mind, we can concentrate on the decisions that will get us there. That's key to finding a way forward that satisfies both of us.

The basics of our Holistic Goal haven't changed since we first took the class. Our quality-of-life statement can be summed up in the adage "Health is wealth." Environmental, relationship, physical, and emotional health are key criteria for us. Production is clear. We are organic vegetable gardener-farmers. Quitting every year is an exercise and a spiritual practice, but this is the work we want to do. Our resource base continues to deepen: the food co-ops, Dave our banker, our ancestral and life lessons, Martin's rich storehouse of relationships, all the people who work on the farm, our children, the rich soil, our region's biological resource, our strong bodies, other farmers.

Then we bring in the external. We make lists of trends in food and farming and hold them against our assumptions and beliefs. This gives us a sharp look at present reality and helps us abandon old ways of thinking that no longer serve our farm, our customers' needs, or us. By day three we begin to shuffle it all together. We list the changes we need to make and ask questions. Will this bring us closer to our Holistic Goal? Will it fix the root cause of the problem it is meant to address? Does it strengthen the weakest link in the chain between dream and reality? What are the possible unintended consequences?

By day five we have created a fifty-one-week action plan titled *2000: The Year of Delivery and Sleep.* Our key objectives are sleeping a minimum of eight hours per night and improving our delivery quality. We will accomplish this by finishing daily no later than 7:00 P.M., hiring more staff and delegating tasks, buying a dock-height refrigerated truck with a lift gate, and hiring a driver. Produce will be loaded the evening before instead of early in the morning.

Our action plan includes who will do each thing, what it will cost, and when it will be done. We sign our names at the bottom of the plan. We write the date. We stand up, look each other in the eye, and solemnly shake hands—then hug.

I am completely aware at this moment that I have chosen how I live my life. I am also keenly aware that I have chosen to farm. We both know a day will come, sometime in the future, when this process will take us to a decision to do something different with our lives, to the decision not to manage a farm. I wonder though, what will it feel like?

The dock-height refrigerated truck is everything Martin ever promised. We should have done this years ago. We were so cautious about taking on debt that we neglected to calculate the cost to our relationship and health. He never buys in singles—when he finds one, a second shows up even better than the first. Before long he rolls into the yard in Hercules, also a ten-pallet refrigerated unit.

Martin and hired driver Billie do the bulk of the deliveries now. I only go in on Saturdays when the order is too large to fit in the two trucks. I drop the Wedge's order and go to the farmers market to buy for the roadside stand. No more 3:00 A.M. truck loading. I just roll out of bed, jump up and down until I'm awake enough to drive, and thirty-seven minutes later I'm backed up to the Wedge Co-op, unloading on schedule at 7:00 A.M. I'm still really tired though.

It's a long, hot season leading up to harvest, but I've had plenty of experience with ignoring exhaustion. It comes pretty naturally. I am driving through the market. Vendors spot my truck and step into the aisle to load: single-source honey and Chestnut crab apples from Ames Honey, paper bags from Fast Freddy, maple syrup from the Sandman. I don't even have to get out of the cab. I pull up behind their stalls; they load the cartons and then come up to my window. I write a check, and I'm on to the next. While they are loading, I close my eyes and take a snap nap. It seems normal to them to tap my arm and wake me when they come to the window for their check. This is the market. Everyone is exhausted.

For flowers, I need to park and run across the street to the auxiliary market. The lot is full, mostly vendors' vehicles, so I park behind a beat-up van that looks like it belongs to a farmer, likely to be here the entire morning. My truck blocks the exit, but there is no one behind me, and I'll be back in just a few minutes.

I never know exactly what I will get when I order from Der, but it is always gorgeous—her bouquets jolt and stir the senses, realign and inspire the spirit—and they always sell. Today's include accents of green millet and balls of mauve globe amaranth. We finish quickly, and I head back with a bucket in each arm. Before I'm even across the road, I see a long line of cars backed up behind my truck. The market manager is standing with the drivers. He points at my truck, the cars, the exit, and back at me. His face is red. "Atina," he yells, "what were you thinking? Blocking the exit!"

"I was only gone a few minutes."

"These people have been waiting for half an hour." He points at a black sedan four cars back. "That's Reverend Billy; he stopped to pick up fresh gladiolas. He's now late for his service."

Thirty minutes? All I did was cross the street and buy two buckets of flowers. I move fast, five or seven minutes, max. But there wouldn't be this many cars, and they wouldn't be this angry over a few minutes. People block the exit here often while they unload. If I was gone for half an hour and it takes only a few minutes to buy flowers, what was I doing the rest of the time? I don't have a clue.

It hits me in the face and gut like a spreader of raw manure. If I am so tired that I lost all sense of time, I have no business important enough to allow me the privilege of driving a truck. This is the *Year of Delivery and Sleep*. Obviously, we haven't taken care of the sleep part yet. The market is full of people just as tired as I am, but that's no excuse. I don't need to think about it. It is right there. My hand is on my heart as I pledge: *From now on, from this moment forward, if I am too tired to drive safely, I will not drive*. Whatever the consequence of this commitment, it is nothing compared to the potential cost of operating a vehicle under the influence of exhaustion.

Then I get in the truck and drive to the stand, too tired to be safe, but thinking, I can't stop right now, right here, there are people behind me. I just have to get through today. Then I will change.

The phone keeps ringing; every food co-op must be down to empty shelves. The product is out there; why not sell it? It's the Friday before Labor Day, and we are looking at the biggest order of our lives.

The only way to get it done is to go absolutely full out. The crew rises to the challenge. We're a force sweeping through the fields, picking; in the pack shed, cooling, cleaning, and packing. Twelve hours later the last box is packed, and the harvest crew leaves.

Every one of our four delivery trucks is going to be jammed from front to back and floor to ceiling. I hold on to the clipboard, call out what's needed, and keep the orders straight. Raul, Julio, and Martin stack the boxes onto pallets and push them into the refrigerated trucks. It is a huge task, and even with lights, it gets harder after sunset. Between the corn and the melons there is a lot of weight. We are long past clear thinking. Martin is stumbling. I tell him, "Go to bed; you have to get up early and drive the hardest route tomorrow."

Julio, Raul, and I finish the last truck after midnight. Then it's just me. I finish writing the drivers' sheets and invoices at 2:45 A.M. When I see the receipts totaled up, I'm a little shocked. Was it worth it? Financially it sure was.

This one day's take, over $21,000, is more than our gross income our first year farming, but there must be another measurement, and I'm too exhausted right now to figure it out. I grew up hearing, "Make hay when the sun shines." It is just part of being a farmer, living with the vagaries of weather and markets and working till the job is done. I can rest up in winter.

I don't want to wake up Martin by getting into bed, so I lie down on the office floor with a wool blanket. I can sleep anywhere right now.

My internal alarm wakes me at the usual Saturday time. I start to dress but have trouble matching the buttons to their holes. I tell myself it will just take a few minutes to wake up. I do jumping jacks, counting to sixty seconds. Oxygen rushes in, waking my brain. I am energized long enough to get into my clothes. I go to the bathroom. Ten minutes later I realize I am sleeping on the toilet. I tell myself, get moving; you're going to be late.

Somehow I remember my promise of the week before. I am definitely under the influence of exhaustion. I do not have the right to endanger others by driving in this condition. The transmission of my mind makes a gigantic shift. In the past I have always just pushed myself into action. The shift is a voice shouting, ENOUGH. It is irresponsible. STOP. Go back to sleep.

I know I could make myself do it, but the word *enough* is still ringing in my ears. I'll just have to skip the farmers market this week. The stand customers will have to do without or go somewhere else for the items I intended to buy. Two hours later I wake up. I'm fine now. I hop in the truck and deliver to the Wedge Co-op—one stop, six pallets—easy. Everyone wonders why I am late. "I was too tired to drive safely, so I slept a little more."

"I'm glad you took care of yourself," and "How are you feeling now?"

I'd be lying if I said I felt fresh, but I'm good enough to drive to the roadside stand. The clerk and I rearrange the displays so there aren't gapping holes where the market items would have been. A few clients ask for flowers or apples. I explain. We don't lose any customers, just a few dollars.

It is our second fall harvest from Bill's land, and there seems to be no end to the sugar-sweet winter squash flowing from the rich valley.

I am a machine, not a woman, as we move through cutting and harvesting. The broccoli on the home farm is also stellar: every plant is a colossal, dense head of sweet greenness. Between the soil diversity of the two farms, there isn't a crop we couldn't grow. But is that what we want? Where is the sanity line, and how will we know when we have crossed it? The market grows, and we grow with it. Despite the fact that we have made harvest more efficient and have great help, by the time the season is over, I've lost touch with reality and my limits as a human. I forget.

I am a woman, not a machine. I wake up predawn. My fingers are numb, white, and stiff. Pain shoots through my wrists, up my forearms, and settles in my elbows. I fill a bowl with hot water and soak my hands. Some of the pain flows out as the blood returns, but part of it settles in my joints, holding them rigid, using aches as glue. This bowl of hot water is just a temporary solution. I know I have to change my life in some way. I keep working on this magic thing that people call balance. I know that our passion for organic farming is part of the equation, but it's not only that. The challenge of the weather and the shortness of the growing season make vegetable farming and a personal life difficult to blend. I haven't yet met a vegetable farmer who claims they have. Mostly we all just complain about working too hard and then defend growing food as the only job worth doing.

Farmers are often annoyed when nonfarmers romanticize our lives. Many of us falsely believe that we have a monopoly on tough ways to make a living. The work is physically hard and endless; we are at the mercy and vagaries of the weather, the market, and seed breeders. What's so romantic about that?

But it's like a good trip. The glow comes in retrospect. Romance in farming is the same: a strange commingling of crazy weather endured, the bond that grows when people pull together, produce more beautiful than anything ever seen, and that moment on a miserable, wet day when the sun busts through the clouds. Romance is about emotional attachment and involvement. It includes loss and redemption. The crop that thrives is all the more beautiful for the mystery of its survival.

This makes just about everything in organic vegetable farming romantic if you wait long enough.

There are different degrees of busy. There is healthy and happy active; in winter I have a full life doing book work and planning, playing piano, cooking meals, enjoying family and friends. Life is rich, satisfying, and relatively balanced. As we enter the growing season, there are certain precautions I take in my attempt to maintain a healthy life, practical steps like laying in enough toilet paper and dish and laundry soap to last until November. But as spring warms and the world turns green, there is a gradual deterioration.

Meals degrade from nutrient-laden three-course dinners to opening a can of pinto beans, to chewing on raw corn and cabbage in the field. Hair brushing goes from daily, to twice a week, to maybe I should just cut it off. Laundry, we won't talk about, and the clotheslines poles are still not put in permanently with concrete.

But then I stop noticing the early morning fog rising up to meet the sunrise and the interpretation of light by the Oak in the front yard. I don't care that the northern lights are racing across the heavens, and I don't catch the smiles on the faces of the eaters. I see only the box to be packed in front of me, and the produce to go in it. I know I've completely lost touch with reality when I find myself using two glasses to drink water. Too impatient to wait, I drink from one partial glass while holding the other for filling, switching back and forth as I slug it down.

It's all a weighing of sorts. True priorities lose their haziness. I find writing is the last thing to go. Normal water drinking is abandoned a full month before I stop journaling while taking phone orders. By the time the season grinds to a halt, I can barely remember who I am or what my interests are anymore. In winter I generate charts of information, gross income per plant, net annual income, assets and liabilities. But what about net me? What's left of me when the season is finished, and does the gain justify the loss?

Winter makes decisions so much easier. I am finally starting to understand Martin's blood farmer theory. We are businesspeople and soil and land lovers; we are passionate about growing food and feeding people.

But we are not blood farmers. It's time to stop acting like we are. I say, "We should focus on the crops that do best in our soils and drop the rest. There are a lot of new organic farmers now. We can pass on our records and provide mentorship to the farm that takes them over. It will increase our efficiency and profitability, and we could let go of Bill's land."

"Cha's family is looking to buy land," he says. Martin has been friends with Cha since the early 1980s when he stopped in Eagan to buy a tractor Martin had for sale out front.

I say, "Every winter we write a quality-of-life statement and talk about balance, then spring comes, and the farm consumes us. When is the last time we lay together in a field and watched the moon? This is an opportunity for us to reduce our workload, for other organic growers to expand, and it's a chance for Cha's family to own land."

"It fits what Bill wanted," Martin says.

Thinking about Bill and his desire to see kids on his land makes me smile. Eliza is a young woman now, in a life relationship, studying nursing and expecting her first child. Maize is a sponsored snowboard artist pursuing his need to be a human bird. Our kids aren't little anymore, and they are developing their own dreams, following their own paths. It's time to step back a little, have another view of life.

The value of our Holistic Goal to guide decisions is evident. We consider hiring more help and moving ourselves out of the field, but that doesn't match our quality-of-life statement. We want to be with the plants, not managing more people.

In an unprecedented decision-making action, we cut a deal. We each get to pick one crop that we will drop. "If I never sort another potato for the rest of my life, I will be very happy," I say.

He says, "I'm through with onions."

We also decide to drop winter squash and leeks. The squash comes as a shock to me—it has been a signature crop for us from the start, profitable, and my crop of passion. Most years we plant it when the crew is off on the weekend, just Martin and I, using the one-row transplanter we bought my second year of farming. We're all alone out there. He drives and I plant. At the end of each row, we refill the water tank, restock the plants, and take off again. We have done this so many times we don't need to look at the name tags on the flats; we can identify all sixteen cultivars by their leaves. We have a picnic lunch lying at the edge of the field, and plant until dark. We're barely walking by the end of the day, but we get it in: ten acres of winter squash. That is romance.

But I know it's the right decision; it's time for a change. Every winter I do recover from the season's exhaustion, but if I push it too far, I won't. As we age, personal balance will require more consistent time for renewal.

Selling Bill's land lifts our debt. Here we are at the First State Bank of Rosemount in President Dave's office, handing him a check to pay off our land mortgage. He knows everything we've been through to reach this moment. "Congratulations, an overnight success after twenty-eight years," Dave says, as he shakes our hands, "and never a late payment."

Driving back to the farm, I ask Martin, "Do you feel like a success?"

"We have been able to create a life based on our values and beliefs outside of the status quo. That's success to me."

When we get home, there is a message on the voice mail from Allen, Eliza's partner. His voice is a cumulus cloud on a summer day.

"It's a boy! His name is Blake. He was born at 11:58." That's right while we were at the bank. Land paid for and our first grandchild in the same moment. I start to cry. Now I feel like a success.

All of a sudden I get something about this balance challenge that I never understood before. Despite my farm definition as a synthesis of the land, people, and business, all this time, we've been acting like the business—the Gardens of Eagan—and ourselves are the same thing. Like the business is an extension of us or, even worse, like we are an extension of the business. But we are not one entity. We own the business; it does not own us. We are separate. The business is here to meet our needs and the needs of the organic community. We provide labor and energy, passion and direction, but our lives are our own, and we need to claim them.

We're in the last stage of our winter planning process. Since we've moved here, I've had a complete diagram drawn of what the farm will look like when the full infrastructure is in: we still need to build a machine shop. Martin resists every time I bring it up, says it's too expensive. I've got it all worked out. What it will cost, where the money will come from, how long it will take to pay back, and, most important, the stress it will lift. Martin says, "We've gotten this far without it," and out of the blue I get it.

He's worked so hard to make it to this point, he's afraid if he lets down his guard, we will fail. "You can take care of yourself too, you know, not just the soil and your family." I hug him and feel his back is quivering underneath the skin, quiet and controlled-like. "No more hauling tools and laying cardboard on the cold, wet ground for Smarty Marty. You're going to have a warm shop," I say. "Grease for Peace. How about *2002: The Year of Infrastructure and Balance.*"

So much for being out of debt. Machine shops are not cheap, but for the first time in my life, I really don't care. We need this building for Martin's health and farm efficiency. Our Holistic Goal makes the decision clear.

I used to think balance was about scale, size of the operation, larger farm equals less balance. But we worked even harder when we were smaller than we do now. We couldn't afford equipment and help, and everything was done by hand. There is never an end to work on a farm, always something that needs to be built, fixed, planted, or harvested. Since we've left Eagan, we've been operating with the belief that the only way we can be safe is by owning our own land free and clear. It's kept us going through hard work and crappy weather, but it's been driving us harder than I'm willing to continue. We don't have to keep living as if there is a bulldozer at our back door.

There is also something else, much deeper, that I am starting to understand about balance. I grew up with the knowledge that a farmer's time is dictated by the seasons and the weather, by the needs of the soil, the crops, and customers. But I didn't understand the role of years and decades in evaluating balance. We can't just appraise from the perspective of exhaustion at the end of a growing season. Martin said it well, "We were able to do work based on our beliefs."

When we are looking backwards at our lives, living our values will be our brightest star. Balance doesn't mean that we will never work too hard or be too tired. We're doing exactly what we need to be doing. It's fine if we choose to work until we're exhausted as long as recovery is possible in the relative present.

That's what present time is, the balancing point between the past and the future.

It is when we steal from our future or burn up the past that balance is out of control. That future and past include our health and the well-being of our crew and children and land and nature.

Balance requires not taking more than can be returned or recovered. It is about loss and renewal, both human and environmental. Our crops take from the soil, causing degeneration. A renewable fertility system returns, regenerates.

Nature is inherently capable of renewal. Balance is the prevention of the tipping point when too much has been taken and health cannot be readily restored. Environmental balance includes preservation, protection, and precautionary principles. We are not outside of the ecosystem. We are part of it.

Balance is all about relationship, which is all about respect.

It's time to recognize how far we've come. Now, with all the buildings finished, we're finally ready to put the clotheslines poles in their permanent location. I start digging with the posthole digger.

It slides easily through the ancient prairie loam. Centuries of prairie grass roots and decomposed oak leaves, fertilized by fire ash, life in this mixed landscape of oak trees and tallgrass prairie must have felt permanent to the sentient beings who lived here. It doesn't take long to carve a hole deep enough to embrace our poles.

The moment has arrived. The dry concrete flows like the passage of life into the wheelbarrow, smoothly at points, with periods of lumps and slowdowns. Stirring in the water to create a smooth mix stimulates the memories of all we have shared to reach this moment. Through it all, the mutual goal of creating this farm propelled us. Somehow, these poles symbolize everything we left behind when the bulldozers destroyed the land in Eagan. We will finally be home again when the concrete dries. I hold the steel clothesline pole fixed in place while Martin shovels the gray concrete into the prairie hole, tamps it, and works out the air bubbles. We are putting our roots of permanence into this soil, unto this land. I think of Maya Angelou, "Making a living is not the same as making a life."

We have been making a living. The struggle since we left Eagan has been to rebuild a life at the same time. No longer are we refugees escaped from suburban madness. We have worked our way back home.

Looking to the Future

Finally, National Organic Standards. Organic production is now defined at the federal level through the USDA. All organic certifiers, producers, processors, and handlers must be in full compliance by this fall, October 2002. Having federal standards feels like the organic community is securing its clothesline poles into concrete. The next generation will be able to build on this solid base.

This is monumental. For the past three decades, numerous private and state agencies have been certifying organic operations, but each certifying organization had its own standards, causing a lack of uniformity from certifier to certifier. One national standard is crucial to prevent confusion in the marketplace and protect against mislabeling and fraud.

It's taken a long time, many people, and a great deal of effort to accomplish. In 1989 the Organic Working Group, made up of twenty-five consumer, environmental, and animal protection organizations, came together to work with organic farmers on behalf of a federal organic label. Then the Organic Foods Production Act of 1990 mandated the creation of the National Organic Program (NOP) and the passage of uniform standards. But passing the bill was just a first step. The act called for the establishment of a fifteen-member National Organic Standards Board (NOSB) to "assist in the development of standards for substances to be used in organic production," and to "provide recommendations to the Secretary regarding implementation."

Over the next five years, the NOSB held public meetings to discuss and develop standards. Martin and I were thrilled in 1995 when the NOSB passed the definition of *organic*: "Organic agriculture is an ecological production management system that promotes and enhances biodiversity, biological cycles and soil biological activity. It is based on minimal use of off-farm inputs and on management practices that restore, maintain, and enhance ecological harmony."

It was clear then that the NOSB understood and supported what organic farmers and consumers have worked so long and hard to create. During the period from June 1994 to September 1996, the NOSB submitted its recommendations for national standards to the USDA's National Organic Program staff. But when the first USDA proposed rule appeared in the Federal Register in December 1997, the organic community was shocked to find this proposal did not adopt the NOSB's recommendations.

The USDA proposal allowed bioengineered crops, sewage sludge, and irradiation in organic production, which became known as the "big three." The organic community responded, making history with 275,000 public comments, shattering the record for any USDA-proposed rule before that. Many positive changes, including removal of the "big three," were made to the final rule before it was published in December 2000.

The organic community had to fight for it and stay involved, and now there is one organic standard for the entire country. It is the only USDA food label with this level of integrity and standardization.

It is so amazing and valuable that we have national organic standards that recognize the importance of biological diversity and soil health. Here we are, living and farming in the midst of an industrial agriculture that endorses production over conservation, a system that believes it is not only OK but also necessary to use toxic substances to grow our food and fiber, a system that has no future, because it is dependent on a finite resource: the stored time and concentrated energy of fossil fuels.

In the midst of this, we have organic. This is our legacy and our future. Farmers and buyers wrote the original standards. They are ours. It is important that we always remember how hard-won the organic standards and label were. They are the only legal protection we have. It is crucial that farmers and organic consumers continue to claim, support, and guard them. Certification does so much more than just educate and assure the customer. It is a contribution to the organic movement. Staying involved as a certified farm helps maintain the integrity of the label and provides a measurement of change in the agricultural system, sending a clear message to the USDA of the growing numbers of organic farmers and the increasing demands of consumers for organic food.

But we've only just begun in our efforts to institutionalize our larger goals of protecting soil, air, water, and biological diversity. Organic farming systems are capable of repairing so much of what is broken in our world: the economic viability of farms, energy-intensive agricultural systems, chemicals affecting our ecosystems and health, access to food, loss of biological diversity, climate change, soil degradation, and water quality. The solution to these massive problems is in how we treat our soil.

Now that we have federal organic standards, one of our next big challenges as a movement is breeding seed specifically for organic systems. Organic growing conditions present different weed pressures, fertility practices, and pest and disease complexes, and conventional seed breeding is continually moving toward genetically modified organisms.

Seeds are all about the next generation—which is exactly what organic is about.

I'm thinking about the next generation of farmers when I open the door. The first thing I notice, before I even say hello, is her crooked bangs. They are as uneven as a jagged dandelion leaf, and they are so short, her forehead is exposed like a gleaming billboard. It's not just the bangs; the back of her hair is completely asymmetrical. I can't imagine where she got this haircut, or what type of person would come to an interview with such a homespun look.

She is a tiny waif, thin and frail looking. Around her neck is wrapped a scarf that looks like it was knit with chopsticks and wool from a recycled sweater. I must be staring instead of greeting her. She says, "Hi, I'm Laura." I notice her smile extends all the way up into her eyes and is beaming with open excitement. I hold the door open and welcome her in. She enters with baby steps; her tube skirt is so tight she can barely move her knees. During the interview I mention that Martin is a barber. She grins and tells us she cuts her own hair. Then adds, "It's really fun. I wish it grew faster so I could cut it more often."

She's barely out of the driveway, and Martin wants to hire her. Usually we mull it over for days and follow up with additional questions and a reference check. He lists her strengths: she speaks Spanish, is intelligent, and is committed to organic. When asked about her favorite part of college, she said, "Frisbee." He says her sense of humor will get her through the tough parts of farming. And he likes her honesty. When asked why she wants to work here, she said, "I know I don't want to spend my life working in a cubicle. I don't know if I want to farm, but I want to explore what it has to offer."

I say she'll never last. Farming is too hard if one isn't completely dedicated. Not only does she look too weak, how would she ever work in outfits like that? The first wind will blow her clear over to the next county. She's living in a fantasy of idealism. Martin reminds me, "That's where we came from, and it got us here. She's a farmer. She just doesn't know it yet."

Our other young farmer for the season, Noah Engel, grew up on an organic dairy farm working like a farmhand most of his childhood. His mother, a homeopathic veterinarian, supported his farming passion by driving him and his brother every week to the Madison Farmers Market, where they sold vegetables and fruits they raised themselves. Martin says, "Noah wants to bust his buttons and go farming."

They want to know and do everything. They are expected to start at 7:30 A.M., but Noah is in the machine shop before sunup helping Martin and absorbing all things mechanical. He has the intuition for this; he mostly needs maturity and business modeling.

Laura walks through the fields before work starts, notebook in hand, studying the plants. She is inefficient in her physical work; this is new for her, but I can see she will learn. She has something more important than experience: determination, application, and passion. The better I get to know her, the more I realize how familiar that is. We have a lot in common.

When they are finished for the day, they cook and eat together, sharing everything they have learned. In the evening they plant a personal garden. Once a week we have a sit-down meeting and discuss one aspect of the farm in-depth. It is here that Laura's deep potential shines. She asks whole questions, and when we don't satisfy her curiosity, she researches and reports back to us all.

Sometimes the inconsistencies of farming are confusing to them. We say, "Never touch a wet tomato plant. It increases the chance of disease." Then it rains all the time, we have to get the fruit to market, and we send them out to harvest a crop that has no chance of drying. I say, "Learn all the rules, the why and the consequences, and then learn when to break them."

Noah wants to know the one right way to do everything. He wants a hard-and-fast rule. He asks, "Why do you plant tomatoes ten feet apart and another farm plants at five? Which is the right way?"

"There is no one right way." I explain that wet tomato leaves are susceptible to invasion by bacteria and fungus. By spacing the plants wide, they dry quicker, and disease is reduced. "Learn the cultural needs of each crop and how different practices affect its growth and health. When you know the consequences, you can make clear decisions based on your circumstances."

One of my first lessons as a farmer was that I needed to learn the laws of nature. It's not humans who set them, and if we ignore them, there can be negative consequences. Even kings do not reign higher.

But I've also learned that sometimes we have to break the rules. This is a fine line, easily abused, but a crucial element of farming success. We need to understand the potential consequences of our actions, and then still be flexible enough and clear enough to utilize the information and experience we have available to us to make decisions based on current reality and conditions. Nothing stays the same in nature or in farming. Remain in the present with connections to the past and consider the future—that's the motto.

Martin takes Noah to a farm auction, and he's right there, absorbing every conversation and piece of equipment. An old-timer pats Martin on the back and says, "Good son you've got there." I realize, now that I've gotten past the haircut, Laura feels a lot like a daughter. They will be feeding the community long after we are gone.

Our grandson Blake—he's three now—and I are lying on our backs in the middle of a sweet corn field. He is snuggled up, tight against my side, his soft little hand clasping my dry, calloused one. We lie still and quiet. The pollen drifts down and coats us with its burnt malt scent and fresh stickiness. The ground is blanketed with a sheet of yellow. Blake sticks his tongue out to taste the drifting gold dust and says, "It's sweet." I follow suit, grateful for the influence of his pure curiosity.

It's a layered sensation; the soil texture against our backs grounds us to the earth. Plant rows on each side create an endless tunnel sensation. The veined, pollen-stained leaves dangle above our faces, narrowing our view. As far as our eyes can see, we are in a world of stalk and cob, leaf and silk, tassel and sky.

The silk is moist and glistening, receptive to pollination and subsequent fertilization. Its scent is green and fresh, welcoming and open, a sharp contrast to the pollen's musky sun-roasted aroma. Over our heads, tassels stretch with brown arms and dangling pollen sacks. They are completely abuzz with a diversity of insects. These are not European honeybees threatened by Colony Collapse Disorder, but native pollinators who require undisturbed ground to nest. The buzz and hum travel through the stalks into the ground. We feel the vibration running through our backs and limbs.

Martin backs the truck through the middle of the cornfield. The plants are tall, over eight feet, and thick, a dense jungle. The stalks bend as the truck passes over, and then spring partway back as they are released.

Blake and I are riding on the back of the flatbed. Corn presses against us on all sides. It's like the vehicle is a cloistered ship, sailing slowly through a world of maize and sky. I look behind; we are closed in with green, forward and to the sides, the same. It swallows us, as we swallow it. The pickers stand next to the sacks to load, but they are shorter than the plants, and Martin can't see them. He shouts, "I can't tell where you are; shake a tassel."

Julio pulls a stalk by the roots, thrusts it high above the ceiling of the field, and waves it. The stirring tassel with swinging anthers is framed in motion against the backdrop of the blue sky. Martin backs up to the pile. The crew loads. I stack. Blake counts. Everyone moves to the next set. "Tequila," by the Champs, is playing on the AM truck radio as the crew on the ground prances, shaking their tassels to the pulse of the music. "It's a dance, the Corn Dance," Martin says.

I look at him and think of all the corn varieties he's grown: from Golden Bantam Cross to the SE Synergistics, they're written like lyrics on the staff of his face. Sweet corn is fully Martin's signature crop, the symbol of his passion for growing food, an attribute and the legacy of him. Changing with the cob has been a tango he's modulated for decades. Howling Mob, Early King, and Golden Jubilee, varieties of his early years, were the ultimate stored sunshine—full, round kernels filled with dense corn flavor. Over the years, market demand directed breeders to switch their emphasis to higher sugar content and longer holding capacity; corn was part of the sweetening of America's table. Now his main cultivars are Temptation and Bodacious.

Just before sunset, we go out to check the maturity of the next corn planting. It is a humid, still August evening; pockets of clammy heat sit stagnant in low spots. The scents are pungent, corn pollen the predominant bass note. Normally corn is a sweet-sour, central aroma, riding high above the kale earthiness but far below the tomato pheromone. But tonight the pollen smells burnt, like it has been roasted on low in an oven all day. Now at half dusk, the heat is off, and the scent pours out. It is gravelly and scratchy, brown and heavy. It catches in the back of my throat and tastes of scorched barley malt and sugar. It rolls off the corn oceans and settles, dense and sultry, in the gullies. It is the overriding fragrance, blocking out the flirtatious sprays of cantaloupe perfume and purslane succulence. I feel it settling into my hair and onto my skin, sugar coating me, as if I too could slide pollen down my silk and fertilize my kernels with the fountain of youth.

Flames lick up the sides of the blackened pot. It only takes a few minutes for the kernels to color to bright yellow. This sweet corn is far more than a way to fill the stomach. This is the starch that binds the community, a great commonality, everyone sharing in the sacrament of being.

I wonder how long this stage of the party will last, eating corn as holy manna, corn as divinely provided nourishment. Melons are cut, and it is the same; the fruit is a connection and ceremony of this most essential relationship we have with nature. The food is the force that sustains us. If the corn was bread, the melon is wine.

This thirtieth anniversary festival of Gardens of Eagan Farm is a parade of relationships. People are here from every period of our lives: grade-school classmates, 4-H friends and teachers, co-op workers from the 1970s to the present, employees, family, and friends. This is a celebration of challenges survived, crop success and failure, food shared, tractors sold, and lessons learned. Martin doesn't look like he has been farming for thirty years; his grin is still that of a schoolboy at play. There have been many times when he's been so exhausted he's wanted to quit, but the passion part of farming has been like recess from adulthood for him. He's still saying, "I'm a gardener, not a farmer." And he still claims the secret to his thick black hair is eating raw sweet corn in the field.

All afternoon people walk the field roads, eat, talk, and laugh. As the sun is setting, the "Pheromones" climb onto a stage made of hay wagons and sing the party into dancing under the Oak.

The lead vocalist, Dr. John Navazio, is a seed breeder who has dedicated his professional career to improving vegetable varieties under organic growing conditions. It's fitting that Gene Mealhow, an agronomist who produces and markets organic heirloom popcorn, is the drummer, and that Glen Borgerding, a soil consultant, plays bass. David Edminster, blowing sax, was here when we burnt down the barn and helps with planting and harvest. Meg Moynihan, on vocals, harmony, and rhythm, works for the Department of Agriculture as the Organic Diversification Specialist. Martin plays lead guitar and sings.

Somehow, all of them being committed to organic agriculture adds synergy to the effect. Usually it takes the first set to warm up an audience, but this crowd surges to the grass floor. The band hops into "Tequila," and Noah, Laura, and I run around handing out freshly cut cornstalks.

It doesn't matter that no one has ever done the Corn Dance before. It comes as a completely natural act, shaking stalks up and down and waving them overhead. Energy surges through the crowd, as if passed tassel to tassel as the tops kiss in midair. Dancers use the stalks as garden hoes, as musical instruments, as waltzing partners. Long lines snake through the throng and slide, bellies up and heads back, under a corn limbo stick. They flow into a liquid spiral, as fluid as the moonlight streaming through the Oak's branches and lighting faces. When the song comes to the bridge, the dancers thrust their stalks to the stars and scream, "Sweet Corn." The frenzy escalates. They offer their tassels to the sky and shout thanks to the Gods of Fertility, the Gods of Maize, the Gods of Nutritious, Clean Food. A circle is formed of waving corn, and people leap into the middle, infused with the pulsing energy.

I look up at the stage and see Martin surrounded by everything that is important to him. I look at myself and see the same. I remember one of our first conversations, when we talked about wanting to prove that organic farming works and about finding a way to make a living at it. We've done both.

Maize says, "Farming is too hot and too much risk. I want to have a job and a life separate from each other. Besides, it's your dream; I want to live mine."

Maize's vision is solar electric systems that power equipment used for farming. While he's explaining what that could look like, I'm imagining Martin's 1950s IH Super C cultivator tractors converted with electrical engines, charging from a solar array. That's not quite what Maize has in mind, but I'm amazed by the elegant blending of his childhood influences: his life experience on the farm, Martin's love of machines, and my aversion to anything dependent on fossil fuels merged with who he is and wants to be.

Eliza is a nurse working in a clinic now. She and her husband, Allen, have two sons, Blake and Chase, and they are pregnant with a daughter, already named Emma Marie. The kids love the land, nature, and plants just as Eliza did before the bulldozers. They live on the south side of the farm, and the grandkids can see our house and fields from their kitchen window. Eliza has changed her middle name from Chicory to Marie, which is my name. She wants to start a family tradition where the women all have the same middle name. Chase has Martin's name, Victor. It's a bridge and, I believe, Eliza's way of making peace with the loss of Diffley land and ancestral continuity.

After a year of working at Gardens of Eagan and a second year working on other farms, Laura and her partner, Adam, want to start their own farm, Loon Organic. We work out an incubator relationship: two acres of land, use of tools, and space in the greenhouse. They plan to purchase their own equipment during this period. When they buy land, they'll be set with tractors and implements. They will also purchase Gardens of Eagan crops at wholesale prices to supplement their CSA share boxes and to resell at the farmers market. This will allow them to increase their income but keep their growing risks small while they are just starting. When they are ready to scale up to a size that will earn them a living, their market will be developed and ready.

Noah is back in his home region of Soldiers Grove, Wisconsin, running Driftless Organics with his brother and building his business. I'm thinking about all these young people and their future while I read the Rodale Institute Farming Systems Trial (FST). Initiated in 1981, it is the longest-running side-by-side comparison of organic and conventional farming systems in the United States.

Results from the FST have been reported in dozens of scientific papers over the years and include this core finding. Corn and soybean yields are the same across the three systems: conventional, livestock-based organic, and legume-based organic.

Although corn yields were lower in the organic systems during the first four years of the study, in subsequent years the organic systems actually outperformed the conventional system under droughty conditions. The results come as no surprise to anyone who has managed soils organically. It takes years to build the soil up, and while the portions of the field under conventional management have suffered further degradation from wind and water erosion, the portions under organic management have shown steady improvements in organic matter, water infiltration, microbial activity, and other soil-quality indicators.

But the finding that really predicts the future of agriculture is that organic systems sequestered 15 to 28 percent more carbon, with a 33 percent reduction in fossil fuel use.

Organic agriculture is crucial for reducing atmospheric carbon, mitigating climate change, and ensuring our food security in a changing environment. It is easy to look at these numbers and feel like we have forever. Gardens of Eagan is more mature and secure than ever. But I am a woman, and Martin is a man—we are mere mortals. We've been so entrenched with putting this farm together and running it, sometimes it is all we can see. There's a big world out there, and we have roles with each other and patterns of behavior; at times I want to shake the whole thing up. Martin often claims he lives two days in one. I want to live two or more lives in one. We still love farming, but there are other things we want to do yet, other skills we want to develop, and other ways to feed people.

Martin says, "I want to be a hobo again, play music, and be at peace with the rain. I want to take care of my hands. I want to be in Montana in summer, in the mountains, and with my Blackfeet friends. I want more time for the grandkids."

We're just discussing ideas, not making decisions. I don't know why my stomach feels like it is full of clunky, spinning rocks, while my head is a balloon floating toward a sharp pin. I say, "What I really want to do is cultivate words like we now cultivate crops. Instead of entering people's lives through food, I want my words to enter their minds, and I want my mornings to be my own."

"If we don't change direction, we're going to end up where we've been going," he says.

Maybe only the people part needs to change. Our kids don't want to farm, but so many others do. Can we find a way to pass this on? We're not ready to quit yet, but it's time to start planning for the day when it comes. We title our plan and commitment *The Year of Excellent Records and Looking to the Future.* When it's time to shake hands and sign our agreement, we both act shy.

Blake and I are lounging in thick grass eating the yellow petals of dandelions. Spring walks are wild tastings; he is particularly excited by the practice of eating flowers. He takes tiny nibbles and rolls them around on his tongue, a contemplative look on his face. He doesn't say good or bad; he doesn't spit out bitter; he doesn't focus on salt or sweet. "They taste like, this is the flavor of spring."

He's right; European immigrants brought dandelions to North America as food and medicine and to provide pollen for imported honeybees in early spring when not much else was flowering. I say, "When you eat this yellow petal, the nutrients and minerals in its cells become part of the cells of your body."

His face lights up. "Oh, it's like recycling." He gets it instantly, lying in brilliant sunshine in a dandelion meadow: nutrient cycling.

That was the last time we saw the sun. Now we are planting cucumbers despite the fact that it is too cold and too wet. It's a gamble but a calculated one. There is a backup set of transplants in the greenhouse if these "go down." If they make it, we'll have an extra two weeks of local organic cucumbers, which means a lot to our customers and our financial bottom line. But the field conditions are abysmal. A cold drizzle has been falling all morning, everything—us, the equipment—is muddy. We are breaking all the rules about staying out of wet fields, not planting fungal-sensitive crops in cold weather, and not touching cucumber plants when they are damp.

The crew is amazingly cheerful; most of them have just started, and they seem to accept this as the normal life of a vegetable farmer. They are going to be so pleased when they learn how much fun planting is in drier soil. We start laying the slotted row tunnels, a season extension system that looks like a miniature greenhouse. Without this system we wouldn't have considered planting in these conditions. The tunnels will provide the crucial heat these plants need.

I can't tell if the mist is getting heavier, or if I am just getting colder. To keep the tunnel layer moving, we walk next to it holding shovels flat against the moving disks where the mud builds up. Everyone is focused on their task. Sara, the group cheerleader, calls out at regular intervals, "We're going to have the earliest damn cukes in the Twin Cities," and "Go Team Farm." Halfway through the last row the rain becomes steady and hard. The tractor tires spin and flip mud up, flecking the crew.

Maybe I'm a real farmer now. I've become just as neurotic about rain as Martin is. When it is dry for three days, I think we're going into a drought, and when it rains, I obsess it won't stop. Rain used

to be God touching my skin. I wonder about the day when we are
no longer farming. Will I ever enjoy rain with open pleasure again,
without worrying about crops?

The cucumbers are thick, vibrant plants now, safe and growing fast
inside the tunnels. We had a few more days of cold drizzle, then the
weather flipped, and we've had hot sun since. Just before bed I walk
the field to check them. They are already vining, and the first flowers
have opened. I consider whether we should remove the tunnels in
the morning so the bees will be able to pollinate, but I decide we can
wait a few more days. There are only male blossoms; the females are
still tightly closed.

All the crops look fantastic. I love this time of year; it still feels
like anything could happen. I go to bed excited about the season's
potential. I am deep in sleep when an explosion of lightning rips
through the room. A crack slams behind the flash. The sky sparks
again, a fused web of jagged lines. Wind jumps in, straight-line from
the west, driving hard rain against the house. I hear tiny pings against
the window. Damn. Not hail, not now. I look at the date on the clock,
June 8, 2005.

Maybe if I go back to sleep, I'll find I'm just having a nightmare. I
pinch my ears closed between my forefingers and thumbs. Maybe if
I don't hear it. But the pings grow louder, harder, and faster.

I am a real farmer now. I think about Laura and Adam, just starting out, creating their dream, then of everything Martin and I have
experienced to reach this moment. I know that whatever happens
with this hail, we're going to be OK.

By fall we are recovering not from hail damage but from the exhaustion of harvesting our best season ever. The plants just want to
reproduce. Losing their leaves was a threat to their future survival,
and they responded with accelerated growth. Everywhere a tomato
branch or leaf was cut by hail, two came in its place. The naked line
of stems grew into massive productive bushes, yielding twenty-seven
pounds of marketable fruit per plant. The peppers recovered as full,

thick shrubs with a yield 45 percent higher. The cucumbers were protected under the row tunnels and reached maturity an unprecedented thirty-seven days from planting. Most of the corn stood up again. Even the tattered kale had a sales increase of 40 percent.

These numbers represent the resiliency of nature and are a testimony to healthy soil. Challenges in my own life act the same way, pushing me to my deepest potential. My roots are deep in fertile soil, and just like the plants, I come back stronger than before.

But not all things come back stronger; some things lost cannot be readily recovered. Biological diversity is one of these. It is not an abstract concept. It is life itself: the life of people, nature, and our planet. When we lose a species, we lose an integral part of the natural world. We lose intact ecosystems, and we lose resiliency. Whether it is lost through toxic pesticides, suburban development, damaging farming practices, patenting of seed, or contamination by genetic modification, all are thefts from the future and from our children.

In grade school I was taught that soil is a nonrenewable resource because on average it takes one hundred to five hundred years for one inch of topsoil to grow. I didn't have any concept of time then. I sat in our garden running handfuls of soil through my fingers and trying to understand how all those years were stored in the brown earth.

Organic farming is so much more than just a set of standards and a marketing label, more than just a way to make money in a competitive industry, more than just a growing system that doesn't use chemical inputs. Organic farming has the potential to be solely based on renewable energy—the sun. We know how to work with the soil, the sun, and plants to manage fertility, pests, and disease through soil health and biological diversity. This is security. This is the future. It is our resiliency and redemption. As long as the sun rises every morning, organic farming systems will remain viable. Our experience is proof of our success, but knowing is not enough.

Martin's favorite adage is relevant here, "If we don't change direction, we're going to end up where we've been going." An agricultural economy based on pollution and the consumption of finite resources is inherently incapable of survival. Chemical and fossil fuel–based agriculture is one of the largest polluters of our water, air, and climate. Imagine if we had agricultural and economic policies based on ecological principles, policies that protect our health and environment, policies that include the needs of the future.

Organic farming systems are the clear choice to protect the gifts of the past that are our natural heritage, to have a relationship with nature in the present time, and to preserve its future potential. We will have reached our dream when we no longer need an organic label because our soil, air, water, genetic diversity, and all life on the planet are no longer threatened.

Kale versus Koch

I'm reading through the week's pile of mail. There are three identical-looking envelopes from an organization called the MinnCan Project. Minn must be short for Minnesota? And the Can, yes you can?

Maybe they are donation requests from a Minnesota food shelf. How annoying that they sent three. I'm about to toss them in the trash but stop myself; it will take only a second to look at one. I am halfway through skimming it before I realize that this is not a food shelf. MinnCan is a crude oil pipeline project owned by the Minnesota Pipe Line Company (MPL), which is operated by Koch Pipeline Company, a subsidiary of Koch Industries. They are informing us that they have filed certificate of need and route permit applications with the Minnesota Public Utilities Commission to install a crude oil pipeline. Why are they sending us a notice?

I keep reading. Then my heart starts pounding in my head. The only thing I can see are the words, black and pulsing, floating off the paper, filling up the room, soaking up the air until there's nothing left to breathe.

Gardens of Eagan is in the proposed route corridor.

It must be an error. It can't be true. I force my eyes to focus and read the date on the letter. February 27, 2006. Today is April 9. Why are we just getting this now? I rip open the second envelope; it is the exact same, and the third also. We own three parcels of land here; there is one notice for each. Along with the letter informing us of the application, there is a time schedule summarizing the Public Utilities Commission (PUC) permitting process and a map of the pipeline route winding out of the tar sand fields of Canada, snaking across Minnesota, and ending in Rosemount at the Flint Hills refinery, which is also owned by Koch Industries. I tear out of the house and down to the machine shop to find Martin.

"They want to put a crude oil pipeline across the farm!"

"Who? What are you talking about?"

"The farm . . . this farm . . . our farm." I shove the letters into his hand, all three of them, as if there's strength in numbers. "You have to call them up and tell them they can't put it through here."

"It's not that simple. They put these things where they want."

"Just tell them," I'm shouting. "Tell them that you are a certified organic vegetable farmer, that you have thousands of devoted customers, that you have been building this soil for years, that they will have to pay for a minimum of three years of high-value crop loss."

"You have the answers. You call them."

"They will listen to you better—you are a man."

Martin just looks at me. He doesn't argue. I don't know what to do, but they can't have this land. Not for a crude oil pipeline.

I don't know anything about pipelines and oil companies. I know about growing vegetables organically and marketing them. I know about soil, food, and health and how strongly they are linked. But that has nothing to do with eminent domain. Or does it? This feels so big; I have no idea where to start. I just want to ignore it, stay in my happy green world, and hope it will all go away.

I download Minnesota Statute 117.48: Crude Oil Pipeline Companies, Eminent Domain. Words and phrases grab my attention: declared to be in the public interest, necessary to the public welfare, the taking of private property therefore is declared to be for a public use and purpose. My head swims with the words: authorized to acquire, easements or rights-of-way, to such end it shall have and enjoy the right of eminent domain.

This makes no sense to me, how a private company has the legal right to force its way across our private property for their personal profit, but apparently they do. I call the Department of Commerce. The public advisor on the project, Deborah Pile, patiently listens to my story about being an organic farm and tells me she once served on the board of the Organic Growers and Buyers Association. She explains the routing permit legal process, but I can't comprehend what she's saying. All I know is they are talking about our land, and I don't even know where. Ms. Pile e-mails a satellite photo with the proposed route through Eureka Township and says, "Call anytime; that's what I'm here for, to provide information to the affected public."

It is a spring photo, a kaleidoscope of farms, woods, and family homesteads. Some of the fields show a tinge of fresh green, and planting lines are still visible. Other fields are brown, bare, waiting for their crop. Our land in the center stands out from the rest with its numerous small vegetable plots, arching waterways, and green buffer strips. The diversity of crops shows in the colors.

A thick red line slashes diagonally across the map, splitting the township in half. It doesn't follow roads or preexisting easements. It rarely stays on property lines, but cuts through the middle of fields. I look at each affected farm and think about the family that lives there—many of them are fourth- and fifth-generation. It seems as if someone in a windowless office drew the shortest path from one point to another without considering what was in between. Where is the public interest in this? Certainly they never walked these fields or met these people. As if tearing the fabric of community in two isn't enough, the Line of No Respect runs boldly over our new town hall.

This arrogant red line rips right through the heart of the Gardens of Eagan, knocking out seven of our most productive fields. We couldn't get through a single season without them. And it would take far longer than my lifetime to return the soil to what it was. During our migrant farming years, we twice rented fields with pipelines running through them; both easements were so badly damaged, even though it was decades since the pipelines had been installed, we couldn't grow a marketable crop on them. The northwest corner of this land is already nicked with an old pipeline easement that is too damaged to produce a crop on. Why don't they at least follow the existing corridor instead of ripping through the center of our farm carving out a new one?

I go to the online PUC docket and download the Pipeline Routing Application. Part of it is technical jargon that doesn't make easy sense to me—I'll have to spend time studying it with a dictionary at hand—but part is very simple. I clearly understand a hundred-foot-wide corridor, consisting of a forty-foot-wide spoil side and a sixty-foot-wide working side, and after construction, a fifty-foot-wide permanent right-of-way that they have the right to disrupt as needed for operation and maintenance of the line. There are also three other documents that grab my attention.

One is a Pipeline Construction Sequence, a diagram with nineteen panels illustrating the pipeline installation process, from clearing trees and brush, scraping topsoil, trenching, stringing pipe, welding, all of the steps involved, until the final panel showing topsoil replacement. But I see beyond the paper to the loss of organic matter and microbial life, the mixing of soil horizons, the compaction and leaking toxins from heavy equipment.

The second document is the Criteria for Pipeline Route Selection. Ah ha! There are some rules to the process of route selection. "The PUC shall consider the characteristics, the potential impacts and methods to minimize or mitigate the potential impacts of all proposed routes, so that it may select a route that minimizes human and environmental impact." Ten criteria are listed, all of which will be violated if they cross the Gardens of Eagan. Clearly they don't know that we're here, and I just need to tell them. That seems pretty simple. One phone call, and we'll be done with this.

The third document is an Agricultural Impact Mitigation Plan (AIMP). With this mitigation plan they claim to return the soil to pre-pipeline conditions. But any farmer, chemical or organic, knows this isn't possible, and since it can't be done, I don't understand the word *mitigate*, so I look it up in the dictionary.

Mitigate. (1) To make an offense or crime less serious or more excusable. (2) To make something less harsh, severe, or violent. Etymology: Middle English, from Latin mitigatus, past participle of mitigare to soften.

They have the right word as far as offense or crime, but I didn't understand it before; now I'm even more confused. To mitigate doesn't fix or solve the problem, just reduces the sting, softens, excuses? Excuse me? They think they can just bulldoze through here and say, "Excuse me"?

Most of the mitigation plan is logical. Commonsense practices like repairing drain tiles and separating topsoil from subsoil, but two sentences jump out at me: "1. D. MPL will not knowingly allow the amount of top cover to erode more than 12 inches from its original level. 2. D. MPL may employ temporary, non-destructive uses of Topsoil such as creating access ramps at road crossings."

As if twelve inches of soil loss isn't enough, they further increase their rights to abuse by adding the disclaimer "Not knowingly," which—I am no lawyer—I believe means they can cause unchecked erosion as long as they don't "know." And calling access ramps a nondestructive use of Topsoil? They clearly know nothing about compaction, microbial life, and soil aggregation. They capitalize "Top" but don't seem to recognize its value. This is not what I classify as an acceptable excuse, nor do I see any softening. I only see offense and crime.

Gardens of Eagan is a federally registered, certified organic, local-market vegetable farm. Thirty-six months of compliance with organic farming standards is required to qualify for certification. We have been building this soil here since 1991. Feeding our soil's microbial life, building organic matter levels, and supporting biological diversity are how we manage fertility, pests, and disease. We grow high-quality, high-value crops. Losing even one acre would be high impact, and they want five acres? The soil, the customers, the farm, the ecosystem—the impact cannot be minimized or mitigated, and certainly not with the plan they presently have.

Enough of this foolishness, I don't need to read anything more. A crude oil pipeline is not compatible with the Gardens of Eagan. No one could be so ignorant as to not understand that it is in the best in-terest of the public to protect and preserve an organic vegetable farm producing for local use. Case closed. Obviously, they don't know we are here. I just need to tell them. I dial the phone number to the MinnCan Project. I hang up after one ring.

I tell myself, a crude oil pipeline is not an act of God. You can't do a darn thing to stop hail or frost. This you can. I breathe in—deep—and let it out. I remind myself that terror doesn't have to mean run; it can mean act. I dial again and ask to speak to the project manager. After twenty minutes of holding and transferring, I am connected to the Right-of-Way Group Leader for the MinnCan Project. My stom-ach is still upside down, but I am a little clearer. I tell her that I need to have a meeting with whoever it is who makes routing decisions. I explain they have made a mistake; their proposed route crosses the Gardens of Eagan, a certified organic farm serving the Twin Cities community with brand-name vegetables since 1973. It will never pass the Criteria for Route Selection. I inform her that there are fifty thousand co-op customers, and many of them will be very upset.

She says, "It doesn't matter if you are organic. We don't change routes. Go to the public hearing and tell the judge."

The line goes dead. Now they do know we're here, and apparently someone is so ignorant as to not understand the best interest of the public. The system is working for the pipeline company; of course they don't want to change it.

I am mad. This oil company with no respect for organic food and healthy soil is not going to get away with it this time. If I have to talk to a judge, I must need an attorney. I sure hope I was right, not just waxing eloquent, when I said challenges in my own life are like hail pushing me to full potential.

"Hello, I am looking for an attorney who has experience with utilities and eminent domain."

"Please hold," and then, after what feels like forever, "Tell me about your case, please."

I tell our story, abbreviated version: local, direct-market, name-brand, federally registered, certified organic vegetable farm, long-term soil damage to our most productive fields, MinnCan crude oil pipeline.

"Please hold," she says. A few minutes later she comes back to the phone, "I'm sorry, we can't help you. We have a conflict of interest."

We are in the middle of the spring planting rush, but every chance I can leave the field, I'm in the house calling law offices. It is the same answer, call after call, "I'm sorry, we can't help you." Could Minnesota Pipe Line Company (MPL) really have tied up every eminent domain attorney in the Twin Cities with a retainer?

After three days of unsuccessful calling, I'm starting to think that maybe I am making a big deal out of nothing. So, it's a crude oil pipeline—so what. Pipelines and power lines have impinged upon agricultural land for decades. Is it really a problem? I sit down and start to write why it matters; writing helps me separate emotion from reality, and really, I'm hoping to find I can just let it go, get on with life and spring planting, back to picking nettles and eating vetch, pipeline and all.

But no, two hours later I have written an eleven-page document titled with a Franklin D. Roosevelt quote: "A Nation That Destroys Its Soil, Destroys Itself: Why the MPL Proposed Pipeline Cannot Cross the Gardens of Eagan Organic Farm." When I show it to Martin, he's not even interested in reading it, just says, "I could have told you you're not overreacting. If a pipeline goes through, we'll never grow on that soil again. Without those fields, we'll shut down. I don't have the energy to move and start over again. It will be the end of Gardens of Eagan."

It's day five when I reach Paula Maccabee, an attorney, who laughs when I give my by now well-practiced spiel. "Gardens of Eagan Organic Farm?" she says. "Crude oil pipeline? Twelve inches of topsoil erosion? This is going to be fun."

"Why aren't you already on retainer with MPL? Every other attorney I called is."

"I don't take polluters," she says.

I call her references. They say she's smart, she has experience with the PUC, she likes to win, and she moves too fast. Perfect—especially the too fast. Martin says go for it. We sign a client agreement and write a retainer check. This is all new territory for us. Little did we know that our *Year of Excellent Records and Looking to the Future* would change to *The Year of Legal Records and Protecting the Future*.

I need a break. We take Blake and Chase out to the vetch field—it's an organoleptic experience for them. They eagerly chomp the delicate leaves Martin and I offer. They have no awareness that most Americans don't know what vetch is, much less eat it. They just trust their taste buds, their body's call for chlorophyll, and their grandparents. Chase, in his meditative state of "I am here now experiencing the world," isn't satisfied with eating pre-picked vetch. He kneels in the sea of green nourishment and nibbles the leaves directly off the plant. We join him on the ground, and for a few seconds the world stops. A pipeline isn't threatening the farm. The only sound is the munching of vetch leaves and laughing. I am completely present in the sensory.

Being with these two gives me so much hope. I think of Frances Moore Lappé, "Hope is not about if things are getting better or worse. Hope is about courage. Hope is coming from the act of trying to shift, or trying to make a difference. It is more verb than noun. You become hope by taking action."

Eleanor Roosevelt comes to mind, "Do something every day that scares you."

I think I'm looking at a long string of scary every days on this one. But then I feel Anita standing next to me, elbow linked in mine. I hear her saying, "You have the power. Use it." I see her smile. She can already see the results of our effort. Suddenly it's less scary.

Paula Maccabee is not what I expected. I knew I would like her, an attorney who laughs at the offer of a challenge and says fighting a crude oil pipeline sounds like fun, who doesn't work for "polluters," and jumps at an invitation to visit the farm. I have read everything I could find online about her and know she is skilled in martial arts. But I didn't know she would be a buff firecracker, dressed in Chico's business clothes, with luxurious, soft black curls that I want to reach out and touch.

We walk down to the fields that are threatened. I show her the young kale and go into my eat-more-kale lecture on its value as a miracle food. We move on to the hairy vetch. I pick a tender tip and say, "Try it. It's delicious."

"It tastes a little like peas," she says. "What is it?"

Yes, like peas, but closer to the beginning, less refined. I must be nervous. It suddenly strikes me as hilarious that I just offered this gorgeous, intimidating attorney something to eat called green manure. I say, "Hairy vetch, it is in the same family as peas; they are both legumes." *Hairy* sounds almost as unappealing as *manure*. "Soil building is the general term for crops used to care for soil, but it provides multiple ecosystem services. It is a catch crop holding nutrients secure and preventing them from leaching into the groundwater or running off, a cover crop protecting the soil from erosion and rain compaction, but most exciting to me, it feeds the microbial life in the soil, increases organic matter and water-holding capacity, and improves soil structure and fertility. We call it a green manure crop."

"Green manure?" She has a funny look on her face.

"Use the term *soil building*." She doesn't ask for more or pick any herself.

She takes charge of the meeting, explaining that it is important to work with the legal process and system. We must put together a combination of efforts. Public clamor alone is not usually effective. For starters, we need to intervene under Minnesota rules as "parties to the case." This will permit us to make discovery requests, file expert evidence, and conduct cross-examination in a contested administrative hearing on route selection. I'll need to write a statement for evidence and ask respected people in the community to write affidavits of support. The process includes submitting an alternative route, and we'll need expert testimony. Here we are, the soil, kale, and vetch standing witness as we plan our strategy in the threatened fields. It strikes me that this soil and these plants are our true experts. It will be my job to translate their testimony.

She goes on to explain that energy infrastructure conflicts are not unique to organic farms, so we'll need to identify what is unique about organic farms. We need to create a record that proves Gardens of Eagan crops are not fungible. And she moves beyond the immediacy of the threat to this one organic farm and says, "We'll want to prove that organic farms are valuable natural resources and should be protected as such."

This word *fungible*—freely exchangeable or replaceable, in whole or in part, for another of like nature or kind—gets my immediate attention. It's one of the key components of our marketing success. In the commodity system, the farmer is just as fungible as his or her crop. Even if the product is a niche item with a specialty clientele— for example, organic milk going into a bulk pool—if it is exchangeable for another of like kind, the farmer can still be treated as disposable. "Gardens of Eagan is definitely not fungible," I say. "Organic farms as valuable natural resources—we can prove that? Like wetlands are valuable natural resources?"

"Yes, we can prove that."

"It's certainly true, and there might be other organic farms on the line."

"We might be able to do more than just move the line off your farm. We can create specific mitigation protections for organic farms." Paula explains, "Pipelines and power lines will likely be an increasing issue. As energy resources ranging from crude oil shale and natural gas to wind turbines and mine-mouth coal continue to develop at locations remote to the communities using the energy, it becomes more, rather than less, likely that there will be land-use conflicts between agriculture and energy infrastructure. There is an implicit assumption that mitigation measures are sufficient to protect agricultural production. These mitigation practices, which certainly represent an advance over historical construction practices, may well be insufficient to protect organic farms."

"Do you think we could stop the line altogether?" I ask.

She looks at me for a second, like she's taking my measure. "How many hundreds of thousands of dollars do you have that you are willing to commit? And even if we had the money, I don't think it is possible to stop it. Just moving it out of your fields is going to be David against Goliath."

Organic farms as valuable natural resources. She's right. We can prove that. The National Organic Program (NOP) standards exclude production methods that are "not possible under natural conditions." And "organic production" is defined as a production system managed by "integrating cultural, biological, and mechanical practices that foster cycling of resources, promote ecological balance, and conserve biological diversity." An organic farm functions not only as a food-production land use but also as a natural environment—an integrated natural system, providing ecosystem services.

Paula tells me that informed-citizen input is not the same thing as public clamor. Public clamor is like anecdotal evidence; it is interesting and it attracts media attention, but it is not effective in a court of law. I like this concept. Informed-citizen input versus public clamor—that is powerful. She says, "If we can get two hundred informed-citizen letters, it would impress the judge."

"Two hundred?" I blurt. "We can get that the first day. People get involved when their personal food source is threatened."

She has that measuring-me look again. "Some people just want to be right, and some people just want to be heard. I play to win." She writes three sentences on a piece of paper.

1. Change the MinnCan Project crude oil pipeline route to avoid crossing of Gardens of Eagan Organic Farm.
2. Require the MinnCan Project pipeline to avoid other organic farms, if such avoidance is feasible.

3. Provide specific agricultural-impact mitigation plan protections for organic farms to minimize production loss
and loss of organic certification.

She says, "This is my understanding of what you want to accomplish.
Is this correct?"

After we shake hands and say good-bye, when she is halfway to
her car, and I'm standing there wondering what the universe is about
to hand us, she turns around and says, "Your job is to provide the
education and teach them about organic farming. I'll take care of
the fight."

I'm trying to write my affidavit about the history of Gardens of
Eagan: how organic farms manage their fertility, disease, and pests
through soil health and biological diversity; how the damage from
a pipeline installation cannot be mitigated for this organic vegetable
farm. But I feel so nervous and jittery, like my entire world has collapsed. My friend Esther calls to check in. My throat is tight, and my
voice comes out in a whisper. I feel absolute sureness that the line
will be moved, that we will succeed, yet I feel so anxious. Originally I
felt nausea, and the tension was in my stomach; now it's in my throat.
She says, "Stomach is power struggle, throat is grief."

"I recognize the feeling of powerlessness, that was before Paula
Maccabee, and the grief is the bulldozers in Eagan. But that is so long
ago, so behind us, I never think about it anymore."

"Just because you don't think about it doesn't mean you don't
feel it," she says.

She tells me she ran into our longtime friend Nick who has been
taking pictures of the farm for the past twenty-five years. He told her
he feels absolutely sick about this. "What if we lose the Gardens of
Eagan?" he said.

"Don't worry about it," she told him. "Atina's on it; it's not going
to happen."

It's great to know that others see me as invincible. But I need to feel it myself. The best place to find my strength is outside in the kale. I take along the route map and the diagram illustrating the pipeline-installation process, a hammer, stakes, tape measure, and tomato-tying twine.

Following the proposed route, I measure out and pound stakes down the center of MinnCan's pipeline corridor. I attach the twine: through the seven threatened fields, stake to stake through the young kale plants, across the lush and tangled nitrogen-sequestering hairy vetch, down into and back out of the grass-covered waterway that also serves as beneficial insect habitat, through the just-planted-yesterday broccoli, the plot ready for watermelon planting as soon as the weather breaks, across the rye and vetch soil-building crop, and, finally, the field where yesterday the crew laid compost in long lines to prepare for tomato planting.

When I get to the end, I look at the installation diagram. "Front-End Grading." I look back at the string line running the width of the farm and see giant machines forcing their way. The kale, broccoli, rye, and vetch lie flattened, trampled—innocent victims. The topsoil sticks to the bulldozer tracks as they lug through mud, compacting a permanent footprint, an indelible mark, forever on the soil.

Again at the paper. "Topsoil Stripping." I look up and see the well-aggregated soil particles crushed. Microorganisms starving, dying. Water channels collapsed. I see a line of Topsoil pushed aside, a long, low ridge. The work zone of the easement is an exposed stripe of bare, brown, skinless subsoil. Veins of erosion scour the surface.

The paper. "Stringing Pipe, Field Bending Pipe, Initial Weld, X-Ray Inspection, Coating Field Weld." Heavy trucks and toxic substances, leaking, dripping, soaking into the soil where we once grew food.

"Trenching, Backfilling." Backhoes digging and beeping and belching diesel smoke. Ripping a seam through the parent material—the mineral source of this landscape. Tearing a hole through the greenness of my life. "Replace Topsoil, Fill-Up, Full Restoration."

Forty feet of the easement width titled "Spoil Side." Sixty feet titled "Working Side." I see a hundred-foot-wide stripe of pasture mix, our attempt to rebuild the soil, but no vegetables growing.

I know what this looks like. I've seen it before. And I know what it feels like. I'm not willing to do it again. I remember the promise I made—it seems like a lifetime ago now—sitting in the Woods Field with Martin, Maize, and Eliza, listening to the first bulldozers flattening trees in Eagan. "We're going to move to a new home and land, and I promise you, no one will ever bulldoze it."

The switch flips. The truth grows bigger and stronger the longer I stand reflecting. I am not a victim, not even a potential victim. I am the guardian here, the human voice for these faultless plants and this generous soil. I am alone right now standing in this field, but I am not alone in this commitment to life. There are thousands of people who will stand up for this kale, for this land, and for this issue. This soil and these plants are not only our witnesses and experts; they are our partners and allies.

I close my eyes and picture the kale spirits. It worked when we needed it in Eagan to communicate with the deer, and we need it now. I imagine them as tiny green fairies with kale leaf hats and gowns resting on the sturdy stems of the leaves. "Kale, you are the organic model. You need to reach for your highest potential and be as healthy and productive as you possibly can. You have the task of demonstrating that organic farming works and for paying the pipeline legal expenses. I will do everything I can to translate your voice and protect you. Together we'll be a powerhouse team."

Maybe it is historically true that pipeline companies don't change routes for landowners. But this time they have picked the wrong plant, on the wrong farm, the wrong woman, and the wrong community.

I take down the string and pull out the stakes; the thought of leaving them up feels like a curse. And that is key. There is no curse.

Not on this land.

Definitely Not Fungible

Martin and I sit down with Dean, the produce manager of the Wedge Co-op, and Lindy, the general manager, to tell them about the pipeline.

I explain that we have hired Ms. Maccabee, how the legal process works, and that we need to do an informed-citizen letter-writing campaign. Lindy is happy to write an affidavit, and she offers the Wedge's help getting the message out. Dean doesn't utter a word through the entire conversation, just sits mute and listens until I'm finished. Then it tumbles out, like water hitting cold rocks. "What should I do?" he asks. "What would you do if it was your farm?"

It is hard to keep from grinning. I think about Paula and her word *fungible*. Gardens of Eagan is definitely not fungible. For Dean, Gardens of Eagan is not exchangeable for another of like kind. He is so committed and engaged; right now he's feeling the threat of loss directly himself.

"Exactly what we are doing, Dean. This is a good thing. By the time we are finished, they will be sorry they ever met the Gardens of Eagan and the Twin Cities organic community. It isn't going to go through. Martin and I are going to fight this with everything we have, and I know that the food co-op community will back us. Gardens of Eagan will not be hosting the MinnCan Project crude oil pipeline. Not only will we protect the Gardens of Eagan, but the Public Utilities Commission will gain an awareness of organic farming systems, and in the future, Minnesota organic farms will have a mitigation plan that includes organic protections."

It is one thing to say it. It's another to feel it. My stomach is a mess of tangled barbwire. My throat is torn steel wool. And it's one thing to speak with confidence, to assure Dean and Lindy. It's going to be a whole lot of work and focus to do it.

But we're not alone. We are completely the opposite of alone. "Whatever we can do to help with this," Lindy says, "let us know."

"An organic farm that ships its food locally should be a model, not a casualty of Minnesota's energy policies." Barth Anderson from the Wedge Co-op is a professional writer, and everything that leaves his pen sounds like smooth honey to me. He says, "We'll get this out on the pipeline." Then he sees my face and says, "Oh, that expression has new meaning. I don't think I'll be using it anymore."

The Wedge Co-op has set up a school desk in the front of the produce department backed by a poster of Martin looking like Clark Gable of the Sweet Corn Patch. His cool expression suggests thoughts along the line of "Frankly, MinnCan, I don't give a damn!" The desk is covered with flyers and information on the issue. Customers can leave their informed-citizen input, and the Wedge will mail it. The staff seems to be spending more time soliciting support than stocking produce.

Mississippi Market Co-op has a letter-writing station at their customer service counter. Eastside Food Co-op has Helen De Michiel's video *Turn Here Sweet Corn* playing on a computer monitor in a rotating loop at the entrance of the store. Signs say: *Once was enough. This time we're keeping the farm. Please write a letter today.* There are articles in every co-op newsletter, the *Mix*, a publication of the Twin Cities Natural Food Co-ops, and the Land Stewardship Project. The Organic Consumer Association sends an e-mail alert to all of its Twin Cities area subscribers. Midwest Organic and Sustainable Education Services (MOSES) sends a letter to their mailing list. And it is not just the organic community. I'm shocked when a story in the *St. Paul Pioneer Press* goes out on the AP wire. I've had reports of newspapers picking it up in Duluth, Fargo, La Crosse, Eau Claire, even Medina, North Dakota. How did this take off so fast?

This morning I mailed the citizen letters that were collected over the weekend at the Living Green Expo held at the State Fairgrounds. For two days, Palmer, the Wedge Co-op sample guy, stood at the booth of the Twin Cities Natural Food Co-ops calling, "Save organic farms. Gardens of Eagan threatened. Write a letter for organic food."

Now the assistant to Administrative Law Judge Heydinger is on the phone to tell me how many letters they have received. Together with the ones I mailed, there are 1,130 letters in the first nine days. These are not statements of public clamor or idealistic rhetoric. The writers clearly understand and articulate organic agricultural systems and the benefits to society and the environment. These are, as Paula requested, informed-citizen input.

This is not about land values or farm income. It is not a NIMBY (not in my backyard). This is about local and clean food production in a world where energy resources are dwindling. As Barth writes, "It is not in the best interest of the public to cut a crude oil pipeline through the center of a premier organic vegetable farm serving its local community with high-quality, certified-organic produce since 1973."

"So just how many food servings does Gardens of Eagan produce in a year?" Barth asks. I never measured it in servings before. I start with broccoli; in 2005 we shipped 117,950 pounds. All in one place, it would have filled 7.2 semis, which sounds like quite a bit of broccoli, but I start to understand the impact a small farm can have in its community when I figure out it's approximately 535,009 servings. It's still abstract until I calculate 133,440 moments of sweet corn pleasure. That is human faces smiling, as are the 618,651 servings of watermelon. I'm laughing when I find 50,439 servings of winter squash. I am amused, because we "don't grow squash anymore" but can't help slipping in a "few" plants. Finally I calculate the entire farm. In 2005, 2,413,115 servings of produce were sold wholesale. Add another 20 percent for the roadside stand. Does that answer the question, why does it matter if we have local organic food?

This is about food security and stability. We need a lot more local organic farms, and we need to protect and preserve them.

Meg Moynihan, the Organic and Diversification Specialist at the Department of Agriculture, tells me she received a call from MPL requesting a list of Minnesota's organic growers. She gives me the name of the other organic grower she knows is on the line, a row-crop farmer in McLeod County. When I call him, he says, "MPL told me there are twenty-three organic farms on the line."

It can't be true. There are only 506 organic farms registered with the Minnesota Department of Agriculture. What are the odds, and why would MPL say that?

Paula asks me, "Is this causing conflict between you and Martin?"

"No, why do you ask?"

"He doesn't come to our meetings or join our phone calls."

"We don't have time for duplication. He's taken on extra with the farm, and he's doing all the cooking and dishes. He shows up wherever I'm working, holds out a plate of food, and insists that I eat. He listens to me and keeps my head straight. I wouldn't do it if he were opposed."

"Doesn't he want to be more involved?"

"Think of it like music. Chord progressions form the spine of music; that's Martin. Melody is the goal-oriented motion; it moves in real time with direction and purpose—that's you and me."

I am awake. I don't know why. Yes, I do know. I hear the ping of hail on the roof shingles and the window glass and the house walls. My heart stops beating. My head takes over and starts to pound. Damn—not hail. I look at the clock to see what the date is, and it says 3:07. No, the date, it is June 9, 2006. Exactly one year and one day from the big hailstorm.

My stomach says, throw up. My logic says, it looked really bad last time, but almost everything recovered, and you had a great year— the best ever. My throat clenches into a wooden stick. My memory says, relax; don't worry about it. My back pulls tight, straining against a wall of frozen ice. My Martin says, "Put in these earplugs. Go back to sleep." Somehow my logic and my memory and my Martin win, and I drift off.

I can tell what bird Martin is listening to by his unconscious tapping on my arm: two quarter notes, followed by three half notes. I take the earplugs out and hear the mourning dove that nests outside our bedroom window. The melody climbs between the first and second tone, then drops off at the third: oo-wah-hoo, followed by a monotone pair, oo-oo. Behind the dove is the simple two-note whistle of the black-capped chickadee. It vibrates a swelling crescendo, then falls, with a break in the middle, fee-bee. It sounds like summer and a mother calling kids in from play. The robins are part of the choir too, "Cheerily cheer-up cheerio," three phases repeated over and over, accented with a staccato interruption, as if the opening measure to the opera is all they can remember.

Then I remember. I go straight to my desk and find an e-mail from Leah Johnson with a link to the *Pulse of the Twin Cities*. The front-page headline proclaims: "Oil vs. Soil—How Not to Treat Soil Like Dirt." Beneath the headline is a photo of Martin and me together in the kale—the quintessential organic farm couple. The article advocates that organic farms should be avoided by utilities if there are feasible alternatives and that special precautions should be taken to protect organic ecosystems and certification. There is a photo of the Flint Hills gas refinery, the final destination of the MinnCan Project crude oil pipeline, contrasted against rows of lush kale in the threatened field. It closes with the judge's address and a request for informed-citizen input. This is perfect. The *Pulse* is free, stacked at the entrance of nearly every coffee shop and food co-op in the Twin Cities.

It's not until I finish reading the article that I remember last night's hail. I run out to check and find a pulsing green world. The damage is minimal, just a few torn leaves. I hope I'll be the same at the end of this experience—just a little tattered but still growing.

Paula has been talking about bringing in an expert witness to write organic protections for the Agricultural Impact Mitigation Plan (AIMP). It sounded great, but I was focused on citizen input, not paying attention to this next step. I'm standing there looking at the hail-bruised leaves, thinking how quickly they'll look whole again, when it hits me: my entire life experience makes me an expert on the subject of organic farming. I don't have to sit back and wait for someone else to write it. I am an expert. I can write the first draft.

I have a ball doing it. This must be what Paula meant when she said this would be fun. I stay up all night combing the AIMP, word by word, concept by concept. Everywhere that I find the mitigation plan is not sufficient to protect organic farming systems, I write procedures to preserve the soils, diversity, and certification integrity of an organic farm. In the morning I send it to Paula, who writes it into legalese. We then send it to Bonnie Wideman and Sissy Bowman, who provide input from organic certification experts. Within a few days, we have a first-of-its-kind draft Agricultural Impact Mitigation Plan with specific mitigation protections for organic farms.

Bob Patton, advisor to the commissioner of agriculture on the AIMP, along with Meg Moynihan, Organic and Diversification Specialist at the Department of Agriculture, are visiting the farm. He's a great question asker. "How will the pipeline's impact on organic systems be different than on a conventional farm?" He listens openly as I explain that the AIMP, as presently written, is not adequate to protect the certification, nor the soil- and biological diversity–based systems of an organic farm. When he asks, "What should I do with this information?" I hand him our amended draft of the AIMP with protections for organic farms.

Paula joins us, and we start to walk between lush, green rows of kale, the umbrella canopy of crisp leaves painting our legs with morning dew. It is intense to move through the crop, describing the impact if the pipeline went through these fields. This isn't a fungible commodity crop. This is food grown for a specific community and loaded with emotion. I say, "Kale has more nutritional value for fewer calories than almost any other food." The kale must have been listening back when I made my request for help. It is always a beautiful plant, but this year it is absolutely gorgeous, and so far it has earned enough extra to pay all pipeline legal expenses.

Following the proposed route, we come to a dense field of waist-high hairy vetch. Bob hasn't seen this before. Paula reaches down, picks a leaf bud, and hands it to him. "Taste it," she says. She smiles at me but doesn't say anything about green manure. She doesn't eat any herself either. We dig up a few plants and admire the root nodules. Bob seems impressed to hear these legumes can fix up to 160 pounds per acre of atmospheric nitrogen, and also that this living plant, creating fertility by using the renewable energy of the sun, will be the main source of nitrogen for the broccoli crop that will be planted here in a few weeks.

We continue on the proposed route, through the tall-grassed waterway, and I explain that we keep it unmowed to provide habitat and nesting for beneficial insects, which in turn provide pest control and pollination—ecosystem services. But it is when we come to the rye and vetch field, just disked in yesterday, that the difference between the impact on a farm relying on chemical inputs and an organic farm is laid out visually like a storyboard.

It is now sixteen hours since the vetch was incorporated. The entire field is covered with a complex network of shimmering spider strands—miles of glistening threads—spun overnight and misted with morning dew. Sticky insect traps, slung like hammocks between the ridges of soil, defend the field. The webs sparkle in the sunlight—a tribute to biological diversity and beneficial insects. We pick up clumps of soil and find spiders in hiding, patiently waiting to eat pests. We dig our hands through the soil. It is loose and well aggregated.

"There are a lot of positive effects from using soil-building crops for fertility instead of fossil fuel–based inputs," I say. "For one thing, it provides habitat for beneficial insects, in this case, all these spiders who eat pest species. Also, adding organic matter to the soil feeds the microbial life of the soil and increases the biological activity. As it decomposes, nutrients are released, humus is formed, and aggregation of soil particles increases. This improves the soil's pore structure, and it can reduce soilborne disease, erosion, and nutrient leaching."

Then I stop talking. Seeing is believing. It is best if I let the farm speak for itself. Intellectualizing will get in the way of him feeling it. The ultimate teacher surrounds us. Now I just have to bring the judge and the Public Utilities Commission out here, or bring here to them.

The legal process includes submitting an alternative route proposal along with our arguments about why our suggested route has a lesser impact. It is a lousy process. A landowner has to submit a map with a line drawn across a neighbor's property. Not an easy step to take in a rural community. "We shouldn't have to do this," I say to Paula. "We should just have to prove how our systems are different, that the potential impact is too great to mitigate on this farm, and the loss to the public is too high. It should be MPL's or the PUC's job to figure out the best alternate route."

"You can take on changing the system after you win," she says. "Right now you don't have time."

We're not going to make any friends in the township doing this; I feel like I am trespassing, and we're just following the process. We consider each of the criteria for route selection and try to determine the route with the smallest impact. Is there a wetland to avoid, a rare natural environment, land of historical, archaeological, or cultural significance? How close are the homes? Are there already existing rights-of-way?

There are many considerations, but there is no such thing as open space. Any route is going to impact someone or something. We draw up multiple options. By the time Paula leaves, I am too emotionally exhausted to do anything. I turn on the television, and there is Robert Kennedy Jr. "The air, the water, the fish, the animals—are all in public trust. They belong to you and me. When someone pollutes, they are stealing from us. They are stealing our right to eat fish, drink clean water, and breathe fresh air. Financial compensation isn't enough. Our health and our children's, children's, children's health is not for sale."

When I was nineteen, I overheard a conversation about me between two women I admired who were ten years older. Louise said, "She's so idealistic."

"We were too before life beat it out of us," Tree Marie said. "I hope she can stay that way as long as possible." Tree is here now. Reminding me to hold my ideals as guide lights. Organic farms are valuable natural resources.

The next morning Mark Zdechlik, a reporter from Minnesota Public Radio, comes out and tapes Martin and me in a voice interview.

After we finish, we walk out to the kale, and he records the birds. They are swooping along the edges of the field and eating insects. He tells us that it's the birds he notices on an organic farm. We look across the buffer strip at our neighbor's field corn. There are no birds swooping and flying—just one fungible mono crop. A truck comes up our driveway. Bold letters on the door say MinnCan Project. Mark looks at us and raises his eyebrows. We walk over to the truck together; he still has his recorder on. It is a pipeline survey crew.

When the story is aired on MPR, Martin's voice is polite but firm, "Hey, hi guys, how are you doing? First of all, this is a private road that you came in on. MinnCan does not have permission to come on this land."

It is true about Paula being fast and smart. Working as a team, we've written and presented resolutions to Eureka Township and Dakota County. They've both passed. Eureka's resolution includes, THERE-FORE BE IT RESOLVED, that 1. The Township of Eureka opposes the current crude oil pipeline route proposed by MPL and requests that any route crossing the Township of Eureka be designed to: ... ii. avoid crossing and irreparably damaging organic agricultural lands.

The county resolution states clear support for mitigation to protect organic farms: NOW, THEREFORE, BE IT RESOLVED, that the

Dakota County Board of Commissioners hereby supports the development of mitigation plans by the Minnesota Department of Agriculture, which recognize the unique characteristics associated with
organic farming; and . . .

BE IT FURTHER RESOLVED, that the Dakota County Board of
Commissioners hereby encourages the Public Utilities Commission
to consider mitigation plans developed by the Minnesota Department of Agriculture to mitigate impacts to organic farms.

That's not all. We've written and filed a Petition to Intervene, a
Notice of Appearance, and affidavits from Dana Jackson of the Land
Stewardship Project; Lindy Bannister, the general manager of the
Wedge Co-op; and myself.

I find that no matter what I am doing and wherever I am, I am
thinking or working on the pipeline issue. Ideas pop into my mind
like explosions all night. I write them down so I can go back to sleep,
but it's not long before the next brainstorm jolts me awake again. It
feels like my entire life has created the essential background. Every
experience, every conversation, every challenge are merging together to be able to do exactly this. I have never been stimulated to
this level before. I can actually feel neuron connections growing in
my brain and bits of data traveling across them. I am scared, however,
of the time when this is over and I return to normal.

My greatest source of energy is knowing we are not alone. Barth
says, "One monster, many heads." I'm seeing it everywhere. After an
interview, reporters will casually say, in passing, a quiet aside, "I had
cancer." Or a staff person at the Department of Commerce will say,
"I shop at the co-op."

Just a few words, a discreet encouragement. This monster has
heads everywhere, in every job, people who are committed to environmental protection and healthy food, all contributing from the
place that they can. Things don't change because it is time or because
it's simply the right thing. Things change because people get involved
and claim their right to speak.

Now the television stations have picked it up. I have to keep reminding myself of Paula's advice: "Teach them about organic farming." We take reporters into vetch and talk about soil health; we show them kale and talk about cancer-fighting glucosinolates. But tonight, watching myself on the ten o'clock news, I see a wrathful warrior standing in the middle of a kale field. My jaw is clenched. I punch my fist in the air to emphasize my words: organic, crude oil, soil microbial life, compaction. The reporter opens with, "The pipeline proposal would cut a hundred-foot-wide path directly through these organic fields. In fact, just four feet below this organic kale, 165,000 barrels of crude oil would flow every day."

The story closes with a pipeline agent, who says, "We want to work with them. We want to walk their land, understand more about organic farming and their unique needs and issues. I think we probably can come up with something that's workable for all of us."

They are not walking on our land, ever.

The segment is finished by a few minutes when the phone rings. I look at the name on the caller ID; it is Julie, the right-of-way group leader for the MinnCan Project. She leaves a message saying she'd like to arrange a meeting on the farm. When I tell Paula to call her back and arrange a meeting in the Cities without me, she is surprised that I don't want to be there. I say, "I'm a little off my kale at the moment. Isn't that why I have representation?"

"Off your kale?"

"Kale equals health. I am too emotionally off base to eat; I'm not going to make it through a meeting with MinnCan without saying something I'll later regret."

All day my emotions are flopping back and forth. I'm absolutely thrilled to think that we might be finished with this. Maybe right now they are telling Paula they are going to move the line. All we'll need to do is write up legally binding documents. We're almost done. But my flip side doesn't want to be finished. I actually feel nausea at the thought of stopping. I have so much rage and momentum built up; we're just getting started, and I don't want to just move the line— I want to push through organic-mitigation protections in the AIMP.

All organic farms in Minnesota need this protective tool. Maybe, right now, they are offering a deal to move off our property if we'll drop the AIMP. How will we weigh that decision?

By the time Paula e-mails in late afternoon, I am completely out of my mind. She writes that I was astute to not allow Julie to visit, that her clear intention was to discuss ways to redirect the pipeline at a different angle across the farm. Julie explained that the company usually "makes accommodations" with landowners within their property so that they don't have to deal with other landowners.

Paula tells me that she made it very clear that neither I nor Martin is interested in any alternative that crosses the farm and that our argument about damage isn't an attempt to enhance monetary compensation. She explained some of the ways that organic farms are different from conventional farms and that we will be providing a route alternative and comments on the AIMP, addressing both avoidance and special practices geared to organic farms. She also made it clear that if they do not come up with a new route that avoids the farm, the administrative law judge will have to decide the issue.

Julie then showed Paula on detailed maps that there are several sections on our farm where MPL wants an additional twenty-five-foot width of temporary workspace in addition to the hundred-foot easement, which adds up to six acres instead of five.

Paula told Julie that the township enacted a resolution. Julie visibly blanched.

And that's it? Now instead of wanting five acres they want six! And they didn't even offer a deal for me to turn down? I plunge into despair. How could I have had thoughts of not wanting to quit? This is going to be way harder than I realized. I go to bed, too miserable to do anything but sink into the deep waters of sleep. I absolutely want to give up.

I am swimming the length of a long, narrow mountain lake in Peru. Steep rocks climb vertically on three sides. At the end, a fertility goddess is carved into the rock and decorated with seeds—different colors of corn, grass, quinoa, beans, and amaranth. Her face is smiling, and her arms are inviting, yet she is intimidating to me. If I climb into her influence, will I be strengthened or consumed?

The water is heavy, dense, and bottomless. It is black. I can't see my hand three inches below the surface. The stickiness of the water pulls and holds me awkwardly. I'm barely moving forward. Solid, dark drops fall from my stroking arms. They plunge into the lake, as loud as the ripples are big.

Her arms are stretched upward holding a temple of the sun high above the lake. I wonder how I can get to the top, and I remember—I can fly. How could I forget that? I wonder if the water on my skin and clothes will weigh me down. I remember to just try. I lift my arms and start to move them; my body follows up and out of the water. It is work, but I pull myself incrementally higher with downward strokes. It is hard, but I can do it. There are power lines above her head, and I have to be careful to not hit them. I see a spot to land next to her neck. I am completely out of breath. From there, it is a short scramble to the top and the temple, which is chiseled out of the center of the rock complete with window holes. The sun streams in: bright yellow waves of heat and light. The light enters my pores and runs a current through my veins. It dries and brightens my body to a brilliant sleekness.

I climb to the roof. It was low risk to start flying from the water; it is a completely different gamble to leap off of a cliff. I'm not sure I can do it. I remind myself to just try. I leap up and glide on a surge of luminosity. Of course I can fly. The power lines are gone; there is nothing to interfere. I fly as high as I want. The flying meets a deep craving. The craving cracks in half and dissolves. I soar—effortlessly—over the water and rocks and trees.

In the morning, when I awake, my first thought is: You can soar. Always remember this.

Soil versus Oil

The stand is open! I stand amid the excited reunion of repeat clients and see a quaint roadside stand, a relic of simpler days, elegant in its pragmatism. Watching the delight of the customers, I see clearly that a fundamental human need is being satisfied. We need food businesses like this in every community.

We are distributing pipeline flyers and letter-writing information. Our customers are alarmed. This crude oil pipeline is threatening them deeper than their food supply. A boy runs up to the corn table and stands there, feasting with wide-open eyes on the produce. His mother tells me he talked about the stand all winter and had trouble sleeping last night. He was so excited that we are opening today.

Last night, 134,000 gallons of crude oil spilled from a MPL pipeline in Little Falls. The news reports oil-coated trees and fields. A wetland and hundreds of acres are contaminated adjacent to the Mississippi River. The Minnesota Pollution Control Agency project manager says environmental restoration is expected to be a years-long process. But there seems to be even more concern about whether the leak will cause fuel prices to rise. I read this with shock. At what point will we choose an economy based on health instead of an economy based on pollution and resource extraction?

I know that MPL-owned pipelines are operated by Koch Pipeline Company, which is a wholly owned, indirect subsidiary of Koch Industries. But who owns MPL? I go online and find Flint Hills Resources (which is wholly owned by Koch Industries), Marathon Oil Company, and TROF Inc. I also learn that Koch Industries is one of the largest privately owned companies in the world. When I tell Martin, he says, "They have deeper pockets, but you have the *food co-op* community." He has a point. Every single one of the thousands of letters that have been sent to Judge Heydinger is in support of protecting Gardens of Eagan and local organic farms.

At the EPA website I learn a lot that I never even wondered about before. "Koch Industries Inc., will pay the largest civil fine ever imposed on a company, under any federal environmental law, to resolve claims related to more than 300 oil spills from its pipelines and oil facilities in six states." In one case, almost one hundred thousand gallons of oil was spilled in Texas and caused a twelve-mile oil slick on Nueces Bay and Corpus Christi Bay. The settlement filed on January 13, 2000, requires Koch to pay a $30 million civil penalty, improve its leak-prevention programs, and spend $5 million on environmental projects.

Closer to home, the website states that Koch received the largest federal environmental fine ever recorded in Minnesota for a spill that released aviation fuel into a wetland and waterway. Other violations in Minnesota include the 1996–97 dumping of a million gallons of ammonia-contaminated wastewater directly into the Mississippi River. This dumping took place on weekends when Koch was not required to monitor discharges. Then I find a Koch brochure that states: "All accidents and injuries are preventable through the application of proper training and knowledge." It makes me wonder, was the dumping an accident or not?

At the Koch website I learn that Koch Nitrogen Company and its affiliates are collectively one of the world's largest producers and marketers of nitrogen fertilizers. They have the capability to manufacture, market, and distribute more than nine million tons of synthetic nitrogen products annually. One thing that many people don't realize is that the synthetic nitrogen, anhydrous ammonia, was originally used to produce bombs during World War I. Today's use of anhydrous ammonia for fertilizer is the peacetime conversion of a wartime chemical. The same is true of many pesticides deriving from mustard gas. In warfare they are classified as "weapons of mass destruction." In agriculture they are called "crop protection."

They do not bring more life, more future to the soil, but death. On the website of the U.S. Chemical Safety Board, I read *December 14, 2001, Iowa Ammonia Pipeline Leak Leads to Massive Fish Kill.* The anhydrous ammonia spill near Algona killed nearly 1.3 million fish, the largest fish kill on state record, Iowa state officials said. More than 58,000 gallons of anhydrous ammonia spilled from a broken pipeline owned by Koch Industries Inc. The contaminated water that reached the Des Moines River likely took about six days to reach Des Moines, where the river is used as a source of drinking water. Koch Pipeline was doing maintenance work on a valve on the pipeline.

All accidents are preventable?

It's not just pipeline spills that pose a threat. It's in every step of the chain, from manufacturing through delivery to application in the field. I read an article describing a toxic cloud of anhydrous ammonia gas from a train explosion. Casualties were likely. A leak from a hose at a grain elevator released deadly chemicals and caused a call for evacuations. Farmers are hit in the eyes and blinded. A blast to the skin can mean blistering and burns within seconds. Inhalation causes severe lung damage; suffocation and death are possible. I read an article in *Chemical Week* about the dangers of transporting anhydrous ammonia. "Every day, disastrous mobile bombs travel at top speeds through densely populated communities across the country. It would take very little for terrorists to turn these transport shipments into an explosive nightmare that could harm hundreds of thousands of people."

And what do the experts say? I read about managing risks and taking extra precautions. "Anhydrous ammonia is one of the most dangerous products that we commonly use on the farm, and farmers need to be prepared for the risk of a hose breaking or valves coming open," says Robert Aherin, Extension Agricultural Safety Specialist, University of Illinois. "A direct blast of anhydrous ammonia in the face can kill, or at minimum destroy lung and eye tissue. Farmers should always wear a full face mask when hooking up the lines to protect their nose, mouth, eyes and lungs."

Fertility has become an intensely industrial business akin to oil refining or chemical production. Instead of talking about safety equipment, why isn't anyone asking if there is a safer fertility? We don't need anhydrous ammonia.

How ironic. A small organic vegetable farm that primarily supplies its nitrogen needs using the renewable energy of the sun with legume plants is threatened by one of the world's largest producers of fossil fuel–based nitrogen fertilizer.

When I check our website counter, I find multiple daily visits from Wichita, Kansas, the city where Koch Industries is headquartered. I am thrilled by the idea of a Koch employee being assigned to monitor our Internet presence, but I'm also terrified. I have nightmares that I will come home and find our house has been ransacked, our computers smashed. Our little organic vegetable farm can't be that big of a threat. But when I tell Paula that I've taken to carrying an external hard drive with me, even in the field, just in case, she says, "That's a good idea."

We file more legal documents. I love the titles, their clear descriptiveness. *Gardens of Eagan Proposal for Alternative Route Alignment to Avoid Organic Farm* provides maps of our proposed alternative route and documentation of why it has less impact than crossing Gardens of Eagan. *Gardens of Eagan Proposal for Modification of Agricultural Impact Plan and Environmental Assessment* is an amended version of the AIMP to include protections for organic soils and certification.

This must be what is meant by the word *representation*. It feels as if Paula is using all of her experience and skill to act as a professional extension of me. As if she has fully absorbed my values, goals, and emotions, added her legal experience, education, and moxie, and acts completely on behalf of my interests. She so wholly represents me that it almost feels as if I am doing the work that she does. I trust her to a depth that I have never before trusted another human. When

I tell her this, she laughs. "This is my dream case. It is so wonderful to have my client also be my expert."

I have completely abandoned any type of normal eating or sleeping schedule. During the day I farm and work on the pipeline project when I can get free of the fields. Most of the night I am at the computer writing documents, reviewing drafts, researching, and doing outreach to the public. I lie down and sleep when I am too tired to continue—wherever I am. In the pack shed I crawl onto the tomato-ripening rack. In the field I lie flat between the rows. I take quick naps on the back of flatbeds, on my office floor, in hedgerows. It doesn't take long. Ten to fifteen minutes, then I am back at it. I eat whatever someone puts in front of me, or vegetables when I am harvesting and packing. When I get discouraged, I inspire my competitive side with a dare, "How many people do you know who have the opportunity to take on one of the largest privately owned companies in the world?"

It is my first time seeing Paula on the stage of law. We are attending a pre-hearing pipeline conference at the Public Utilities Commission. MPL, the Department of Commerce, and Gardens of Eagan are the only parties to the case. Paula has a seat at the table and the same rights to speak. She is a brilliant performer, choosing her words with precision, and she understands the importance of branding and the power of name recognition. She says "Gardens of Eagan Organic Farm" in its entirety about ten times in five minutes.

It's also my first time seeing the representatives of MPL. They fill the front two rows of the left side of the room, big, serious company men in black power suits. They are a contrast to Paula and me, two short and fiery women, she in red and black, I in green and blue.

The MPL oil spill in Little Falls seems to be tainting everything that is said. Even with the best precautions, the probability of a leak exists. I am impressed with Judge Heydinger; she is facilitating with intelligent thoroughness. She makes a point of including everyone who wants to speak and makes certain that the public isn't left out or confused.

When the hearing is finished, one of the pipeline men comes over and shakes my hand, "I buy your sweet corn at Lakewinds Co-op. It's the best." Is it possible our monster has a head sitting at their table? Sweet corn does have a powerful lure. Paula introduces several of the staff from the PUC and the Department of Commerce. One of them tells me that he heard the story on MPR so he came out and drove past. "Nice-looking farm. What was that tall grassy plant growing along the road?"

"Sorghum-sudangrass. It's unrivaled for adding organic matter, up to four tons of biomass per acre. It feeds the microbial life, fluffs the soil, and increases water-holding capacity. It can even choke out thistles." I can't turn it off. I want everyone to know how elegantly organic systems work. "It also has allelopathic properties. While growing, it exudes sorgoleone and other organic acids that inhibit weed seed germination and growth."

"I've never seen it before," he says.

"You should have come in and introduced yourself. I would have given you a tour."

"I was scared to, might get kicked off," he smiles.

I think he's joking, but I'm not sure. Then I am talking to the next person. It's all a blur. I can't remember who anyone is past the handshake, even though I am really trying. Afterward, Paula says, "Everyone wants to meet you, unreal."

Since I'm in town, I stop off at the administrative law judge's office to read letters and e-mails from informed citizens. There is an e-mail from Dr. Deon Stuthman, University of Minnesota professor of agronomy and plant genetics. He writes, "I have just finished reading the summary of the *Gardens of Eagan Proposal for Modification of Agricultural Impact Mitigation Plan* and the *Environmental Assessment*. I have also read the summary of the *Alternative Route Alignment to Avoid Organic Farm*. In both instances I find neither *biological* or *agronomical* misstatements or overstatements. If it was my research plots being run through, I'd make just as big of a fuss."

I call Paula and read her the letter. She says, "Expert witnesses don't usually drop out of the sky to give unsolicited testimony or send e-mails to the judge."

"It gets better than that, Paula. I've met Dr. Stuthman. Judge Heydinger has some passing familiarity with him. Years ago he did some work with her husband."

I go back to reading and find one from Gary Zimmer of Midwestern Bio-Ag. He writes, "Organic farmers access nutrients in the soil by working with and enhancing the natural soil system. This soil food web is an intricate system requiring billions of tiny creatures in the soil interacting with plants. This soil life, which includes six basic categories: the microscopic bacteria, fungi, protozoa, and nematodes, plus the larger arthropods and earthworms, is found almost exclusively in the top few inches of the soil. Taking apart this well-established, natural soil system and then mechanically putting it back in place will certainly disrupt the vital biological world the organic farmer has taken years to create, nurture and protect."

From Bill Hinkley, "It was with shock and grief that I read of the proposed building of a crude oil pipeline through the Gardens of Eagan. I wish you could see the care, research, and planning that goes into the raising of each crop, see the diversity of the fields, and the use of the natural watershed in determining the approach to husbanding the land, and taste the sweetness of the corn and the tomatoes and the cabbage that grow."

Dr. Carl Rosen from the Departments of Horticultural and Soil Science, University of Minnesota, writes, "The many years needed to develop soil to the condition required to produce high-quality produce will be lost in the vicinity of the construction. . . . In addition, the installation of a pipeline will permanently alter the soil temperature above the pipeline, making it impossible to restore the site to a natural condition. In my opinion, constructing a crude oil pipeline through a certified organic farm is an oxymoron."

This is crucial testimony from a respected soil scientist. Soil temperature affects diseases and pests and causes numerous growing issues.

Rick Christianson of Co-op Partners Warehouse informs on the loss to organic eaters: "It is very important to realize that locating the pipeline through Gardens of Eagan would harm much more than just their farm. The entire regional organic supply of produce would be severely affected. From a consumer demand perspective, Gardens of Eagan is a source of quality food that is irreplaceable in this marketplace."

There are letters from University of Minnesota soil scientists, plant geneticists, agronomists, and geologists; from organic certifiers, restaurant owners, produce managers, doctors, and musicians; from third-generation Gardens of Eagan corn-avores and chemically sensitive clients. They talk about the importance of preserving organic farms, about peak oil and food security, soil building, and renewable fertility systems. They tell stories of family traditions and multiple generations eating Gardens of Eagan produce. They say, "We have a treasure here that cannot be replaced."

They show what would be lost if the Gardens of Eagan no longer provided local organic produce. They urge the judge to require MPL to choose a route that avoids the Gardens of Eagan, and to recommend that the AIMP be amended to protect all organic farms in Minnesota. I am getting ready to leave when the staff attorney comes in with a box sent over by courier from Mississippi Market Co-op containing 1,003 letters. To date, more than 3,000 letters have been sent!

Last winter during our planning week, Martin and I asked, how much goodwill does the Gardens of Eagan have? I didn't have any idea how to measure it, or even a tangible understanding of what goodwill is. Now it is very clear. Goodwill is a savings bank of support, and Gardens of Eagan has a very full account. Goodwill is true wealth.

When I tell Paula about the letters, she says, "I am blown away by the level of love that I see in this case. I've seen organizing that feels like it is based on anger and fear. This seems to be based on caring and protection."

"That's because organic farming is based on love, caring, and protection," I say.

But even so, despite our intervention and all this informed-citizen input, despite the Criteria for Route Selection and the amended AIMP, MinnCan has not changed its route.

It's August, busy and hot, 104 degrees. Adria and Emi pick watermelons the entire day, heads bent to the vines in the heat. Field conditions are so miserable that in the evening, after they shower, I pay them a bonus based on the peak temperature.

In the middle of the morning, Judge Heydinger hovers over our fields in a helicopter. She is viewing the entire proposed pipeline route from Rosemount to Clearbrook. I picture her peering out of the window with a notebook and pen in hand. Gardens of Eagan must look different from most of the farms she is flying over. Instead of large tracts of corn or soybeans, she is seeing forty-three small fields, a multitude of plant shapes and colors, laid out according to water flow and topography, with beneficial insect habitat between them. There are eighteen people spread out in small crews harvesting. It is likely she can see more people working outside on this small farm than she will see in the next hundred miles. A tractor in the monoculture would be a sign of life. I don't expect her to see the sweat on our skin, but can she see where the birds and insects live?

A 2005 sampling of wells in Dakota County reported an 82 percent detection rate of nitrates or pesticides, with 9 percent of samples exceeding drinking water standards. As she flies the route over Minnesota's rural landscape, can she see where the nitrates and pesticides came from and how they flowed into our aquifer?

Has she read the report from the U.S. Department of Health and Human Services that states that pesticides are now found in the blood of 95 percent of Americans tested? Does she know that levels of these pesticides are twice as high in the blood samples of children than in adults? Can she look down and see the link between pesticide exposure and hyperactivity, behavior disorders, learning disabilities, and developmental delays in children? Does she know that the study *Pesticide Appliers, Biocides, and Birth Defects in Rural*

Minnesota found the birth defect rate for all birth anomalies was significantly increased in children born to pesticide appliers?

Does her position looking down allow her a glimpse into the future?

Can she read the "2008–2009 Annual Report," from the President's Cancer Panel, which recommends food grown without pesticides, chemical fertilizers, and growth hormones and warns that our lackadaisical approach to regulation may have far-reaching consequences for our health? "Only a few hundred of the more than 80,000 chemicals in use in the United States have been tested for safety." Can she read on page 43, "The entire U.S. population is exposed on a daily basis to numerous agricultural chemicals. Many of these chemicals are known or suspected of having either carcinogenic or endocrine-disrupting properties. Leukemia rates are consistently elevated among children who grow up on farms, among children whose parents used pesticides in the home or garden, and among children of pesticide applicators."

She's up in the air, looking down at the land, but can she see these children and how their lives are affected by pesticide use? I trust she will make the best recommendation she can, based on the information that she has at the time. Our job is to provide her with relevant and credible testimony. We'll have expert witnesses who will testify with research. We'll also collect information from MPL for the record.

As intervening parties, we have the right to serve "information requests" on the other parties. We ask MPL for details: describe all chemicals, material, and equipment used in pipeline construction maintenance. For any epoxy, development chemical, coating, fertilizer, pesticide, or herbicide, specify the chemical compositions and product name. Specifically identify if any materials are radioactive. Explain how a crude oil seepage or leak from the MinnCan pipeline on an individual farm would be identified.

Their responses usually start out the same: "MPL objects to this request on the grounds that it is overly vague, overly broad, and unduly burdensome." Sometimes they add: "Seeks information not relevant to any issues properly before the Minnesota Public Utilities Commission in the Route Permit proceeding, and is not likely to lead to the discovery of relevant information." Then they go into their response. Sometimes it is informative, sometimes not. They can serve information requests on us also, and they do . . . they ask for our Organic System Plan.

Organic Integrity

Brilliant information request!

For us. Our Organic System Plan (OSP) is a federally registered document. Every certified organic farm is required to submit the details of how their individual operation is managed organically and in compliance with National Organic Standards. Having our OSP on the legal record provides credible evidence of our organic practices and the difference between organic and conventional systems. I hadn't thought to include it, and now they will do it for us.

Ours is forty detailed pages. Every practice on the farm is documented. I start to review it and come to "Has your water been tested?" Oops—for them. I realize the pipeline trench will be a water runoff conduit from a chemical farm to an organic one. Mitigation protections on water need to be added to the organic amended AIMP. I missed that. "MPL will not allow trench water from adjacent land onto Organic Agricultural Land."

But it is in Module 11—Weed, Pest, and Disease Management: Field—where it all comes together. "What management practices do you use to control weeds, pests, and diseases?" The principles of organic farming are clear in practice after listed practice. Soil building and the integrated use of natural habitat to support biological diversity: soil, insect, bird, and wildlife. It talks about disrupting the life cycles of pests, weeds, and disease and allowing the waterways and the "beetle bank" strips between the fields to be unmowed, for beneficial insect habitation and nesting. Managing weeds as an asset and a green manure is included, along with preventing compaction and minimizing equipment in fields.

Sixty-four cultural practices are listed, and they each validate the same truth. The management decisions on an organic farm are subject to the laws of relationship in nature. When we change one component of the farm ecosystem, there is a ripple effect throughout.

Then I come to "Prohibit tobacco smoking and prohibit people who have smoke on their clothes or body—human vector."

Tomatoes, potatoes, eggplants, and peppers are susceptible to the fungal disease tobacco mosaic. Plant pathologists F. L. Pfleger and R. J. Zeyen at the University of Minnesota address the disease in an online document. Tobacco mosaic is the most persistent virus known. It has been known to survive up to fifty years in dried plant parts. Handling cigars, cigarettes, and pipe tobaccos can contaminate the hands. The most common method of transferring the virus is on contaminated hands and tools. To date, there are no efficient chemical treatments that protect plants from the virus infection. Control of tobacco mosaic virus is primarily focused on reducing and eliminating sources of the virus and limiting the spread.

Our Organic System Plan is a federally registered document of how we manage Gardens of Eagan. If MPL comes onto the farm, I expect them to act in accordance with this document.

Dr. Deborah Allan, a professor in the Department of Soil, Water and Climate at the University of Minnesota, has volunteered to be our expert witness on soils. This is a huge gift. Hiring an expert can be prohibitively expensive. She will provide specific written testimony on the unique characteristics of organic farms, highlighting the vulnerability of organic vegetables to impairment of soil qualities. She will also review and comment on our recommendations for organic mitigation protections in the AIMP.

Paula and I meet with her at the university. I am mesmerized as she explains the microbial food web in soil. Her words draw an image of bacteria decomposing plant material and providing a first step in the soil food web of nutrient cycling. She describes the mycorrhizal fungi, how they bind soil particles into healthy aggregates, thus improving drainage and preventing erosion, and how they grow in a zone around and into the plant roots, functioning as an extension of them and increasing their nutrient and water uptake. She is not surprised when I tell her our pepper yields increased 50 percent when we inoculated the seed with mycorrhizal spores in the greenhouse.

Most important, she tells us that our documents accurately portray the reality of soils in an organic system. This confirmation from a soil scientist is what we need from her. I know soil through my relationship as an organic farmer, but credible research evidence is necessary in court. Dr. Carl Rosen attends our meeting also, and he confirms that tobacco mosaic is transferable from smoke on human bodies and clothing and that it is logical to include the prohibition in the organic mitigation protections for the AIMP.

Dr. Allan's sixteen-page testimony focuses on soil: "The quality of soil on a successful organic farm is usually quite different from that on a conventional farm. This difference can be measured in terms of soil compaction, soil aggregation, organic matter content, particulate organic matter and soil microbial biomass."

I am struck by her use of the word *successful*. Our soil has changed significantly since we first started building it fifteen years ago. This is a two-way relationship. We would not have reached this level of success if we hadn't given the soil what it needed. Dr. Allan writes, "I believe that the losses to an organic vegetable farm from diminished soil quality are of a different character and order of magnitude than on a conventional crop farm. To start with, the value on a per acre basis of conventional field crops is only in the range of two to three hundred dollars per acre. Atina Diffley has explained that the Gardens of Eagan yields per acre range from $4,000 to $70,000. This is consistent with a well-run premium organic vegetable farm in the Midwest."

The simple truth is that healthy soil is required for our success. She continues, "The market for premium organic produce is unforgiving.

Sub-standard organic vegetable products cannot be marketed. If organic sweet corn, melons or other vegetables are below quality standards, the crop will be a total loss."

Theoretically, the financial loss of farmers can be compensated, but any such compensation would not protect the organic consumers. Craig Minowa, environmental scientist and representative of Organic Consumers Association (OCA), has volunteered to testify regarding the interest that organic consumers have in the protection of organic farms. OCA represents over 850,000 members, subscribers, and volunteers. His testimony states, "Many members of the Organic Consumers Association perceive that preserving an organic food supply is necessary to protect themselves and their children from health risks associated with pesticides and food additives."

The loss of Gardens of Eagan as their food source is a real and significant threat for them. Mr. Minowa addresses the challenge of finding pesticide-free food in his testimony: "According to the United States Food and Drug Administration, half of the produce tested from grocery stores (1994–2002) contains measurable residues of pesticides. Researchers have reported that in blood samples of children aged 2 to 4, concentrations of pesticide residues are six times higher in children eating conventionally farmed fruits and vegetables compared with children eating organic food. The United States Centers for Disease Control reports that one of the main sources of pesticide exposure for United States children comes from the food they eat."

I'm relieved that I eat organic food when I read, "The United States Department of Agriculture prohibits mixing different types of pesticides in disposal due to the potential of increased toxicity from chemical interactions. On a consumer product level, pesticide mixtures are common in multiple-ingredient products. Sixty-two percent of food products tested contain a measurable mixture of residues of at least three different pesticides." I'm picturing the typical American child's diet. What long-term price is being paid?

We also have an organic certification expert, Jim Riddle, the

Coordinator for Organic Outreach at the University of Minnesota Southwest Research and Outreach Center. As the former chair of the National Organics Standards Board and the founding chair and lead trainer for the Independent Organic Inspectors Association, he is well qualified.

"Organic farms, unlike conventional farms, are intended to be maintained as a 'natural environment.'" He gets right to the point in his testimony. Organic farms are valuable natural resources and should be protected as such. He backs up his message, quoting federal organic standards: "National Organic Program (NOP) standards exclude production methods that are 'not possible under natural conditions.' NOP, 7 C.F.R. §205.2. Under NOP standards, the features of an organic farm are specifically recognized as 'natural resources.' The 'physical, hydrological, and biological features of a production operation, including soil, water, wetlands, woodlands and wildlife' are defined as natural resources of the operation. NOP, 7 C.F.R.§205.2. Organic producers are specifically required to 'maintain or improve the natural resources of the operation, including soil and water quality.' NOP, 7 C.F.R. §205.200."

Then he points out what is obvious to me but not to MPL: "The customary three-year time frame to prepare land for organic certification is intended for a situation where the prior land use was agricultural. Land used for pipeline construction would be like an industrial usage."

There will be seventeen public hearings around the state, spanning three weeks. It would be cost prohibitive to have our expert witnesses at all of them, and they can't miss that much work. Paula files the Gardens of Eagan Request for Exemption for Availability of Witnesses. It proposes that our expert witnesses testify and be available for questioning at the Dakota County public hearing and exempted from appearing at the other hearings, which are not the subject of the Gardens of Eagan's intervention.

I'm focusing all my attention now on outreach to our informed citizens. It's important that we pack the public hearing. Then from

Paula, this e-mail: "Please take deep breaths before you read this. We'll have to wait and see what the judge decides."

I open the attachment and find, Minnesota Pipeline Company's Memorandum in Opposition to Gardens of Eagan's Request for Exemption for Availability of Witnesses. Their argument is that one of the more significant responsibilities of a full party to a case is to ensure that each of its witnesses who pre-files testimony be available for cross-examination by interested persons at each hearing on the matter. They also argue that our Proposal for Modification of Agricultural Impact Mitigation Plan has gone beyond our scope of participation as represented in the Petition to Intervene.

Without our experts we have no chance to move the line or push through the organic mitigation protections. Take a deep breath? I haven't taken a deep breath since this started.

I remind myself, they may have money on their side and the largest privately owned business, but as Martin said, we have the food co-op community, and the best part is, we'll win either way. If we win legally, the farm will continue, and Minnesota will have organic mitigation protections. If we don't win—if Gardens of Eagan is gone—the loss will grow awareness of the value of local organic farms.

Judge Heydinger sets up a telephone conference call with Paula and the MPL attorney to settle the matter. The call goes well. Dr. Allan and Mr. Riddle need only attend the Dakota County public hearing on September 5. Craig Minowa will testify at a hearing up north, closer to his home. If citizens wish to submit written questions, an expert for Gardens of Eagan will respond in cross-examination at the hearing.

When the deadline comes for pre-filing our experts' testimonies, everything is ready. Along with the testimonies, we file a soil-horizon diagram to illustrate Dr. Allan's testimony, three maps of route alignment modifications, our updated Organic Appendix to the AIMP, and the curricula vitae of our experts. We've come a long way since Paula first outlined our three goals.

Most important, the Minnesota Department of Agriculture has

been very supportive in the goal of providing mitigation protections for organic farms. Drafts and discussions have gone back and forth with Bob Patton at the department, who worked with and brought in the suggestions of MPL. Paula and I have revised it numerous times. Our experts Dr. Allan and Mr. Riddle have reviewed drafts and added their expertise. Through the process, the document format has changed from the Amended Agricultural Impact Mitigation Plan to the Organic Appendix to the AIMP. But the purpose hasn't changed.

Now it's up to the judge and ultimately the Public Utilities Commission. We have filed our version, the Department of Agriculture will make their comments, MPL will present their statement, the judge will write her recommendation, and in the end, the PUC will make the final decision. The public hearing is in two weeks, and we need to pack it with informed citizens. The timing is tough, though, the Tuesday after Labor Day, and traditionally our largest wholesale order of the season. I figure the best way to inspire public-hearing testifiers is the visual of the green farm overflowing with food. Nine days before the hearing, we throw a Harvest Party and Public Hearing Energizer: organic field day, corn feed, and the new, to-be-unveiled "Pipeline Dance."

Martin and I are rooted under the canopy of the Oak all afternoon, greeting and hugging, handing out flyers with public hearing information, thanking people for their support, and asking them to testify at the hearing. Visitors write their names and e-mails on a list and check if they plan to attend.

As the sun is setting, Martin's band, the Pheromones, stirs the party into motion. They start into "Tequila," and Paula and I run around handing out stalks of corn, sunflowers, and amaranth. The Corn Dance comes naturally; many of the guests have danced it here before. Everyone jumps into the rhythm, moving in and out of a ring, using the plants to illustrate the cycle of planting, harvest, and eating. Every time the song comes to the bridge, the dancers thrust the stalks to the sky and yell, "Sweet corn." The shouting increases the frenzy, and the dancing escalates. The band slides into playing the melody of "Ghost Riders in the Sky." Robin hops onstage to sing the newly penned lyrics of "The Pipeline Song."

Once upon a time Koch pipeline threatened GOE.
Their disregard for healthy soil evoked the Diffleys.
When called they said, organic huh, it matters not at all.
This is where, they made their mighty fall.
Soil verses Oil,
Kale verses Koch,
No pipeline on GOE.

The dancers shout, "No pipeline on GOE." Long pipelines form and wind through the moon shadows cast by the Oak. Paula and I run between the dancers, breaking the pipe. The shouting changes to "Go, pipeline warriors, go." Children dart through the crowd, poking with corncobs, pollinating heads with tassels. The dancers wave the stalks in the air and pound out ancient rhythms to the Gods of Soil and Biological Diversity. I stand in the center of the whirl and look up through a sky of flying corn plants.

Back when I was a young mother trying to get our farm and family through bulldozers and development, I had no idea that someday we would be here, surrounded by supportive community. I look at the line of dancers and imagine them prancing up to the microphone at the public hearing. People committed to health and the protection of nature, speaking up, one by one, together for organic farms and farmers. I can't say what the end result of this will be, whether we will succeed in our effort or whether MPL will push their crude oil pipeline through, but I wouldn't take it back for anything, and I have no doubts about the public hearing. We are going to pack the house.

It is the Thursday before the hearing, and everything is "in" on the farm—harvest peak—it's now or never. Bins of watermelons and pallets of tomatoes fill the pack shed; the walk-in cooler and every truck are jammed with sweet corn, broccoli, and kale. I'm back and forth all day between the computer, responding to Paula's e-mail requests for schematics, and the pack shed, sorting tomatoes. I've been operating on reserves for a long time now. I don't dare stop moving. Once I do, it's going to be a long while before I start again.

Late in the day, I manage to get up to the judge's office for a last look through the letters. I tell myself I need them for the hearing, but really I just want to absorb energy from them. There is a packet of letters and drawings from the kids at the Seward Peace Garden. Crayon pictures of round faces eating bright yellow corn on the cob and smiling watermelon slices. I slide down in the chair and start to sob; this is the first time all summer that I have cried.

I count up to 4,200 letters, and then, even though there is another box, I stop counting. The number is so over the top, and for every person who found the time and energy to write, I know there are ten more who meant to. I am so proud to be a member of this community of people who are willing to speak up for what they value. The point has been so well made.

Organic farms are valuable natural resources and need to be protected as such.

The next day, in the middle of the morning, after we've already had eighteen e-mails between us, Paula calls and says, "The MPL attorney has approached us with a stipulation."

"As in they may agree to what we want instead of letting it go to the public hearing?" I ask.

Nothing she is saying makes any sense to me. I don't think I understand the word. I have learned from this experience to always keep a dictionary handy: Noun 1. stipulation—(law) an agreement or concession made by parties in a judicial proceeding (or by their attorneys) relating to the business before the court; must be in writing unless they are part of the court record.

I still don't understand. Why now, the last business day before the public hearing? And I don't believe it, even though the e-mails keep coming. MPL sends their draft stipulation. Paula responds with ours. I think it is a bluff to distract us from preparing for the hearing. I'll believe it when it's signed.

The Labor Day order is huge. The phone is ringing with order additions from the food co-ops. Harvest trucks are backing up with loads of produce. I focus on washing and packing. Paula's got this one, and I'm sure she's having fun. In late afternoon she calls and says, "Off in the distance I can hear singing."

She e-mails the final version of the agreement, which paraphrased and condensed into layperson's phraseology says: 1. The MinnCan crude oil pipeline will not cross the Gardens of Eagan certified organic farm at any point; and 2. MPL has agreed to include and implement the Organic Appendix to the Agricultural Impact Mitigation Plan.

"As soon as I hear from you with your approval to the terms, I will meet the MPL attorney and we will sign," Paula writes.

I don't even have to be there? Our representation can sign for us? That's great, because there is so much work to do here, but it's really anticlimactic. I slog back to sorting tomatoes. The fax rings and spits out the signed stipulation. I read it but still don't believe it's true. I hand it to Mike, who is waist deep packing watermelons. First he says with his brow furrowed in a scowl, "You're not going to settle after all that." Then he reads that the stipulation includes the Organic Appendix to the AIMP. His face switches to a beaming grin.

The crew goes wild. They are putting together tomato boxes, and instead of the fifty we need, they stack a pyramid to the fourteen-foot ceiling. Mike climbs the apple-picking ladder and hangs a cardboard sign on the top box, *CONGRATULATIONS!*

Why am I not jumping up and down? All I want to do is walk down the driveway, without looking back, alone and away. I can hear them whooping and laughing. I see them hugging. But I don't want to be any part of it. I stand at the sorting table and just keep moving, one tomato at a time. It gives me a simple decision to focus my hands on, and it's my anchor to the farm for now. Is it a number one? I place it gently, stem side down in the cardboard carton for tomorrow's co-op delivery. If it's a number two, it goes in the wooden flats for the roadside stand. Number threes I pack into twenty-pound lugs to fill the waiting list of people who want to can tomatoes for winter.

Martin is like me. He just keeps packing cabbage. I hear the clink of the metal scale every time a box reaches fifty pounds.

I send a notice to every e-mail address I have: Congratulations and thank you for your help and support. There is no need for you to come to the public hearing. We have just signed a stipulation with MPL: no pipeline on Gardens of Eagan, and MPL has agreed to implement the Organic Appendix to the AIMP.

This wouldn't have been possible without the support of over four thousand people who spoke up in favor of Gardens of Eagan and organic farms. The testimonies of our expert witnesses, Dr. Deborah Allan, Jim Riddle, and Craig Minowa, and the affidavits of Dana Jackson and Lindy Bannister were extremely valuable. Barth Anderson and the Wedge Co-op were so helpful with writing and a poster. Mississippi Market members sent over 1,250 letters! All the Twin Cities food co-ops and the *Mix* got the word out through newsletters and in-store information. Leah and the *Pulse* article! Organic Consumers Association, Land Stewardship Project, and MOSES kept people informed. Organic certification organizations ICO, MOSA, and ICS provided support and input on the Organic AIMP. Bob Patton and Meg Moynihan at the Minnesota Department of Agriculture and the Organic Advisory Task Force worked very hard and played a positive role in identifying the differences between organic and conventional agriculture and supported the need to be more protective of organic lands. Attorney Paula Maccabee—may she live forever.

My e-mail in-box is instantly jammed with congratulations.

This is great news. I am sure we will want to do a follow-up article. We publish next September 14. Let me speak with my colleagues to figure out what approach we want to take.
Dan, NewFarm.org

Congratulations to you and your entire team, staff, organization, posse, whatever on a well-organized and righteous campaign. By the way, Judy said that at the party, Atina looked like she just stepped out of a Maxfield Parrish painting.
Bill and Judy

You are a dragon-slayer.
Greg

Everyone at the Farmers Market was overjoyed and flabbergasted at the news. Many congratulations are sent your way from farmers, customers, chefs. Way to go! We think that now you have to write a book chronicling your victory and how you did it!
Laura

The advantage of land is paramount. Even a king is subject to the soil.
Ecclesiastes

Thanks, Atina.—I'm squealing with glee like a little girl!
Roxanne

But Martin and I are not squealing with glee. I don't trust any of it. I just want to unplug the phone and the computer. I don't want to see anyone, think about public image, or how to articulate a thought, but I can't back off. I lie awake writing e-mails in my mind and reviewing documents. I ask Paula what their next move will be.

Martin, who has been an unbreakable wall of support through the entire effort, dives into complete obsession rebuilding a propane John Deere 4020—like the engine is a sea of peace where he can float undisturbed.

We should be on top of the world. We succeeded with a first-of-its-kind Organic Appendix to the Agricultural Impact Mitigation Plan. We had tremendous support from thousands of people.

I keep thinking about the other organic farms on the line. I know of four now. They will have the organic mitigation protections as a tool, but they still have to face the pipeline. None of them joined the legal process or attempted to reroute it. Maybe I could have done something more. And just because MPL signed the stipulation doesn't mean it's over.

We still have to follow the process through to the end. Even if our support people don't need to come to the public hearing, Paula, Martin, and I have to go. Who knows what will be said there?

Hail Thaws into Life

Paula says, "We'll wear clothes that are peaceful colors, not scream-ing victory." I arrive in tranquil blue, she in blinding red. Martin wears all black.

The public hearing is a formality and a blur. Bob Patton, from the Department of Agriculture, testifies in support of the Organic Appendix to the AIMP. The MPL attorney shakes my hand and says, "I'm glad we reached the stipulation. It was the right thing to do."

Paula says, "How does it feel to have kicked ass of the largest pri-vately owned company in the world?"

"Did we do that?" I ask.

She knows just when I need a little encouragement. This morning it is in the form of an e-mail: "It may not have sunk in yet how much your life energy has been threatened by the fight for Gardens of Eagan. I am feeling very good about preserving the victory through the final vagaries of the process. But, you have been in a fight for your survival with some very negative forces, not only the pipeline com-pany, but also the jealousy and fears of neighbors and other farmers. This requires healing. I hope that you and Martin are starting to be-lieve that this is real. That sometimes good deeds and good people create positive change in the world." She closes with, "Remember, you've done something incredibly unique with your life on this farm, and you were able to get me to eat 'green manure' the first time I met you."

I take a deep breath. Through this entire campaign, every time I've checked my breath, it was barely there. All my years of striving to create balance, I've never been this drained in my entire life. Is it really possible I can come back stronger than before? I don't know.

But if I can't, if I've stolen from my future, this one time, it was worth the price.

A neighbor comes over. He wants to know how to transition to organic. He asks about the market and where to get production information. This is the second neighbor with this question in a week. They're not interested in organic for philosophical reasons; they want the protection. Laura Paine, the Organic Agriculture Specialist at the Wisconsin Department of Agriculture, calls to say that she is working on organic mitigation protections for Wisconsin.

Then the realities of vegetable production and the weather slam me out of my funk. When cold weather comes in fall, the frenzied dance of spring planting can feel like child's play in comparison. This isn't just first frost. It's a hard freeze, a month earlier than normal. The forecast calls for four nights of 19 degrees and daytime highs below freezing. We have 44,000 broccoli plants still maturing in the field; five acres of storage cabbage, cauliflower, and kale are unpicked. They can survive a freeze but not that low, and multiple nights will cause cell rupture and dry and rubbery produce. It's not just the money. I hate to see the food wasted. People are counting on it.

In a raw, cutting wind we harvest what we can. The next morning the growing season is over, but the pipeline case isn't. I don't understand why Paula says we've been successful. I'm receiving just as many e-mails from her as before, and my attention is still focused 100 percent on the pipeline. I ask her what will happen next, and she tells me that MPL will submit final route alignments. The Department of Commerce will have until October 6 to respond. There will be a briefing with the judge. Even though we have reached an agreement, we will submit proposed Findings of Fact and Conclusions to justify the changes in the route alignment and the mitigation plan.

Are we still fighting, or is this just the aftershock?

....

November 17, 2006. Administrative Law Judge Heydinger has filed her Findings of Fact, Conclusions and Recommendations. Not only does she affirm our agreement, but she has also added conditions of her own. She recommends that MPL be required to retain an organic certifier to assist any landowner to negotiate terms to the right-of-way agreement for any farm that is Organic Certified, that MPL be required to notify each landowner annually of the opportunity to register organic farms and the landowner's or tenant's Organic System Plan, and that MPL be responsible for the damage caused by any maintenance practice that is inconsistent with the landowner's or tenant's Organic System Plan.

The judge's supportive recommendation is fantastic, beyond our hopes and objectives. Not only does it provide protections to organic farms, it empowers a farm's Organic System Plan as a document of integrity. But this is a process.

MPL will file exceptions. We'll submit in response. The Department of Commerce will file comments and recommendations. There will be another hearing before the Public Utilities Commission. Members of the public will have opportunities to speak to the record. We won't be able to relax our vigilance until the five public utilities commissioners make the final decision, and they don't have to follow the judge's recommendation.

They could decide something completely different.

There's really nothing left of me now. I go to bed wishing I could sleep for months, until I'm either revived or this is finished—whichever comes second. We are deep in sleep when the pinging starts. I wake with a shock, panic soaking into my chest.

Now? In November? What the hell is the purpose of hail anyway, and why is it part of nature? Is it some kind of test or character-strengthening agent? Does it symbolize everything that is destructive and evil in the world? Does it lead us intact through the experience of loss, illuminating what we most value and must protect? Is the recovery a demonstration of the immense power of life, able to rise again after being beaten down?

Or is it just hail? Deal with it. All of our hard-made plans, we don't control the weather. It truly is an Act of God. There is no farmer prerogative here. No rights. No privileges. No mitigation. Just reality.

There aren't any crops in the field to worry about anymore anyway. Most of the birds have migrated. The trees have given up their leaves and gone into dormancy. It really doesn't matter, and there is something so completely outrageous about balls of ice pelting down from the sky. We start to giggle and can't stop. The weather and the pipeline fight seem equally ridiculous and bizarre. We lie in bed and snort and kick and squeal. The pounding of hail on the wall and window intensifies, an unwelcome guest demanding entrance at the door. We laugh even harder.

We answer the call by cranking open the window and howling into the darkness. Our voices echo back to us transformed—bigger than life and full of power. Hail bounces in and covers our pillows with a sheet of frozen memories. We lie facedown on the ice and feel it melting to liquid against our warm cheeks. Not just the hail thaws into life-carrying water, but everything unmoving and hard within us dissolves and becomes a river gushing, carving bedrock into pure, fresh form. Tears are pouring out of Martin's eyes as he says, "I wouldn't change a single thing."

We pick it up and throw it with full force, all of it—the hail, the fear, the exhaustion—soaring out into the air, never to land again in frozen form. "Take that you crazy weather," we scream. The hail quickens, as if fighting for one last chance to be all-powerful. It zings through the open window, hitting us back, roaring as if this is a battle it can and must win. We laugh even louder as we watch it melt into the wool blankets—its cutting hardness is nothing against the warm force of life. Soon it is gone, transformed into water, no longer a trickster and teacher, no longer a destructive element.

But most important of all, I let out the breath I've been holding since receiving MinnCan's letter. And far beyond, the breath I've been holding, all the way back, through crop after crop, storm after storm, and co-op after co-op. Through working until there's nothing left of me and I'm only a machine but not a woman.

Through finding our relationship with this new land; detoxing the soil out of chemical dependency, burning down buildings, and blowing up the silo; learning the land's personality and adjusting to the new synthesis of land, people, and business. Through wanting to be what we once were before, a family farming, and accepting we might never be again.

Through migrant farming all over Dakota County and searching and wanting new land to call home. Through the grief of bulldozer destruction, the disregard for soil and nature, and the blow to ancestral continuity; through Maize's and Eliza's irretrievable loss and Martin's buried heartbreak; through learning the sacred will not always be protected. Through frozen pumpkins, fleeing wildlife, and sterile emptiness.

Through drought and brownness, learning that God is still present, even when there are no raindrops or weeds. Through discovering and healing my dirty farmer shame. Through finding the way to merge Martin's past and my future into our present, healing in love, and learning to trust a two-way relationship.

Through picking periwinkles and climbing into the fiery summit of loneliness. Through gritty-dirty divorce, and that first touch when the universe shifted. Through crossing the Mississippi and giving away my rights and self-respect. Through Anita's influence, Grandma's cancer, Grandpa's leaving, and the sale of family land. All the way back, to god reaching down and touching my skin, elderberries, and following Dad in the garden, stepping into his big prints. From now on, from this moment forward, be it resolved, I am breathing.

When the hail is finished, somehow I am finished too. When we awake, I am spring, bursting through the earth's covering, ready for another go at life.

Every breath is claimed as mine now.

I spend the morning tallying up sales for the year. When I come to kale, the number is approximately 182,000 servings of kale from one and a quarter acre of land. All of it was sold within forty-three miles of the farm. The pipeline battle was for the kale, for the vetch, for the soil, for organic farms and the people who support them.

Normal Process

MPL files exceptions—arguments against the judge's recommendation. I read them without strong emotions. Now the process is just that—process—and interesting. Today I receive an e-mail from one of the organic farmers who rents land on the pipeline route. She is relying on the Organic Appendix to the AIMP to protect their soils and certification:

> Atina, I just thought I'd check in. A guy from the pipeline came out to meet with the landowners. At first, the pipeline guy was trying to say that everything will be the same as conventional, blah, blah, blah, but as soon as I showed him our thick, three-ring binder of field records, our Organic System Plan, and a copy of the Organic Appendix to the AIMP, his tune changed. He said that he will be putting in a request to have the route moved over to the road. Also, the landowners are now looking more seriously at organic as well. Again, thanks for your help.

April 13, 2007. Here we are at the final hearing before the PUC, and the only parties to the case the entire time have been the Minnesota Pipe Line Company, the Department of Commerce, and Gardens of Eagan. It is astonishing to me that there is no ombudsperson provided to protect the average landowner. It is an onerous task to follow the process and have a meaningful impact. It should not be this hard for citizens to have a voice.

Paula is at the table, and she seizes the opportunity to speak for all landowners. I am proud to be a client and friend of this woman with integrity as she argues for conditions to minimize landowner and environmental impacts of routing, making certain that the protections in the permit apply to all relevant properties on the line, whether or not MPL had a contract with the owner before the final order was issued.

Despite strong objections by MPL, in nearly every instance the PUC rejects the arguments of MPL and provides protection to the environment and to landowners. Specific to organic farms, the PUC not only accepts but also improves on the judge's conditions by requiring MPL to hire an independent third party to assist organic landowners with site-specific practices to minimize damage during construction.

This is the final order. Case is closed.

April 25, 2007. Not quite. MPL has filed a Petition for Reconsideration of the Commission's Routing Order. The company is arguing against the issues that were central to our post-hearing advocacy: landowners' rights.

June 8, 2007. The PUC votes unanimously not to reconsider its past decision. Now. Case is truly finished. The kale will be ready to harvest in one week. I go out and thank it for supporting the pipeline case and close with, "This year, how about a solar photovoltaic system?"

I'm certain its leaves are waving, "YES!"

When I bring up the solar system with Martin, he asks why. This is our normal process. But I veer from tradition. "I could go through my list of justifications, but the real reason is, I've always wanted to. Is that good, or do you want the long explanation?"

"That's a great reason. I don't need anything else."

Seventeen years after the first night that we slept here on this land, I write on a piece of paper and slip it under my pillow: What is the most important message this book needs to tell?

Martin and I are awakened in darkness by coyote voices held solid in a single, unwavering tone. An opening statement of consensus—it is stamina itself, long and unified. The suspense is charged further when each pulls loose with lifting-high, wailing plaints. Smashing, short bursts of falsetto yips—an opus of free speech—catching each other with quickness, then sliding into hoarse blackness, while others rise higher. Their sharp calls shatter the frozen air and fall like ice, slicing into our memory; once there, exposing forgotten knowledge. This is a language from far before, one that all of nature knows.

They are right outside our bedroom window, stamping the ground with rigid forelegs, embossing the land with their urgent message. There is a pattern to their dance. One jumps twisting. Another pounds. They move in mystery, like the web of ecosystems, the weaving of species. This is not a victory call after killing meat. It is not a mating ritual or a friendly chat. It is a directive. A decree. They are performing a law of nature. Telling us of relationships lost that must be restored.

Since their visit the first night, when they circled our house furious at our presence, the coyotes had never returned. They have come again now, to remind us of our obligation as caretakers and advocates. The land was here long before us, and it will be here long after we are gone. We live on the land, and the life upon it sustains us. Everything we do has consequences in nature; all of life is connected; only our relationships redeem us.

Someday our businesses and enterprises will cease to exist. They do not need to live eternally. But the land does.

The land and nature are forever.

Postscript

In January 2008, the Wedge Community Co-op purchased the Gardens of Eagan name and equipment and began leasing the farmland for organic vegetable production. The Wedge-operated Gardens of Eagan continues to provide organic produce to the local community. At the end of the 2012 growing season, the Wedge Co-op will move the Gardens of Eagan to their own farmland. For current information and opportunities at Gardens of Eagan, visit www.gardensofeagan.com.

In addition to managing the farm, the Wedge Co-op has started the Organic Field School at Gardens of Eagan, a 501(c)3 educational nonprofit dedicated to transforming our food and farming systems by providing organic and ecologically based practical education and research to farmers and the public. To learn about education opportunities or to support the Organic Field School, visit www.organic-fieldschool.org.

Since the implementation of the Organic Appendix to the AIMP in the Gardens of Eagan/Minnesota Pipe Line Company case, Minnesota environmental inspectors have been trained to oversee the organic mitigation plan on projects. The organic appendix has been applied to other projects in Minnesota, including the Enbridge Pipeline, the Northern Natural Gas Pipeline, and the Cap-X transmission line.

In Wisconsin, the Federal Energy Regulatory Commission required mitigation specific to organic farms for the Guardian Natural Gas Pipeline. In addition to mitigation, decision makers may also include the presence of organic farms as a factor in determining route selection. In Wisconsin proceedings regarding routing of the Guardian Pipeline, two route alternatives were rejected by the Wisconsin Public Service Commission for a portion of the pipeline, based in part on the concern that the organic farm crossing could raise issues that make these alternatives not practicable.

To read pipeline case documents, the Organic Appendix to the AIMP, and a *Drake Law Review* article about the pipeline case, visit www.atinadiffley.com.

In 1991, filmmaker Helen De Michiel's award-winning documentary *Turn Here Sweet Corn* was released. Filmed in 1988 and 1989 on the original Diffley family land in Eagan and in the surrounding community, the film focuses on the loss of greenbelt farmlands to suburbia. More video essay than documentary, it interweaves the specific story of our family and the Gardens of Eagan Organic Farm with an evocative contemplation about the future of family farming in a new era of rural culture. To learn more about the film or to purchase a DVD, visit www.thirtyleaves.org.

Eliza now lives with her husband and three children in a small town near the farm and enjoys visiting often with her family. She is a lead nurse in a family clinic and finds her childhood lessons about relationships at the roadside stand and in nature to be invaluable in her work with patients. Maize worked as produce staff at Valley Natural Foods Co-op and the Wedge Co-op through college; he is now married and beginning his solar career as an electrical designer.

Martin and I provide consulting services and educate consumers, farmers, and policymakers throughout the United States about organic farming and related issues through our business, Organic Farming Works LLC. Our current on-farm projects include breeding of sweet corn cultivars specifically adapted for organic systems, mentoring beginning organic farmers, and transitioning conventional farmland back to organic. Our future land-use plans include increasing the biological diversity on it, hosting research, outreach, seed breeding, and incubating beginning farmers. I enjoy calling my mornings my own, and Martin plays guitar every day and continues his passion for farm equipment.

To contact Martin or me for information on public speaking, workshops, equipment, consulting services, links to research and recipes, or to download reader discussion questions and organic farming information, visit www.organicfarmingworks.com.

I just can't leave you without a kale recipe. This is our grandson Blake's favorite. If you are feeding a child who resists eating greens, try starting with exercise. Hunger makes the most delicious sauce.

Sesame Kale

> Two to four servings, depending on appetite and
>   level of kale passion
> 1 bunch of organic kale, stems removed and
>   coarsely chopped
> 1 to 4 cloves of garlic, minced; adjust according to
>   your taste and social life
> 1 tbsp. olive oil
> ¼ cup water
> roasted sesame oil
> ume plum vinegar

Heat olive oil in a heavy pan. Sauté garlic for 20 to 30 seconds, stirring. Mix in chopped kale. Add water and cover. Steam on low for 5 to 10 minutes, until desired tenderness. Spread on platter. Sprinkle with roasted sesame oil and ume plum vinegar to taste.

Compliments for this recipe go to Strider Hammer, produce manager at Just Food Co-op, who inspired it when he said to me during an early morning produce delivery, "You could eat gravel with roasted sesame oil on it."

Gratitude

When people ask what I most cherish about farming, what comes is the depth of intimacy—with plants and nature, with coworkers in the field and at the stand, with produce buyers and customers.

Hundreds of people have worked at Gardens of Eagan over the years. This farm would not have thrived without their labor, sweat, ideas, and commitment. The Twin Cities natural food co-ops and wholesale distributors, produce buyers, and tens of thousands of people supported this farm through purchasing its produce. Thank you all. A major challenge when writing this book was choosing between stories and characters. Endless pages would be required to tell all.

Thanks to Minnesota, an early leader in providing state support for organic farming, including such measures as passing state organic standards in 1985, and support for the Organic Mitigation Appendix to the AIMP in 2006.

I am grateful for information from "The Role of Time in the Organic Agro-food Chain" by Bernhard Freyer, *A Language Older Than Words* by Derrick Jensen, *The Voice of the Coyote* by J. Frank Dobie, and "Rocks into Sand" by singer Bill Kirchen: all articulate our relationship with nature. Thanks to *Building Soils for Better Crops* by Fred Magdoff, Harold Van Es, and SARE; *Managing Cover Crops Profitably* by SARE Outreach and Andy Clark; *Manage Insects on Your Farm: A Guide to Ecological Strategies* by Miguel A. Altieri, Clara I. Nicholls, and Marlene Fritz; *Weeds and What They Tell* by Ehrenfried Pfeiffer; *Weed the Soil, Not the Crop* by Anne and Eric Nordell;

Kris Olsen, Marilyn Larson, and the Minnesota Historical Society for food co-op and OGBA documents; and George Kuepper and ATTRA for organic history. Thanks to nonprofits MISA, MOSES, OCA, LSP, OSA, the Rodale Institute, and the Xerces Society. Ed Brown, your commitment to organic farmers changed the Twin Cities organic community. Roger Blobaum, your lifelong contribution and passion for organic agriculture is a never-ending endowment.

Thanks to Robin Mittenthal for serving the farm as a working/walking world encyclopedia; Nick Lethert and Liz Welch for photo documentation, for transforming our autumns from labor to love, and for filtering the farm through an artist's lens of beauty; Clean Up the River Environment in Montevideo, Minnesota, for providing an artist's retreat space; the Loft Literary Center and writing instructor Mary Carroll Moore: you were crucial in my learning the craft of writing. And thanks to unidentified singer-songwriters and poets, whose phrases and lyrics have become a part of my thinking and vernacular and are present in this text.

I received tremendous support and feedback on this manuscript from friends and colleagues. I thank Esther Ouray, my lifelong friend, for seeing me with clarity and for remembering and repeating back to me years later the important things I say and then promptly forget; Pat Cumbie for teaching me it's OK to be vulnerable on the page— you brought out the inner story; Beth Dooley, so astute, who knows when to and when not to answer my questions, so in the process I find the answer myself, which is most powerful and true; Dr. Carrie Jennings, an endless fount of caring, intelligence, and integrity, of bright light and sharp focus; Audrey Arner, for devotion to the same spirit; Kate Gaynor, for perspectives from a local organic eater; and Mr. Paul Maccabee, for the final punch.

Todd Orjala: what more could an organic writer-farmer ask for than an editor who freezes sweet corn, cans tomatoes, and sends unsolicited e-mails; Mary Keirstead for patience and attention to detail; Kristian, Laura, and the entire staff at the University of Minnesota Press, I appreciate all that you have contributed to this book.

Paula Maccabee: a relationship that comes only rarely and to the most fortunate of lifetimes. You draw me out to my fullest potential.

Thanks to the entire Diffley clan; Mom and Dad, for raising me with real food and in an environment where nature was my greatest teacher; Maize and Eliza, for allowing me free rein to always grow; Blake, Emma, and Chase for laughter.

Martin, without whom this story and this book would not have come into existence: beyond my wildest dreams, I've been with you. That is the greatest gift of all.

Atina Diffley is an organic vegetable farmer who now educates consumers, farmers, and policymakers about organic farming through the consulting business Organic Farming Works LLC, owned by her and her husband, Martin. From 1973 through 2007, the Diffleys owned and operated Gardens of Eagan, one of the first certified organic produce farms in the Midwest. To contact Atina or Martin Diffley, visit www.organicfarmingworks.com.